W: Faithorne sculp:

THE LIFE OF DOM JOHN DE CASTRO

THE FOURTH VICEROY OF INDIA

THE LIFE OF DOM JOHN DE CASTRO

THE FOURTH VICEROY OF INDIA

WRITTEN IN PORTUGUESE BY

JACINTO FREIRE DE ANDRADA

TRANSLATED INTO ENGLISH BY

PETER WYCHE

GYAN

Published by

Gyan Publishing House
5, Ansari Road
Daryaganj, New Delhi-110002
Phone: 011-47034999, 9811692060
E-mail: books@gyanbooks.com

Distribution Network
gyanbooks.com
India, USA, Canada, UK, Australia, France

ISBN : 978-81-212-3719-2 (PB)
First Published, London 1664

2nd Impression 2020

Printed at: Gyan Press, Delhi.

The Life of Dom John De Castro the Fourth Viceroy of India
Author: Jacinto Freire De Andrada

THE

LIFE

OF

DOM JOHN DE CASTRO,

The Fourth Vice-Roy of *INDIA*.

Wherein are seen the *Portuguese*'s Voyages to the *East-Indies*; Their Discoveries and Conquests there; The form of Government, Commerce, and Discipline of Warr in the *East*, and the Topography of all *India* and *China*.

Containing also a particular relation of the most famous siege of *DIO*, With a Map to Illustrate it.

BY

JACINTO FREIRE DE ANDRADA,
Written in PORTUGUESE,

AND

By S[r] PETER WYCHE K[t].
Translated into English.

Φήμη δ' οὔτις πάμπαν ἀπόλλυται, ἥν τινα πολλοὶ
Λαοὶ φημίξωσι. Θεός νύ τις ἐστὶ καὶ αὐτή.

Hesio. ἔργα καὶ Ἡμέραι.

London, Printed for *Henry Herringman*, and are to be sold at his Shop at the Sign of the *Anchor* on the Lower walk in the New Exchange. 1664.

TO THE QUEENS Most Excellent Majesty.

May it please your Majesty,

EVery Man's way of paying his Reverence and Devotion, being particularly his own, and as peculiar as any thing he derives from his Temper; and the Splendor of Your Majesties Vertues and Perfections (of which to name any first were to fail in Ceremony to the rest) being as Glorious and Unquestionable as Light in the Sun, who, daily Prodigal of his Benign Aspects, is yet above being the Theame and Subject of Praises; I have thought it suitable to my Zeal, and first Imployment had in *Portugall*, to tell my Fellow-Subjects in plain English, the Greatness and Glory of that Crown and Kingdome, which are Contractedly drawn in the Life of one particular *Portuguese*,

since

ſince the Miniſters Actions have their Spring in the King's Inſtructions, and the Prince's Zeal makes the Subjects Apoſtles. And now *Madam*, the Praiſes of your Native Country, will come with advantage to the Eyes and Ears of the *Engliſh*, ſince your Majeſty, ſo Endear'd before, as to make them Hope in Deſpair, and Joyn (ſuch is the Miracle of your Goodneſs) in one *Form of Common-Prayer* for your Happy Recovery, (when ſo many thouſands ſo Sacrifize to their own Opinions as to be willing with their Lives and Fortunes to pay for their Non-conformity) will be now look't upon as the Queen of every particular Man's choice. The Life of the great *Portugueſe Dom John de Caſtro*, Dedicated in the Original to Prince *Theodoſius* of Happy Memory, Your Royal Brother, hath Suggeſted the preſumption of Begging for the Tranſlation, your Sacred and Auſpitious Patronage, which only (in ſo Cenſorious an Age) can protect in Print, and in Safety,

Madam,

Your Majeſties moſt Loyal Subject,
and moſt Dutifull Servant,

PETER WYCHE.

THE

Authors Dedication

To Prince

THEODOSIUS,

Of Happy Memory,

Who was Heir of *Portugall*, and Eldest Brother to Our Most Excellent Queen *KATHERINE*.

Most Serene SIR,

THE Scipios *have met with their match in their Actions, not in their Fortune; There were in* Asia Darius's *for* Dom John de Castro *to Conquer, in* Europe *not a* Curtius *or* Livy *to propagate his Fame. The Bishop* Dom Francisco de Castro, *perswaded me to write this History, (which the Press now publisheth) though in a Style inferiour to the deserts of a Man,*

 who

who came to be Great amongst the Greatest, whose Vertues blossom'd so soon, that they seem'd rather Hereditary, then Acquir'd; He Liv'd not out the Years of his Government, (in which almost the same Numbers stood for Days, and Victories) though he was long Liv'd to his Country; short to Nature. Yet now his Memory is under your Highness's Protection, 'tis a question, if he were Happier in his Life, or Posterity, being always a Conquerour, then over his Enemies, now over Time. I might here take an occasion to publish your Highness's Vertues, but an Epistle is too short, (as the Book would have been) for such a Subject. The general Cry of the World, is to be the Book where all shall read them in a more impartial Character; since our Hopes are, that your Highness uniting to the Pleasantness of Study, the Glory of Arms, will for Fame and Courage be the first on the File amongst our Portuguese *Princes.* God preserve the most Serene Person of your Highness. *Lisbone* 15th. of *March* 1651.

Jacinto Freire de Andrada.

THE

THE PREFACE.

1. PORtugall, given by Alphonsus *the sixth King of* Castile (*after a signal Victory obtained against the* Mahometans, *Anno* 1089.) *in Dowry with his Daughter* Therasia *to Count* Henry, *Grand-child to* Robert *Duke of* Burgundy, (*in Recompence of his extraordinary* (*though but personal*) *assistance in the Battail, and to have there so considerable a Strength, where the incursions of the* Moors *were most frequent and terrible*) *hath been maintain'd, enlarg'd* (*at home and abroad*) *and recovered, by Courage and Policy not below those Deserts which got so unusual a Match and Portion for a Stranger.*

2. *Count* Henry *took* Viseu *and* Lamego *from the* Moors, *yet left* Portugall *with Neighbouring Frontiers, for Southward it was bounded with the River* Mondego, (*infested with the Invasions of the Infidels*) *Northward with the River* Minho, *towards the Rising Sun it had the Province* Beira, *and towards the Setting, on the Sea-side the City* Porto, *which being the only Port, unpossess't by the* Moors, *and chiefly frequented by the* French, *seems more reasonably then some other Etymologies, to give the name to the Kingdome of* Portugall.

3. Alphonsus Henriques, *Son to Count* Henry (*as the fatal greatness of* Rome *made its first King* Romulus *a Souldier*) *was not second to any in Story, in Courage and Action; He defeated* Albucaran *King of* Badajos, *and took the City, raised the Siege of* Coimbra, *besieged by King* Eujunius, *with three hundred thousand men: In the year* 1139. *at the Battail of* Orique (*where impartial and concurrent Histories count an hundred* Moors *for every* Christian) *he overcame* Ismarus *and four more* Mahometan *Kings, on which he was* (*as some affirm*) *after the Fight saluted King by his own Souldiers; from that Action also, the* Virgil *of* Portugall Luis de Camoens (*in the* 53. *and* 54. *Stanzas of his third* Canto) *derives the bearing of the Arms of the Kingdome, which are five small shields Azure, in a great shield Argent, left plain by his Father.*

* 53. Aqui

53.
Aqui pinta no branco escudo usano,
Que agora esta vitoria certifica,
Cinco escudos azues esclarecidos,
Em sinal destes cinco Reys vencidos.

54.
En estes cinco escudos pinta os trinta
Dinheyros, porque Deos fora vendido,
Escrevendo a memoria em varia tinta,
Da quelle de quem foy favorecido.
Em cado hum dos cinco cinco pinta,
Por que assi fica o numero comprido;
Contando duas vezes o do meyo
Dos cinco azues que em Cruz pintando veyo.

Which the Right Honourable Sir *Richard Fanshaw* late Embassadour to *Portugal*, in his Excellent Translation of that Heroique Poem thus renders,

53.
In his broad Shield which he till then wore plain,
A badge eternal of this glorious day,
Five small shields Azure he doth now include,
In sign of these five Kings by him subdude.

54.
In these five Shields he paints the Recompence,
For which our Lord was sold, in various Ink,
Writing his History who did dispence
Such favour to him more then heart could think.
In every of the five he paints five Pence,
So sums the thirty by a Cinque fold cinque,
Accounting that which is the Center twise
Of the five Cinques which he doth place Cross-wise.

Though the more venerable Testimony of a Latin Record made of the Oath Alphonsus Henriques *took in the year* 1152. (*before the Bishop and Magistracy of* Coimbra, *and the Bishop of* Braga) *about the Vision he saw before the Engagement, saith, he was proclamed King before the Fight, as was fore-told by Christ, who at the same time commanded him to take for his Arms what he paid for the Redemption of Man, and what he was sold for to the Jews, to which the King added for his Crest* Moses's *Serpent, A Type of Christ; The words under the King's Oath are,* Gentem tuam invenies alacrem ad bellum & fortem & potentem ut sub Regis nomine in hac pugna egrediaris, Nec dubites, sed quicquid petierint liberè concede. Ego enim Ædificator & Dissipator Imperiorum & Regnorum sum; Volo enim in te & in semine tuo Imperium mihi stabilire ut deferatur nomen meum in exteras gentes; Et ut agnoscant successores tui datorem Regni, Insigne tuum ex pretio quo ego humanum genus emi, & ex quo ego à Judæis emptus sum, compones:

compones: *This Record also sets down a famous Prediction delivered at the same time by an old* Hermit *to* Alfonsus (*as he then affirm'd upon Oath*). *concerning the Succession, Alienation and Restauration of the Crown of* Portugall; Bono animo esto, Vinces, vinces, & non vinceris, Dilectus es a Domino, Posuit enim super te & super semen tuum oculos misericordiæ suæ usque in sextam decimam generationem in qua attenuabitur proles, sed in ipsam attenuatam ipse respiciet & videbit, *which this Age hath seen fulfill'd precisely and to the Letter, by the King of* Spain's *seising on the Kingdome of* Portugall *after the Death of King* Henry *the Cardinal (who succeeded the unfortunate Sebastian) the seventeenth King, and by the happy Restauration of the Royal Family in King* John *the Fourth of Glorious memory, Father to our most Incomparable Queen* Katherine. *This Record was found engross'd in Parchment with five Seals annex'd in the Royal Monastery of* Alcobaca, *the Original was carried to* Philip *the Second King of* Spain, *and is now in the Escurial; there remains in* Lisbone *an Authentique Copy, and* Dom Antonio de Sousa de Macedo *hath Printed it in the second Proeme of his* Lusitania Liberata, *pag.* 96, 97, *and* 98. *This first King took Saint* Iren *from the* Moors, *and (by the help of the* Northern *Fleet sent to the Holy Land under the Command of* William *Long-sword) got from them, after a long and bloody Siege,* Lisbone: *Afterwards* Beja *and* Evora, *and the greatest part of the Country on the South-side of* Tagus, *by the* Portuguese *called* Allentejo, *he Died in the year of our Lord* 1185. *of his Reign* 73. *and of his Age* 91. *a King so extraordinary in his own Person, in the unusual length of his Life and Reign, was necessary for the fast Rooting that Monarchy, which was so gloriously to spread it self, as far as* East *and* West *extend.*

4 Alphonsus *was succeeded by his Son* Sanctius *the first, from whom the Crown continued in the direct Descendency for above two hundred years, till* John *the first Brother to King* Ferdinand, *the last of nine Kings, who in continual Warrs had imployed their Pious and Victorious Arms in driving the* Moors *out of* Europe, *so long so stoutly did they defend their Possessions.*

5. *King* John (*seeing all clear behind him*) *did then, Prudently and in Compliance with that Innate hatred the Crown of* Portugall *had against the* Mahometans, *pass over to* Africa, *where he took from the* Moors *the City of* Ceuta, *as Emulous and Troublesome a Neighbour and Competitor to* Spain, *as* Carthage *was once to* Italy. *After this advantage on the* Africans, *his third Son the* Infante Dom Henrique *Commander of the Cavalliers of Christ (an order founded by* Dennis *the sixth King of* Portugal *against the Infidels, on the Dissolution of that of the Knights Templers) incited by the obligation of his Office and Family, set upon the Discovery of the* Western *Coast of* Arabia, *of which, in the expedition of* Ceuta (cujus pars magna fuit) *and other passages made over thither, he had got the best Information he could find amongst the* Moors; *He began his design* Anno 1420. *by sending forth every year two or*

three

three Ships, which were to pass Cape Non, *the furthest of the* Spanish *discoveries, and by them so named, like* Hercules *pillars, from their despair of passing further; In all the Voyages of twelve years they came but to the Cape* Bojador, (*so named from its Launching out*) *which no man had the boldness to double, because finding that Cape to shoot out* Westward. *about forty Leagues further then the rest of the Coast, and at the beginning of the Cape a Bank of Sands to run the same way, the unexperienced and raw Pilots (used then to Sail by the Shore) durst not stand off six Leagues (which had avoided the Flats) and go so far* Westward. *The* Infante *undaunted by the consideration of expence or danger, continually set out Fleets and gave Orders to the most skilfull and stout Commanders to adventure the passing that then so formidable Cape; In these Voyages* Porto Sancto *was, after a great Storm, recovered and found out, (and so named from the Preservation), afterwards the Island* Madeira, *so called from the thick Woods upon it; with Resolute and Magnanimous perseverance, Vast and Prodigious expence, unheard of Suffering and Danger, he at last past the Cape, and in forty three years carried on his Discoveries from* Cape Non *in twenty eight degrees and an half, of* Northern *Latitude to Cape* Sierra Lione *in* 7¼. *of the same Latitude, which makes on the Shore* 430. *Leagues. In the Sea, besides those already mentioned, were found out in his time the* Canary *Islands, and those of* Capoverde; *He laid the foundation of that great Design, not thought of by any of the Antients, but* Semiramis, Bacchus, *and* Alexander *the Great, and till now, above the narrow Souls of so many succeeding Ages; the* 13th. *of* November *in the year* 1463. *was the Day of his glorious Memory.*

6. Alphonsus *the fifth, Grand-child to* John *the first by his Son King* Edward, (*who Reigned but five years*) *set to Farm at a certain Rate the Trade of* Guinney *for five years to* Fernaon Gomes, *on condition, that beginning from the Cape* Sierra Lione *he should every year discover one hundred Leagues on the Coast; In* January 1471. *he first came to the place in* Guinney, *by him called (and yet of the same name) the Mine, and there began to truck for Gold; His discoveries fell not short of his agreement, for they reached to Cape Saint* Katherine (*so call'd because first seen on her Day*) *which lies in* 2 *and* ½. *of* Southern *Latitude. From this most famous discovery of the Gold Coast he had (according to the first rule of Sirnames) by Patent from the King given him that of* Da Mina, *and for his Arms in a field Argent three* Moors *heads with Gold Rings in their Ears and Nostrils, and Chains of the same about their Necks. In this King's time were discovered in the Sea the Islands of Saint* Thomas, *of the Prince, and of* Anno Bon; *He went* Anno 1458. *in Person with a Fleet of* 220. *Ships, and about* 25000. *Men, and took* Alcacer Leguer *from the* Moors; *In a second expedition got* Anafe, *in a third* Arzilla *and* Tangier.

7. *King* John *the Second took the Title of Lord of* Guinney, *and Built on the Gold Coast the Fortress call'd Saint* George *of the Mine,*

thereby

thereby to take Possession of the past and intended Discoveries, and to lay the first Stone of a Church for the Conversion of the Pagans. Diogo Cam by his Commission came in the year 1484. to the Kingdome and River of Congo, where (according to his Orders to raise Pillars of Stone (in stead of Wodden Crosses used before) in the most Eminent places of his Discoveries, fixing to them an Escutcheon Royal, and about it an Inscription in Latin and Portuguese, declaring the King, the Time and Person employed in the Discovery) He set up a Pillar on the South-side of the River, (how much more Glorious then the Imaginary ones of Hercules) which was therefore call'd Rio do Padraon, (i. e.) the River of the Pillar; the Discovery of the Kingdome of Congo was so considerable, as Diogo Cam returned with the news to the King, who in a little time fitted him out again; in this Voyage he went 200. Leagues beyond Congo, and planted two Pillars, one called Saint Augustines in 13. degrees of Southern Latitude, another which named the place Capo do Padraon, in 22. degrees of the same Latitude. About this time was discovered by Fernaon Do Po the Island yet called by his Name, and the Kingdome of Benim, whence the first Guinney Pepper came into Christendome.

In the year 1486. there came into Portugall an Ambassadour from the King of Benim, to desire some Priests to instruct that Kingdome in the Catholique Religion, this Embassadour told King John, that twenty Moneths Journey (according to the slow Travelling of their Caravans) Eastward of their Country was a Prince call'd Organé, who amongst the Pagan Princes of that Coast was esteemed as the Pope is in Europe, by whom (according to antient Custom) the Kings of Benim were Confirmed in their Succession to the Crown, who instead of a Scepter and a Crown, sent them a Staff, and to wear on their Head a Cover of Copper, like an Helmet, and a Cross to wear about their Neck; The King comparing this Relation with what some of his Friars had heard at Jerusalem, from the Abissines, of their Prince's being a Christian, and his Kingdome Southward of Egypt, upon consulting with Ptolomies Mapps, and his own Discoveries, and the distance Eastward, concluded Ogané to be the Presbyter John then so much talkt off, that by his means he might get into the Indies, and that by his Fleets following the Coast they might arrive at Ptolomies Prasum Promontorium, now Mozambique.

8. This Story heightning his hopes and desires of getting to the Indies, he sent May 1487. over Land Pero de Couilhaan to endeavour that way to come to India, and Alphonso de Paiva with Letters to Presbyter John; the first going from Grand Cairo in the Company of some Moors to Adem, (in the Streights mouth of the Red-Sea) thence cross'd over to the Coast of India, and was at Cananor, Calicut and Goa; at his return to Cairo, finding his Companion Dead, and meeting with fresh desires of the King that he should find out Presbyter John, he went again to the Red-Sea, and from thence got to the Court of Presbyter John, where the welcome Ceremony of his Reception was great, but his Return was (according to Custom there to retain Strangers) out of hope. The prosecution

cution of the Discoveries on the Coasts was continued by sending out a Fleet, in 1486. under the Command of Bartholomew Diaz, *he placed his first Pillar in the height of 24. degrees* Southward, *in a place then named* Serra Parda, 120. *Leagues beyond the last of* Diego Cam's, *pursuing their Voyage they came to* Angra das Vottas, *which lies in 29. After five days stay here putting to Sea again, bad Weather kept them 13. days with their Sails half-Mast high; when the Storm ceas'd, concluding the Coast according to former Observation to run from* North *to* South, *they stood in for the Land with an* Easterly *course, but being some days without making it they went* Northward, *which brought them to* Angra dos Vaquieras, (North *of the Cape) not having here any Intelligence for want of an Interpreter, and the fearfull* Moors *leaving the Shore at the sight of so unusual men, returning to Sea with the same course, they came to an Island in 33 ¼.* Southward, *where they planted a Pillar call'd the Cross, which also gave the name to the Island. Here the Mariners weary and fearfull of the great Seas they found, began to complain and desire not to be put to tempt Fortune further, but to return, having found a thing more considerable then any of the former Discoveries, which was, That the Land being now observed to run* Northward, *there must be in their Stern some great Cape which they ought to strive to discover: The Counsel of the Chief Officers of the Fleet rose in this Resolution, hardly granting* Bartholomew Diaz's *earnest request, to hold the same Course for two or three days, and then finding no encouragement to proceed, to Tack about; at the end of the Limited time, they came to a River 25. Leagues* Northward *of the Island of* Cruz, *in 32 ½. call'd* Rio do Infante, John Infante *Commander of a Ship being the first who went on Shore. Hence, the Mariners renewing their Complaints, they returned and came in sight of that so famous Cape, hid for so many Ages, which now did not only Discover it self, but a new World;* Bartholomew Diaz *from the Storm and Dangers he met with in doubling it, call'd it* Cabo Tormentoso, *but the King at the return of the Fleet gave it the more Illustrious name of* Bona Esperanza; *They returned* December 1487. *having in sixteen Moneths seventeen Days discovered 350. Leagues on the Coast. In this King's time was the* Astrolabe *found out by two of his Physicians, (to whose thoughts he had recommended the Improvement of* Navigation) *and one* Martim of Bohemia, *Scholer to the Great* Regiomontanus.

9. *King* John *Dying without Lawfull Issue, the Kingdome came to* Emanuel *Son to the* Infante Dom Ferdinand, *Brother to* Alphonsus *the Fifth; This was that great Fortunate and only* Emanuel *of* Portugall, *so call'd not only from being Born on* Corpus Christi *Day, 1469. but from his Mothers being delivered (after a sharp and dangerous Labour) as the Procession came before her Palace; * He was Born; with Arms so long, as standing upright, and holding them down, they reach't to his Knees; on which the Astrologers concluded his coming to the Crown, and the extent of his Dominions, according to their* Axiome, Brachia usque ad genua extensa imperare desiderant, & aliquando imperant. *Some pretend without any force to the words to apply to him the* Sybilla Cumea's

* On which 'twas said, If at Christ's Birth the Angels, at *Emanuels*, Christ himself assisted.

Cumea's *Prophecie in* Virgils *fourth* Eglogue; *He began to Reign at 26. years Old 1495. and Fir'd with the high design of his Predecessours to Sail through the Ocean to the* Indies, *he the next year concluded to send the great* Vasco do Gama *to try for them; This year was spent in Councils and Preparations, and in the following 1497. in the beginning of* July, *an unseasonable time, (but that great Actions expect not Opportunities) the Fleet consisting of three Ships and a Victualler, (after a solemn Procession of Prayers and Tears and general Benediction) set Sail, the first Land they came at was (after five Moneths) the Bay of Saint* Helena *lying in 32. degrees* Southward; *On the* 20th. *of* December, *they doubled the Cape of* Good Hope; *On* Christmas *day they pass'd by the* Costa do Natal, *not arrived at before, and so call'd, from the time they came to it; On* Twelfth *day they entred into a great River, therefore call'd* Rio dos Reys; *following on their Voyage they came to another great River 50. Leagues* Northward *of* Sofala, *where the Natives freely and friendly Convers'd with the Fleet, furnish'd them with fresh Provisions, and told them that* Eastward *there were men of their Colour who Sail'd in such Ships, whom they often saw pass by that Coast. On which* Vasca do Gama *call'd the place* Rio dos bons Sinaes, *and set up a Pillar there call'd Saint* Raphael, *with this good news and security (the best warrant they ever had of their Hope) they came to* Mocambique, *where they were at first well received by the* Xeque, *after assaulted by his Permission, and betray'd by his Pilot;* Palm-Sunday *they came to* Mombaza, *thence went for* Melinde, *where they made Peace with that King, and had from him a Pilot who carried them in 22. days cross that great Gulf of 700. Leagues, which is betwixt this Coast of* Africa *and that of* Malabar; *the first place he arrived at was* Calecut, *the design of his Voyage and end of his Instructions, having particular Letters and an Embassage for the* Samorin *(i. e.) Emperour, who (as* Portugall *was inform'd) was the greatest Prince and Lord of all the Spices of those Parts;* Vasco da Gama *had twice Audience of the* Samorim, *setled the Trade with him, and having plac'd five Pillars in his peculiar discovery of 1200. Leagues from* West *to* East, *returned safe to* Lisbone, 23 August 1499.

10. *The news* Vasco da Gama *brought from the* Indies *of the hopes to recompence so many pass'd difficulties, by the propagation of the Gospel, and the Spices and Jewels of the* East, *encouraged the King to set out in the year 1500. a Fleet of thirteen Ships, under the Command* Pedralvarez Cabrall, *who meeting with a Storm at* Capo Verde *went out to Sea, to make sure of doubling the Cape of* Good Hope, *and after a Moneths Voyage, came first to the other great Continent of* America, *where (from the solemn Planting of a Cross) he named his new discovery* Sancta Cruz, *but the common discourse of Interest, prevailing against Devotion, the profit of the Wood brought from thence call'd it* Brasilia. Pedralvarez *setting out from* Porto Seguro, *(so call'd by him from the goodness of it) lost by foul weather four of his Ships, in that great Ocean between* Brazil *and the Cape, and after the extremities of a bad Voyage,* came

came but with six torn Ships to Sofala, *thence Sailing along the Coast got to* Quiloa *and* Melinde, *where he took two Pilots, with whom he cross'd over for* India, *deliver'd his Letters to the* Samorim, *Laded two Ships there, the rest in* Cochim *and* Cananor, (*where he began Factories*) *and from those two places brought Embassadours to settle a Peace and Trade, arriving safely with them in* Portugall. *After so great Discoveries, the probability of a Trade, and a Resolution to set out every year a Fleet for the Discovery and Commerce of* India, *King* Emanuel *enlarged the Title of the Crown, by Styling himself Lord of the Navigation, Conquest and Commerce of* Ethiopia, Arabia, Persia *and* India.

11. *In the year* 1502. *this now so great a King, knowing Protection not to be less glorious then Conquest, made* Vasco da Gama *Admiral of all the Seas in the* East, *and sent him with twenty Sail to the* Indies, *whereof five were as a setled Fleet to continue there, to protect the new Factories, and to go some Moneths in the year to the Mouth of the Red-Sea to hinder the* Moors *of* Mecca *from coming out, who were the fiercest Enemies the* Portuguese *had, and who most Laboured to hinder their progress in* India; *for these getting into their hands the Trade of Spices, the* Moors *who before furnished* Christendome, *by the way of* Cairo *and* Alexandria, *fore-saw the ill consequence of their loss. This Voyage made Tributary the King of* Quiloa, *placed new Factories, revenged Injuries, protected Allies, and made the* Portuguese *so famous in the* East, *as their coming thither was not in a few Kingdoms and Provinces taken for the* Æra.

12. *The Acquisitions and Trade arrived to that height, as in the year* 1505. Dom Francisco d' Almeyda, *was sent thither with the Title of Vice-Roy, the first so eminent Title given in these Parts; with him went divers Gentlemen to serve there, with the Obligation then begun and always continued to stay there three years; in his Voyage he took* Quiloa, *built a Fortress, and left a Commander there, burnt* Mombaza, *built also a Fortress in* Anchediva, *he sent his Son* Dom Lorenzo *to find out the Island* Zeilan, *and the* Maldives, *which he performed, and to intercept the* Moors, *who after the* Portuguese *coming into* India, *and keeping a Fleet on the Coast of* Malabar, *carried the Spices laded at* Symatra, *a new way they had found out,* South *of* Zeilan, *and through the Islands, whence to avoid the Coast of* India *they cross'd over the Gulf, till they came to the Mouth of the Red-Sea, or* Persian *Gulf:* Dom Lorenzo *was afterwards Kill'd in a Sea-Fight, which the Vice-Roy's Vengeance made dear to the Infidels.*

13. *On* Palm-Sunday *in the year* 1506. Tristaon d' Acunha, *parted from* Lisbone *with a Fleet of fourteen Sail, and on it thirteen hundred Souldiers, after a great Mortality caus'd by a Plague which hapned among the men, the bad Air was observed to cease, and the Sick and Infirm to recover in their crossing the Line; in the Voyage they made Cape Saint* Augustine *in* Brazil, *and crossing the great Ocean before they came to the Cape, discovered the Island then named, and yet called* Tristaon d' Acuna;

Acuna; *One of the Ships, parted from the rest by a Storm; first put in at a Port of* Madagascar, *call'd* Maratana, *where he got so good Information of the place, as the News put* Tristaon *on the Discovery, which he perfected, and going afterwards for the* Indies, *in his way took from the* Moors *a Fortress in* Socotora.

14. *After the business of* Socotora, *the great* Alphonso d' Alboquerque (*who came with the Fleet from* Lisbone) *with seven of the Ships designed to go along the Coast of* Arabia, *and after so many Ages to revenge on the* Arabs *their Incursions and Possessions on the Continent of* Spain; *the first place he arrived at in the Kingdome of* Ormus *was the City* Calayate, *where he accepted of their Friendship, and forc'd four more to take his upon his own Terms, went on persuing his Victories, and sending fear (his* Harbinger*) before him, till he came to* Ormus, *where he made Peace with the King, upon condition to turn Tributary to the King of* Portugall, *and permit him to Build a Fortress on the Island; By the great Fleet which parted* 1509. *the Vice-Roy received orders to return, and* Alboquerque *was possess'd of the Government, which he Eterniz'd by taking the Cities of* Calicut (*the greatest and most powerfull Enemy the* Portuguese *had in* India) *and* Goa, *seated in the heart of* India, (*therefore judiciously made the Residence of the Vice-Roys and Governours*) *went in Person to* Sumatra, *and possess'd himself of* Malaca, *so famous among the Antients for its Scituation in the* Aurea Chersonesus, *and then the great Mart of all the* Eastern *Merchants; In the time he spent here, he received Embassies and Offers of Friendship from the Kings of* Campar *and* Java, *and from the King of* Siam *upon the Continent, sent an Embassadour to the King of* Pegu, *and Ships to discover the Spice Islands of the* Maluccoes *and* Banda; *He made the first expedition into the Red-Sea, and entred that Streight, Coasting* Arabia *till he came to the Island of* Ccibam, *in the middle of that Gulf, being returned from setling* Ormus, *he Died full of Glory and Deserts on Ship-board, at the Barr of* Goa, *in the year* 1515. *and his own Climaterical.*

15. *The same year King* Emanuel *designing an honourable Repose, for* Alboquerque *after so much Sweat and Toyl in Warr and Victory, had sent Governour to the* Indies Lopo Soarez d' Albergaria *with a Fleet of thirteen Ships, and Instructions to make a Fortress upon the Island of* Zeilan, *whence according to his Intelligence came all the Cynamon of those parts. At his first coming to the Island in* 1518. *the King of* Columbo, *on the noise of the* Portuguese *Arms and Justice, readily consented, but altered by the Jealousie and Interest of the* Moors *of* Calicut *and* Malabar, *was afterwards forced to yield a Fortress, and become Tributary; In his Government* Perez d' Andrade *with four Ships went to discover the Gulf of* Bangala, *and the Coast of* China; *He was succeeded at the end of three years, by* Diogo Lopez de Sequeira, *who made a Voyage to the Red-Sea, according to his Instructions from the King, to find out the Coast of* Presbyter John, *he came to the Island* Macua, *Inhabited by Christian* Moors; *and to* Arquico *a Fort of* Presbyter Johns,

Johns, where with mutual Tears and other Expressions of Joy was the first solemn meeting of the Eastern and Western Christians, of which, (that it was to come to pass) the Abissine Friers, said, they had by them, antient Prophesits.

16. King Emanuel Died in December 1521. after a glorious Reign of 26. years. The first sent to the Indies by his Son King John the Third, was he who discovered them, Vasco da Gama made Conde da Vidigueira, he went with the second Title of Vice-Roy, which was not given of course to those who went to Govern India, but (as the Romans chose their Dictators) bestowed on Men of Eminent worth, or for extraordinary Emergencies and Atchievements, so the Turks preparations at Sues, and giving out, he would drive the Portuguese out of India, were the cause Dom Garcia de Noronha was sent thither 1538. with the Relief of four thousand men on twelve Ships, and the Majesty and Terrour of the Third Vice-Roy, as our Dom John de Castro was made the Fourth, upon his signal Victory against the King of Cambaya, and raising the second so famous Siege of Dio.

17. Dio famous for twice Baffling the Power and Policy of the East, and scituated at the entrance of the Sea of India, and in the passage thither from Africa, Arabia, and Persia, was (according to some) Built by Alexander the Great, intended to be the Mistress of the Sea and Land, and so called from the word Διος, which his Flatterers gave him as the Son of Jupiter Ammon, others (without Searching into the reason of the Name) give it a more Ignoble beginning, by saying it was only antiently Inhabited by Fisher-men, but afterward, like Venice grew great, rich, and formidable; It was a constant part of King Emanuel's Instructions to those who serv'd him in the Indies, (knowing a Fortress here would be to India such a Curb as Argos in the hands of Strangers was once to Greece) to try always to get footing in this place. It was accordingly often (but in vain) attempted by all the ways force or stratagem could suggest, but was only that, the Fortune and Grandeur of so great a King could not atchieve; Dom John the Third, not so Covetous of the Kingdoms, as Virtues and Victories of his Father, commanded the Governours not to lay aside the design, without engaging for it in whatsoever expence or difficulty, who were all so blindly obedient as to lye with great Fleets before it, observing the places of advantage, sometimes falling on by open Force, sometime by Design, yet all unsuccessfull; On which advice the King ordered the Warr to be carried on in other places of Cambaya, that by desolating his Cities, annoying his Ports, and obstructing the Trade, that King might be forc'd to purchase his quiet by granting him a Fortress there; The Execution of the Portuguese's Arms, and Crys of his Subjects, brought him to seek Peace by giving, first the City Bacaim, with its Jurisdiction and Revenues to the Governour; afterwards being press'd by so terrible an Enemy as the Mogul, and the Rebellion of his own Subjects, he bought Protection and Assistance from the Portuguese, by giving them leave to choose a place there, to Build a Fortress on, which Martim Al-

phonso

phonso de Sosa *Admiral of the Seas of* India, *imployed by the Governour to compleat the Treaty, placed on the point which commands the Haven; This was in the year* 1535. *It was not long before the King of* Cambaia *perceived the* Portuguese *by their possession here to have their Feet upon his Neck, and all the* East *to complain of the interruption of their Pilgrimages, and the loss of their Trade and Commerce to* Mecca, *upon which the King listned greedily to* Coge-Sofar's *perswasion of Besieging the place, on the security of being assisted, by a great Fleet from the* Turk, *who design'd to drive the* Portuguese *out of* India. *This Siege began (* Antonio da Silvera *being Governour of* Dio) July 1538. *the first Army which came against the place consisting of six thousand Horse, and thirteen thousand Foot, under the Command of* Alucan, *and* Coge-Sofar; *and in* September, Solomon Bashaw *Admiral of the Turks came to their Relief, with a Fleet of seventy six Vessels, full of Choise men, and a suitable preparation of all other necessaries. There was not wanting by Sea or Land, the personal and constant gallantry of Assaults, the subtilty of Stratagem, and uninterrupted Battery of great Guns, against a few men taken unprovided; yet did the Enemy raise the Siege himself, at the end of* October, *and the Vice-Roy* Dom Garcia de Noronha *found him gone when he came to their Relief with one hundred and sixty Sail.*

17. *The subjection all* India *was in, under the Fortress of* Dio; *the old Animosities for the first Baffle received at that place, and* Sultan Mahumed's *revenge for the Death of his Father* Badur, *kill'd by the* Portuguese, *begot the second Siege of* Dio 1546. *the chief Story of our History, which, (if not much prejudiced by a lessening Translation) may probably appear one of the greatest Actions on Record. Here Envy cannot fasten that, with which she so disparagingly blasted* Alexanders *Expeditions and Conquests in* Asia, *That he had to do with unarm'd and unpolisht Men, master'd to his hand by Vice and Luxury. Courage, Discipline, Design and Arms were here in that height, as they seem'd not to be newly learn'd in the* East, *and must have prevailed against any one but a* Dom John de Castro, *one so singular in all Vertues as he might Cope with any of the antient* Heroes, *and challenge a place in the Kalendar of Saints, whose constant Carriage and Influence over all* India, *is (besides the universal consent of History) a strong argument for some successes, which might be otherwise startled at as improbable; if any can be so, to that Magnanimous and Hereditary preseverance in difficulties, which we have shew'd to be Entaild for above an Age upon the* Portuguese. *To Atone the imperfections of the Translation, and help the Reader in the passages of so famous and memorable a Siege, I have procured, (and gratefully acknowledge it as an eminent favour) the Mapp of* Dio, *from his Excellency the Marquess of* Sandé, *now extraordinary Embassadour in* England *from the King of* Portugall, *which I have inserted in the proper place.*

18. *The Death of our great and glorious* Dom John de Castro, *left not* India *so destitute, but the following Governours added Conquests to the*

out of Lisbone, *was acknowledged King of* Portugall, *and went in Person to* Lisbone *in* June 1581.

20. *The Restauration of King* John *the Fourth, to the Kingdome and Crown of* Portugall, *Anno* 1640. *is eminently observable; That the Possession of the King of* Spain *for threescore years, had not made the* Portuguese *loose their Courage, or Hopes to effect their desires; That the King of* Spain *should make the Duke of* Braganza, (*whose pretences to the Crown and affections of the People he very well knew*) *Grand-master of the Artillary, who in discharge of his trust seemed to refuse the offer of the Crown; That a secret intrusted with six hundred should not miscarry; That the design should be perfected with only the Death of the Secretary: And that its influence should be so general and powerfull, as the* Castillians *were every where, and almost at the same time laid aside particularly in* Brazil, *where they were totally extirpated; And where afterwards the States of* Holland *found this policy of the* Portuguese, *seconded by the Courage of their Ancestors, in taking the* Reciffe *in* Pernambuck, *January* 1654. *a place the States with a Fleet of fifty Ships had taken from the* Spaniard 1630. *of such consequence, That whilst the Crowns were united in one, the Recovery of it, was the great Debate of the Councils; attempted by the Admiral* Dom Antonio de Oquendo, 1631. *Afterwards for many years, by the greatest Preparations and most eminent Persons of both Kingdomes; yet the complicated Strength of Nature, and the* Hollanders *Fortifications* (*whom their Experience had made the great Masters of that Art*) *made it impregnable against all Attaques. The taking in of this by the* Portuguese *alone, when a King of their own made them act like and for themselves, and the keeping of it against the Force and Fleet of Count* Maurice *of* Nassau, *may at the end of a long Preface excuse the Recital of many more performances of the* Portuguese, (*after their Restauration*) *Notorious for the Wisdome of the Contrivance and Gallantry of the Execution.*

Peter Wyche.

WHITEHALL, *Aug.* 12. 1663.

Let this Tranſlation be Printed.

Henry Bennet.

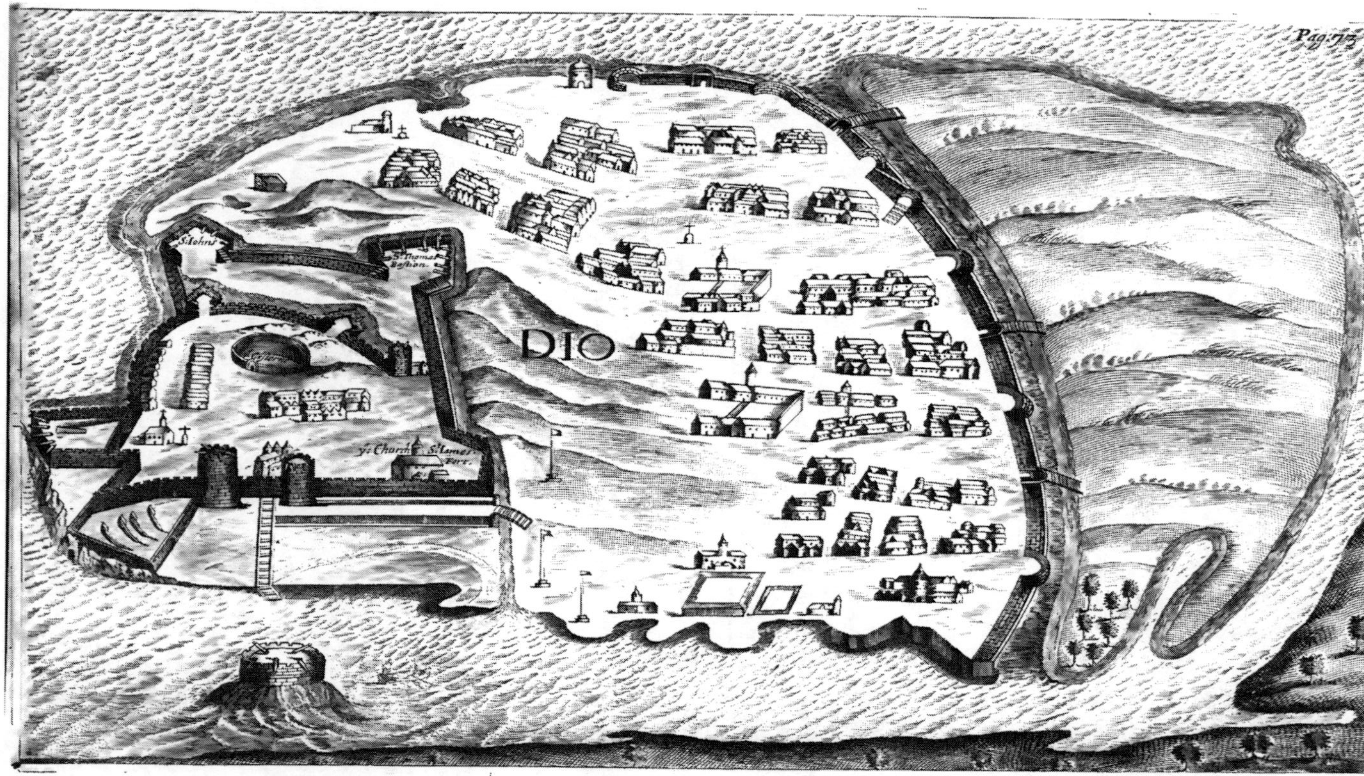
Pag. 73
DIO
S.t Iohns
S.t Thomas Bastion
y.e Church
S.t Iames Fort.

THE LIFE OF

DOM JOHN DE CASTRO.

The First Book.

I Am Writing the Life of *Dom John de Castro*, a Man greater then his Name, greater then his Victories; whose Memory is yet fresh in the *East*, descending from Father to Son, a successive Book, wherein the Fame of his Actions is preserv'd always Alive; and we will add to the general Acclamations of his Glory this little shout, since Records keep not so well in Tradition as Writing.

1. *Dom John de Castro*, was, a Renown'd Branch of an Illustrious Family: But first we will tell his Vertues, then his Stock; the Nobility a man raiseth by his Actions, being greater then that he acquires from his Ancestors. He spent his first Years in that Learning and Vertue, his Age was then capable of; being so naturally inclin'd to Learning, that he needed not be forc'd, but only put in the way. *Dom John*, not being the Heir of his House, was intended for Study; Learning being always the second Birth-right amongst the best Houses of this Kingdome. *Dom John* obey'd, not having then Liberty to refuse, or a School to take another Lesson in.

The first Studies of *Dom John de Castro.*

2. He Learnt Mathematicks of *Peter Nonnius*, the greatest Man *Portugall* knew of that Profession, and came to be such a Master in the Science, as if he had intended to profess it. In this School he was Companion to the Infante *Dom Lewis*, whose Familiarity he

He learnt the Mathematicks.

 got

got into, both by his Quality and Ingenuity: but as *Dom John* embrac'd Learning out of Obedience, and Arms by Destiny, he look'd upon the glory of the Schools as small, finding himself intended for the Warrs, both by his own Inclination, and by his fore-fathers Example.

3. The repute of *Dom Edward Menezes*, Governour of *Tangiers*, was at that time great, whose Name the *Africans* heard with terrour, and we with respect; *Dom John* look'd more upon his Victories, then the Schemes and Circles of *Euclid*, loving the Arts only as they waited on Courage.

He goes to *Tangiers*.

4. Being eighteen years Old, finding himself more grown in Spirit then in Age, making an escape, he Embark'd for *Tangiers*, where (contrary to the Custom of such places) he bore Arms nine years, as if he intended to spend his Life, in what was only a beginning: on all occasions, in that Warr he behaved himself with Courage equal to his Blood, and above his Years, deserving the joy of it from his Friends, and envy from the Souldiery.

Dom Edward de Menezes Knights him,

5. *Dom Edward de Menezes* respected him, as if he had then read in this History; his Victories in *Asia* we are now Writing; he would needs with his own hands give and receive the honour of Knighting him, being proud so long before of this Son of his Discipline; and considering, that so great Bravery deserv'd to be encouraged by the favours of Princes, desiring that Valour should have due Rewards, equally favouring the King, and Subject, he writ to the King *Dom John* the Third, that *Dom John de Castro* had so serv'd, that now no Place or Reward could be too great for him; that his Highness ought to conferr some honour on him, because Kings make Souldiers by taking notice of them, and it was just, that in the sight of so great a Prince, Vertue should not remain unrewarded.

and informs the King of his Desert.

The King sends for him, and rewards him.

6. The King immediately sent for *Dom John*, by so honourable a Letter as if he had intended him no other

recom-

recompence, with that *Dom John* came to the Court, where he was as much Envy'd for his wounds as for the favour shown him; The King made him Commendatory of *Salvaterra*; awaking Deserts in others by the Value he had for them in him.

7. *Dom-John* spent some time in Court, without being drawn away to any youthfull Vice, either by his Years, or Example, appearing truly a Man all along, taking so well his Measures, that neither his Maturity made him ill-humour'd, nor his Civility facil: He knew how to play the Philosopher amongst the Varieties of the Court; shunning in that kind of Life what had any shew of Idleness, not any thing that argued Discretion.

His behaviour at Court.

8 He altered his course of Life by Marrying the Lady *Leonore Coutinho*, his Cousin German once removed, the Daughter of *Leonel Coutinho*, a Gentleman of the Illustrious House of *Marialva*, Nobility so known and so auntient, that our knowledge of that and the Kingdome bear both the same Date: He had no other Portion but the Qualities and Vertues of his Bride; yet without the propps of an Estate, did so maintain his Honour, that he was by all treated with the respect of a Rich, and the pitty of a Poor man.

He marries *Leonore Coutinho*.

9. Then presented it self the Battail of *Tunis*, an Action more famous for the Victory, then Advantage, in which, *Dom John de Castro* had no little share, in the Honour or Danger. We will give a larger relation of its success, The King *Dom John* having engaged in it his Forces, the Infante *Dom Lewis*, his Person. That notorious Rover *Barba-Rossa* had infested all the *Mediterranean* with more Strength and Boldness then is ordinarily heard of in a Pirat, finding Fortune so ready to assist his Daring, that, amidst the Triumphs of *Charls*, only *Barba-Rossa* was the scandal of his Victories; Seeing himself every day more advanc'd in Opinion, and Forces, he went to serve the *Turk*, with whom, the report of our injuries had given him credit; and buying his

The Battail of *Tunis*.

The occasion of it.

his favour with the most Valuable things he had, got to be Admiral of the Seas; coming often with great numbers of Gallies, he very much infested the Ports of *Naples* and *Sicily*; the Valour of the Natives, or the Protection of the Empire, (to which they were Vassals) not being able to defend them; He made Slaves of infinite numbers, (whereof divers truckt their Faith for their Liberty.) laid waste Provinces, and burnt Ships, getting a very great Name amongst the Infidels, by the miseries of the Christians, till forgetting his beginning, his Prosperity made way for his ambition of Reigning, and he usurp'd the Kingdome of *Tunis* by diverse Artifices, which Story belongs not to our History. *Charls*, looking upon this Tyrant, having so much force of his own, that he was abetted by a far greater Power, and that his Kingdoms being so near, it was not fit he should root himself at the Gates of his House; that the *Moors* (who wanted not Valour, but Discipline) being set on work by so experienc'd a Souldier, would come to know their own Strength to the prejudice of his Kingdoms; resolv'd with a very strong Navy to find him out, and to divest him of the Protection of *Tunis*, because at the best scaping from thence he must to Sea again, where, as a Pirat, he could only offend with stragling Forces, which the weather, and fortune, might more easily Destroy. He drew his old Souldiers from the Garrisons of *Italy*, (whom he suppli'd with new) made great Leavies in High *Germany* and *Flanders*, Listed *Italians* and *Spaniards*, besides Gentry and Nobility which serv'd without Pay, and the Enterprise being so usefull and justifiable; and where the Emperour ventur'd his own Person, there came many Voluntiers to joyn with so pious and valiant Arms. The Emperour Mustered the men he rais'd, in *Sardinia*, and found five and twenty thousand Foot on the List who received Pay, besides very many others who serv'd without it, who made up a great part of the Army; every day he receiv'd diverse Succours which increast his Camp.

10. The

10. The Infante *Dom Lewis*, a Prince worthy of designs matching his Courage, resolv'd to accompany the Emperour his Brother-in-law in the expedition, and though very much disswaded by the King *Dom John*, with diverse Arguments, some taking in his affection to a Brother, others the care for his Person; yet the Infante apprehending the King's inclinations forwarder to excuse his Courage, then to accept his Obedience, did with some Gentlemen depart privately; which when the King knew, he sent him to *Barcellona* (where the Emperour then was) large Credit, and ordered the Equipping 25 Carvels, and some other Ships, amongst the rest * one Galleone, which carried two hundred Brass pieces; the greatest that till then ever Rode in our Seas: that, under the Command of *Antonio de Saldanha*, they might be in readiness for the Fight, and out of respect to the Infante all the Vessels of the Fleet were entrusted with Gentlemen of eminent Quality, of whom *Dom John de Castro* was one, who in this Action did equally despise Danger and Covetousness, as will presently appear by the ensuing relation.

The Infante *Dom Lewis* is there in Person.

* This was the Vessel which in the invasion 1588. was call'd the *Caca-foogo*.

11. Those Gentlemen who Embark'd in this expedition, and who are come to my knowledge, were (besides *Dom John de Castro*) *Dom Affonso of Portugall*, Son and Heir of the Earl of *Vimioso*, *Dom Affonso de Vasconcellos*, Son of the Earl of *Penella*, *Lewis Alvarez de Tavora*, Lord of *Mogadoura*, with his Brother *Ruy Lorenco de Tavora*, who was afterwards Vice-King in the *Indies*, *Dom John de Almeyda*, Son of the Earl of *Abrantes*, *Dom Pedro Mascarenhas*, who also was Vice-King in the *Indies*, *Dom Diogo de Castro*, Governour of the Castle of *Evora*, *Dom Fernando de Noronha*, *Dom Francisco de Faro*, *Dom Francisco Pereira*, Embassadour from King *Dom Sebastian* to *Castille*, *Dom Affonso de Castelbranco*, Lord High Bailiff of *Portugall*, *Pero Lopez de Sousa*, *John Gomez de Sylva*, Page of the Lance, and *Dom Lewis de Attayda*, afterwards Earl of *Attouguia*, and

Gentlemen who were at the Fight.

and Dy'd in the *Indies*, being the second time Vice-King there. All these Gentlemen serv'd at their own Charge, carrying with them Servants and Souldiers without any pay; their Cloaths also and Liveries show'd with what delight they went to the Warr. All the Fleet came to Anchor in the Port of *Barcellona*, and saluting the Emperour's Admiral, made a warlick and pleasing sight. The Emperour came to the *Portugall* Embassadors House, (*Alvaro Mendez de Vasconcellos*) which being on the Sea-side was fitter to honour and entertain the Entry.

12. The Dukes of *Alva* and *Cordova*, with many other Lords, came to the Sea-side to find out the General, and the Gentlemen with him, they all went to Kiss the Emperour's hands, who received them with all the honour and welcome befitting his place, very glad to be accompany'd with our experienc'd and stout Souldiery, to whom the half Moons, and Lances of *Africa* were no strangers. The Emperour acquainted the Infante *Dom Lewis* with all his weighty Resolutions; not only out of respect to the greatness of his Person, but to that of his Judgement, well seen both in Court; and State; of whom I must here tell a pass of Civility, for the valew the *Castillians* put on it. The Emperour and the Infante were together one Night, and at the going in of a Door both Complemented for the precedency, the one would have the Stranger go foremost, the other would put it upon Majesty; The Emperour taking him by the Arm forc'd him to enter first, The Infante not willing to accept the honour, nor able to refuse it, snatch'd a Torch from a Page. The Infante knew so well how to please the Emperour, as he resolv'd to give him the State of *Milan*, finding in him Qualities to deserve it, Valour to defend it. But the claims of *France*, made the Dominion of that State so uncertain, as it lay many years under the Decision of Arms.

Civility betwixt the Emperour and Infante.

13. I will not tell the success of that Warr, because the

the Story is from my purpose, though *Dom John de Castro* behav'd himself so in't, as the Emperour would fain have Knighted him; an Honour, from which he justly excus'd himself, as having had it before from other Hands, which, though not so Royal, suppli'd that defect by their stoutness. The Emperour Commanded two Thousand *Crusades* should be given to every Captain of the Fleet, which *Dom John* alone accepted not, serving more Ambitiously for Renown than Reward.

The Emperour would have Knighted *Dom John de Castro*, who refus'd it.

A *Crusade* worth 3 s. 8 d.

As the reward of Money.

14. *Charls* now Triumphing, like an other *Scipio*, after the Warr of *Africa*, saw Himself at rest, amidst the Applause and Acclamations of *Europe*, styling himself more fitly the Founder, than the Heir of his Empire. Our Fleet return'd to the Port of *Lisbone*, where *Dom John* found in the Embraces of the King, and Salutations of the People, a greater reward than he had refus'd from *Cæsar*; and as one who knew how to despise his own Fame, he retir'd to his Country House at *Sintra*, desiring to Live to himself, having so carry'd himself in his Country's Service, that he neither forsook it, as an Unprofitable, nor Courted it as an Ambitious Person: Here he past his time in a strange and new kind of Husbandry, Cutting down Fruitfull Trees, and Planting in their stead Wild and Barren ones; by this perhaps shewing, that in all he did he was so dis-interess'd, that from the Earth he Till'd he look'd for no return of benefit: but 'tis not much, if he so little valew'd what the Rocks of *Sintra* could produce, when he scornfully Trampled upon the Rubies and Diamonds of the *East*.

He retires to *Sintra*.

15. *Dom John* in the prime of his Age, found himself put upon Service by the Examples of his own Family; and, as the Warr in *Africa*, by the new Conquests in the *East*, was either slighted or forgot, (the World most Valewing the Fame which is far-fetch'd) He resolv'd to go for the *Indies*, whose Conquests stored the Kingdome with Glory and Victories; He went on Board, without asking any employment or reward,

He goes the first time for the *Indies*.

See *John de Barro's* History of *Asia*, Decade .. Lib. 3. Cap. 8. N°. 10.

reward, counting that Honour more his own he went to winn, than that he might carry with him.

16 In that expedition, *Dom Garcia de Noronha*, his Brother-in-law, went Governour to the *Indies*, who look'd upon *Dom John de Castro* as one fit to succeed him, though he then past but for a private Souldier; as soon as the King knew *Dom John*'s resolution, he ordered him a Thousand *Crusades* yearly all the time he serv'd in the *Indies*, and by his Letters Patents the Government of the Fortress of *Ormus*, which he, I know not if with greater ambition or temper, refus'd; the Memory of rewards rejected being rarer than of those accepted: an Action more easily prais'd than imitated.

The King profers him a Reward, and now he accepts it.

Ibid.

17. *Dom John de Castro* took Shipping with his Son *Dom Alvaro* then about thirteen, giving him for the pass-time of that Age the Dangers and Tempests of so long a Voyage. *Dom Garcia*'s Fleet arriv'd prosperously at the *Indies*, where he found the Governour *Nuno de Cunha* going with a Fleet to the relief of *Dio*, and to Fight the *Turks* Galleys which lay before it; in that famous siege, *Antonio da Sylveira* held out. *Dom Garcia* at once with the possession of the Government took on him the Obligation of succouring the place, in which service *Dom John de Castro* offer'd himself, and as a Souldier of fortune earnest upon't, put himself on the first Ship, as if he fore-saw those future Triumphs *Dio* call'd him to: but the retreat of the *Turks* lost *Dom Garcia* the Victory, or rather gave it him without Blood-shed, if less glorious, more secure.

He carries his Son *Dom Alvaro.*

He embarks himself for the relief of *Dio.*

18. *Dom Garcia* Dy'd in a little time, to whom succeeded *Dom Estevaon da Goma*, one who had in the *Indies* the Reputation of his Family, and was likely to have had the Fortune, had not his Government been so short; He engag'd in an Action, great in the danger, and the glory of it, which was to pass the streight of the *Red-Sea*, and burn the *Turks* Galleys which were Building at *Suez*, with intent (as'twas given out) to drive

History of *India*, Dec. 5. Lib. 7. Cap. 1.

drive the *Portugues* out of *India*: a design the *Turk* thought worthy his Power.

19. When all the Fleet was under Sail, there was not any Souldier of Courage not inspirited by the hazard of so extraordinary an action of as much Fame in the undertaking as Victory. *Dom Estevaon de Gama* set Sail with twelve great Ships, and sixty small Boats the first of *January* 1541. here *Dom John de Castro* had the Command of a Gallione, and pursuing their Voyage with Easterly winds, they all, though scattered, saw the Coast of *Arabia*. The Governour *Dom Estevaon da Gama* made it about *Monte Felix*, and arriv'd at the mouth of the Streight, expected the other Ships of his Convoy; here they had notice that the Enemies Galleys were drawn on shore, and so watch'd that there was no Burning 'em, without open force; which (for the Flats and Shelves of that Port) would be impossible to our Round-bottom'd Ships. Yet *Dom Estevaon da Gama* slighting the advice and danger, went forward with some small Barks, (one of which, *Dom John de Castro*, (leaving his Ship) Commanded.) They past by the *Primero* Islands, which lye in twelve degrees and ½ and by the Bay of *Velba* which is in almost thirteen, they Anchord in the Bay of *Fortune*, which is in the same heighth. In all the Creeks and Bays from the mouth of the Streight to *Sues*, was *Dom John* taking the height of the Sun, and making a Journal, discoursing, sometimes like a Natural Philosopher, sometimes like a Sea-man; showing how blind the bare Experience of Pilots is, without the rules of Art; here with as much Judgment, as he had Courage, he Learnedly canvas'd the Reasons why the *Red-Sea* was call'd so, and the Natural causes of the over-flow of *Nile* in the Summer; a Theme which hath kept many Wits awake, yet hath Nature for so many years kept her own secret; but we reckon as the least part of this Mans greatness, that which the *Romans* with so swelling Rhetorick write of their *Cesar*, that he manag'd a Pen as Judiciously,

History of *India*, Dec. 5. Lib. 7. Cap. 5.

He goes to the *Red-Sea* with *Dom Estevaon da Gama*.

Ibid.

Ibid.

as he did a Sword Couragiously. This and other Tracts, (of which we promise you more Light) writ at Sea in Storms and Winds, he Dedicated to the Infant *Dom Lewis*, presenting him with the Fruits of that Learning they suck'd in together.

Ibid.

20. From this Harbour they had a sight of Mount *Sinai*, where the Angels laid the Reliques of St. *Katherine* in a famous Repository of their own Building; at the sight *Dom Estevaon da Gama* Knighted *Dom Alvaro de Castro*, who in memory of so great a Sanctuary took for his Crest the Katherine-wheel, which his Family doth Religiously give to this day; we will give no particular account of that design, because the Vigilancy of the *Turks* hindered it from taking effect.

Dom Estevaon Knights *Dom Alvaro.*

History of *India*, Dec. 5. Lib. 7. Cap. 8.

21. *Dom John* returning to the Kingdome, (as if designedly giving the *Palms* of the *East* time to grow, which were afterwards to Crown his Victories) brought no other Riches on shore but the Fame of his Actions; and being yet in his Sea-cloaths, (those too scarce dry) was by the King chosen to be Admiral of the Navy of the Coast; putting him on new Employment in recompence of his former Services. *Dom John* immediately put to Sea in the year 1543. to Convoy those Ships which were expected from the *Indies*, and plying too and again in his Station, spy'd a French *Corsaire*, who had with seven Ships infested those Seas, and had made Prize of some of ours, which had Emboldned and Enrich'd him; as soon as *Dom John* saw him, with his Fleet before the Wind he made up to him, and setting on the Enemies Admiral, Boarded him, and after a brave Defence made him yield, two Ships he sunk, the rest by the advantage of the Night sav'd themselves; the Circumstances of this Fight are not to be found in Writing, the Carelesness of other excusing our silence.

Dom John returns to the Kingdome.

Is made Admiral of the Coast.

Defeats seven Ships of the *Corsaires.*

22. *Dom John* in a few days saw our Ships, when by Saluting one the other they rejoyc'd for the overthrow of

Brings in the *Indian* Fleet.

of the *Corsaire*; they came together over the Barr of *Lisbone*, the applause of his reception being so general, that he seem'd to have already weathered the storms of Hatred, or Envy; an Happiness, or Misery, which Great men in their Graves only purchase or avoid: In this success *Dom John* had no other reward than that of the Victory; for when the Debt is great, Kings, not to be thought Niggards, chuse rather to appear Ungratefull, being more willing to confess the Vices of their Person, than their Majesty.

23. 'Twas but a little time *Dom John* had to rest in the content of his Victory, being forc'd for a business of greater moment, to put on his Arms again, as I will (though against my Custom) more largely relate, taking it higher, not to Disjoynt the History. That famous Pirat *Haradin Barba-Rossa*, found himself almost quite broken with the loss of *Tunis* and *Goleta*, and more after the loss of his Galleys, losing by Land the power of a Tyrant, and by Sea the strength of a Pirat; yet was not this Arch Enemy so much shaken, but that *Italy* many years after sighed under his Lash; He had laid up in diverse places the best part of his Booty, as an other plank to save himself upon; this he presented to *Solyman* the *Grand Signior*, of Valew enough to efface, or excuse, the disgrace of his Fleet, and Flight at *Tunis*; which was yet fresh in *Solymans* grief, and memory; withall represented what he could do against the *Christians*, that taking the Sea at first with only two Galliots ill fitted out, his Valour and Success had made him so formidable and powerfull, that with their own spoils he entertain'd them with a sharp Warr, that the Jaols of *Africa* would not hold the Slaves; that in the Kingdome of *Naples*, in all *Apulia*, and the *Terra de Lavoro*, he had committed such Outrages, that neither their Blood, nor Tears were yet dry; that the Galleys of *Sicily* out of fear rotted at Anchor; That, that *Andrea Doria* (so much sought to by the Princes of *Europe*) could not but confess how oft he was forc'd

to Row for't, to escape *Barba-Rossa*, that he fear'd not to Cite his Enemies as witnesses of his Actions; that the Emperour *Charls* (Nettled with so many Losses, seeing *Barba-Rossa* only over-cast his Victories) did more like the impatient Man, than the Souldier, joyn all the Forces of *Germany*, *Italy*, *Spain*, and *Flanders*, to Destroy him, rashly exposing the best of his Kingdoms, to the chance of his either losing or getting the Day, and though his old Fortune left him not, he only got the credit of the Battail without any profit, (for Dispossessing one Enemy of *Tunis*, investing an other in't) neither was the Victory so entire that it Cost him not Ships and Men, and with the expence of so great a force he had exhausted the Exchequer of *Spain*; that now was the true time to ruine *Christendome*, weakned with a great Warr, and grown careless with a seeming Victory; that in the Streight of *Gibraltar* was the famous City of *Ceita*, (the Port whence heretofore the *Africans* with Victorious Arms entred on their Conquest of *Spain*) which the *Portuguese* held with weak Walls, and a poor Garrison, more bent upon Disturbing their Neighbours, than securing themselves from 'em, because heightned with their prosperity in the *East*, they slighted things at home, like Rivers that are largest at their greatest distance from their Spring-head; that if the *Grand Signior's* Majesty were inclinable to bring under his Dominion that so considerable a part of *Europe*, He would undertake with a reasonable number of Galleys to possess him of *Ceita*; by which those who were farthest *West* should Live in awe of his Empire. Thus discourst the *Corsaire*, endeavouring with an others force to recover the Credit and Station from which he was fall'n. And as in Princes Courts, great Designs more than possible are listned to, and *Barba-Rossa's* Experience and Valour had so good security, proud and warlick *Solyman* began to give ear to a design of so great Importance, and so well laid for the peace and prosperity of his Empire: He willingly heard

heard *Barba-Rossa* perswading him that the Benefit of this Action would out-weigh the Difficulty; The *Moors* of *Africa* too kindled the *Turks* indignation, who Lamented they could not breath quietly but in peace with us, some bewailing their lost Liberty, others the Effronts of their Prophet in their ruind *Mosques*; for the remedy of these grievances, they strove to engage the *Turk* upon his Zeal, and Greatness, which Motives concerning Religion, and Majesty, might veil over the Ambition, and justifie the Action.

24. *Charls* the Emperour Sollicitous what *Barba-Rossa* did in *Constantinople*, knowing that that Stock (whose Branches he had Lopt) was not so Dry, but that it might with anothers warmth, produce fresh Poison, did all he could to know what the *Turk* resolv'd about the invasion of *Spain*, and though the first Blow was aim'd at *Ceita*, yet (Victory never stopping where it begins) and unwilling to be crush'd in our ruins, He ordered the providing of Ships, Listing men, and the doubling those Garrisons which were in the Ports of the *Streights* mouth, writing to the King *Don John* his Brother-in-law the News he had; that they might joyntly provide for the resisting the common Enemy.

The Emperour adviseth the King.

25. The news coming to *Portugall*, the King immediately fell upon Fortifying *Ceita*, whose Defence was only after the rate of those Times; and we being Conquerours in *Africa*, kept our Garrisons by our Neighbours fear. *Dom Affonso de Noronha* was then Governour of *Ceita*, who was by the King entrusted with the Fortifications, and had sent him Men, Materials, and Engeneers. The Emperour desir'd the King, that our Fleet might come forth and joyn with his at *Cales*, under the Command of *Dom Alvaro Bacaon*, and so expect the Enemy in the *Streights* mouth, where, happen what would, the protection of his Ports would secure their Retreat; upon Debate, the joyning of the Fleets seem'd reasonable, that

Desires aid of him against the *Turk*.

all the weight of the Warr might not lye upon our Forces.

26. The King was busie in finding out one to Command the Fleet, and though there were men enough in our Kingdome, whom the Experience and Dangers of our Conquests had made Souldiers, yet *Dom John de Castro*'s Name made it self room amongst the first; t'was his Pride neither to ask or to deny any Service for his Country: We know that though King *John* lov'd his Valour, he car'd not for his Right, so that what he got by one Virtue, he lost by an other; and we observ'd not that he had any Place or Preferment about the King, because so free a Spirited man might be endured as a Subject, not as a Favorite. The Fleet was ready to Sail, a great part of the Nobility of the Kingdome on Board, and the Souldiers expecting who should Command in so considerable an Expedition, when on a sudden *Dom John de Castro* was nam'd to be the Man, to the general satisfaction even of his Competitors.

The King makes *Dom John* General.

27. The King sent for *Dom John*, acquainting him with the News from the Emperour, and with the Designs of the *Turk*, expressing to him with what Envy he sent him upon so Honourable an Employment; but since it was the Royal Prison of Kings, to conferr Honour, and not to be in a condition to deserve it; He entrusted him with that Fleet, in confidence he would, with the Arms of the *Castro*'s quarter the Banners he wonn from the *Turks*; and leave them more Honourable to his Posterity, than he receiv'd them from his ancestors; *Dom John* kist the Kings hand with a sence of his Favours, knowing how much better it was to be esteem'd, than countenanc'd by Princes.

He joyns with the Emperours General.

28. On the Twelfth of *August* 1543. all the Fleet set Sail, and in few days with favourable Winds came in sight of *Gibraltar*, where they found the Emperours Fleet at Anchor, which receiv'd ours with all the Ceremony of the Sea, by their often repeated Salutations

tions Rejoycing and Affrightnings on the place. *Dom Alvaro Bacaon* with the Chief Officers of the Fleet, came presently to Visit *Dom John de Castro* on Board, where (when the Complements were ended) he gave him an account of what he heard of the Enemy, and that according to Intelligence, his first Onset would be upon *Ceita*; they then fell upon't, that the Fleets of two such great Princes being joyned, it lay upon both their Honours to Fight the Enemy, though he should be much stronger; that we Fought in our own Seas, and in sight of our own Ports, which would be able in the Fight to furnish us with fresh men, and our battered Ships would have a refuge at hand; that though the *Turks* should get the Victory, they would be so broken, as not to be able to set upon any place in the *Streight*, which, by Fighting, let the success be what it would, they should secure; Besides, the Orders they had under Seal to find out the Enemy, could not be understood otherwise with safety to their Honour and Obedience. Having taken this so precise and bold Resolution, the Souldiers were all on Fire, and the Chief Commanders Sollicitous in giving out their Orders, and disposing for so great an Affair; when on a suddain advises came thick, that *Barba-Rossa* with his whole Fleet was coming towards the Streight. *Dom John de Castro* presently sends for his men who were on shore, Commands the Captains to fit and trim their Ships, and sends word to *Dom Alvaro* he was weighing, who coold of his first heat by an imaginary sight of the Enemy, writ to *Dom John*, that new accidents must have new Counsails; that by the Spies intelligence, he knew *Barba-Rossa*'s Fleet was double to the *Armados*; that 'twas neither according to the Intention or for the Service of their Princes, to lose themselves in so apparent a Danger; that while their Fleets were entire, the Enemy could undertake no great matter, and if in the Fight they should have the worst of't, all the places of the *Streight* would be the reward of the Victory;

They discourse about the Battail.

Resolve to Fight.

The *Spanish* General changeth his mind.

Endeavours to bring off *Dom John*.

ctory; that 'twas much against his humour to desist from Fighting, but the Service of *Cesar* was to be minded before the Gallantry of particular Persons; that he desir'd him to bring all his Fleet into Port, and as the *Turk* mov'd, they would more safely conclude what was to be done. *Dom John de Castro* answer'd the *Spanish* General, that he alter'd not his Opinion at the sight of the Enemy, that their appearing timorous would encourage the *Turks*, whose design being to get footing in *Spain*, the Fleets ought out of honour to engage, much more out of a sense of the Effront; what would the World say, if the Forces of two such great Princes joyn'd only to manage a defensive Warr against *Barba-Rossa*, letting the *Turkish* Banners Lord it in our Seas, in sight of the Eagles of the Empire, and the Cinques of *Portugall*; that he was resolv'd to expect the Enemy, not fearing to be Blam'd however the day went, because, if worsted, lost men answer'd nothing, and no body would call Conquerours to question.

He persists in Fighting with the *Turks*.

29. But neither had this Resolution force enough to sway the *Spanish* General *Dom Alvaro Bacaon*; we are not certain whether he thought it the better or the more secure way. *Dom John de Castro* put himself in the *Streights* mouth, where he lay three days: here he had advice, that the Enemies Fleet steered another course, by Dissentions of the Chief Officers, or (as other Memorials have it) *Barba-Rossa* had received new Orders from the *Turk*, to bring back the Fleet; yet the Gallantry of *Dom John de Castro*'s staying in the *Streight*, deserv'd envy from the Living, glory from Posterity, since for the obtaining a memorable Victory, not Courage, but Occasion was wanting; though this so generous resolution was diversly tax'd in *Spain*, those Branding it, who call all extraordinary actions Temerity; yet I believe, those who most condem'd it, would have been content to have it themselves.

And stays for 'em three days in the *Streights*.

30. *Dom John* seeing, by the Enemies retiring, those places above their fear, went to *Ceita*, to communicate

some

some part of his instructions to *Dom Affonso Noronha*, who receiv'd him with so many Shot, as the *Spaniards* in *Gibraltar* thought the Fleet had been engag'd, yet would they not weigh Anchor and come forth; so alterable were they in their first, so firm in their second resolution. Here *Dom John* had news that the *Moors* had laid close siege to *Alcacere Ceguer*, a place our men kept in *Africa* at an unnecessary charge and danger; the Governour was a Gentleman of the Family *de Freitas*, he immediately sent his Son *Dom Alvaro* with part of the Fleet, and Orders to put relief into the Town, and to continue in the Port till the Enemy sail'd out first, which he did, providing the place with Victuals and Ammunition; and the *Moors* Army consisting of Hot-headed men, the heat of their first Onset being cool'd, they rais'd the siege. *Dom Alvaro* return'd to the rest of the Fleet, which, (having secur'd *Ceita*, and freed it from fear of the *Turks*) return'd to *Lisbone*, where the Fame of both his adventures was arriv'd before, which was the greater, by lighting on Valour so unquestionable; but *Dom John* who counted nothing great, and despis'd his own Actions, avoided popular applause by retiring to *Sintra*, either out of Modesty, or Hight, not Valewing any thing he did worthy of himself.

He sends his Son to relieve *Alcacere Ceguer.*

He returns to *Lisbone*, and retires to *Sintra.*

31. The King *Dom John* was about finding out one to Govern the State of *India*, *Martin Affonso de Soussa* having staid out his Time, and instantly desiring a Successour, the affairs of the *East*, upon diverse Emergencies declining, and he unwilling that the glory of his Actions should be foil'd by a mis-carriage in the Warr, very well knowing that the Peoples ignorance might occasion such a disgrace as might discredit many Victories; for so considerable an employment, the King look'd upon men differently qualified, upon some, who for the antiquity of their Blood, without respect to their Deservings, us'd to Inherit the great places, a second piece of Tyranny of the Nobilities invention,

upon others, who were mean in their Birth, but famous in Themselves; who lost what was due to their Merits, because others had none; so as for so eminent an employment deserts not well Born, or a bare Title would not do.

Is propos'd by the Infant for Governour in the *Indies*.

32. The King on these reasons irresolv'd whom to chuse to trust with the weight of so great a Government; ask'd the Infant *Dom Lewis*, whom, (as affairs now stood) He should make Governour in the *Indies*: He told him the opinion he had of *Dom John de Castro*'s Temper, that, though in the business of the *Streights*, many thought he had behav'd himself too Daringly; yet 'twas certain, there's no Souldier but would be glad to have been guilty of so Honourable a fault; that, though those who envy'd him, accus'd him of being High and Cynical, because he begg'd no Rewards, or Courted the Ministers of State, these faults were of so good a kind, that *Dom John*'s Vices might be more Valew'd than others Virtues; that he knew none but *Dom John de Castro*, who could keep up the first Discipline of the *Indies*, who serv'd so unconcern'd for his own interest, as if he despis'd all earthly Rewards, and his Majesty were not a King of Men, but a God of Vassals; that he did very much love *Dom John de Castro* for his Qualities, but so impartially, that he should Valew his Deserts (though separated from his Person) in any other.

See *John de Barro*'s Hist. of *India*, Dec. 6. Cap. 1. Fol. 1.

The King chuseth him, and speaks to him.

33. The King, (with whom the Infant's opinion had no little credit, seeing him prize *Dom John* with a Zeal for his Prince, and Knowledge of his Friend) lik'd the Hint the Infant gave him, (whose Authority too had an influence over the minds of others) and sending for *Dom John de Castro* to *Evora*, where the "Court was, in the publick Hall, told him, I have of "late been Sollicitous to provide one whom I might "send Governour to the *Indies*, and was of opinion I "might find him in the Family of the *Castros*, from "whose Stock the Kings my Predecessors have always

" tane Generals for their Armies; and Regents for " their Provinces; I too flatter my self that the Fruit " of so generous a Root cannot degenerate; and that " the rather, by guessing what you will do by your " former Actions, which have given you so just a repute " in the Kingdoms opinion, and my esteem, and for " which I confidently put into your hands the Govern- " ment of the *Indies*, expecting that you will so carry " your self there, as I may give what you do, for a pat- " tern to those who succeed you. *Dom John* kist the King's hand, better pleas'd with the Honour, than the Employment, in so great a charge only Valewing the not seeking it: There were diverse Opinions in the Court about this Election, some found fault with it out of Envy, others out of Custom, and where they could not tax any Defect in parts, they charged the excess; yet was it so lik'd of the most, and best, that the King was glad he had pitch'd upon one, who so much pleas'd every one.

34. The King gave him Orders presently to provide the Fleet, not letting any Body else have to do with it, as is falsly writ by one Author, who tells us, that *Dom John* went Discontented to the *Indies*, because he was not Comply'd with in some particulars; a thing so thwarting our certain information, and the little ambition of this Gentleman, who was more busie in what to deny, than what to ask, as if the King had met with one he was not to entreat but obey.

35. He resolv'd to carry with him his Sons, *Dom Fernando*, and *Dom Alvaro*, who being the Eldest, had bespoke some rich Cloaths, allow'd of by his Years and Quality; *Dom John* passing by chance through the *Jubiteria*, saw a pair of Embroidered Breeches hang out, and stopping his Horse ask'd whose they were? the man answering, that *Dom Alvaro* the Governours Son of *India* bespoke 'em, *Dohn John* ask'd for a pair of Cisers, and cut 'em in pieces, leaving this word with the Master of the Shop: Bid the Boy buy Arms. We read not that

He finds fault with his Sons rich Cloaths.

A street in *Lisbone* where the Whole-salemen sell Cloaths.

that the Discipline of the old *Romans* was more exemplary or severe.

The Ships and their Commanders.

36. *Dom John* quickly made ready the Fleet, without the oppression and complaints of the Poor, the Extorsion which great Officers carry out by their Princes favour, being then not us'd, or not known; the main of the Fleet was six great Ships, on which went two thousand paid men. The Admiral call'd the Saint *Thomas*, on which the Governour went, who gave her that name which he afterwards call'd upon in the Field, justly imploring the protection of the Apostle of the *Indies* in all his undertakings; the other Captains of the Convoy, were *Dom Jeronimo de Menezes*, Son and Heir of *Dom Henrique*, Brother to the Marquiss of *Villa Real*; *Jorge Cabral*, *Dom Manoel da Silveyra*, *Simaon de Andrade*, and *Diego Rebello*.

What time they set Sail.

37. All the Fleet set Sail the seventeenth of *March* 1545. and in a few days they had been at Sea, 'twas told the Governour, that in his Ship there were about two hundred who had their allowance of Diet, and nothing to do there; some were not receiv'd because useless, others were offenders who got on Board by stealth: The Officers were importunate with the Governour to put them on Board the Hospital Ship, so to rid his own, and keep their Provisions for the Casualties of so long a Voyage; but the Governour (more Compassionate than Cautious, making his and the poor mens case the same) follow'd on his course; in a little time Provision began to be scarce, on which the Mariners and Souldiers were forc'd to complain of the Governour, who with so Venturous compassion would to save a few, hazard all; most were of opinion to Land those men on the *Cape de Verde* Islands, where the Offenders would be out of the reach of Justice, and the Necessitous kept from Starving; but the Governour upon Reflection, that the Air and Soil of the Islands at that time of the Year, were in every ones opinion unhealthfull, resolv'd to protect the poor men

The Governours compassion.

When the Winds do not blow.

in his own Ship, hoping to preserve both himself and them, saying in their behalf, It would be unhumanly done to deny them the Sea who fled from the Land; They had but little Winds, till they met with the Trade winds on the Coast of *Guine*, where the Governours Ship striking upon the ground, was like to overset, those Seas, in the judgment of Mariners being clear, and where the Card mark'd no Sands. Every ones Confusion was like his who drinks in Death unexpectedly, the season and fear too heightned the danger, when the Ship being all on one side, and not feeling the Rudder, began to be on float again; it might be chance, but seem'd a miracle. The Governour commanded 'em to shoot off three Pieces, that the Ships which were on stern him might avoid the Sands, which, not understanding the Warning came upon 'em; but with better Luck, than Skil, though of the same Burden with the Admiral, scap'd the Sands, finding in the same place other Fortune, the cause of which pusled the Seamen.

The danger his Ship was in.

Not feeling the Rudder.

38. The Governour, with the whole Fleet got together, pursuing his Voyage arriv'd at *Mocambique*, where the Landing of, and the procuring conveniencies for, the sick men was what he chiefly minded, being in that assisted by his two Sons, *Dom Alvaro*, and *Dom Fernando*, who then were Heirs apparent of his Charitableness, afterwards of his Valour; the time he staid at *Mocambique*, he observ'd, the Fortress the State hath there to be ill contriv'd in being too far from the shore, by which, with difficulty it provided and reliev'd our Fleets, and being in a bottom was commanded by many Hills, which also hindring the good Air, made it unwholsome; He put this to those who either by Study, or Experience, had any Skil in this Science, and all agreed that the faults in the Fortification were judiciously observ'd; what was Debated was immediately put in hand, and with the choice of a convenient Situation he ordered Materials and Work-men for a new defence;

He arrives at *Mocambique*.

Changeth the Fortress, seating it better.

defence; and this going on in the Governours sight, the Gentry as well as others carry'd Stones, some for Flattery, others to promote the Building.

He departs for *Goa*.

39. The Fortress made tenable, and the Sick recover'd by the fresh Air and fresh Provisions on shore, the Governour set Sail again, and having the Winds always favourable, cast Anchor on the 10th. of *September* at the Barr of *Goa*; where, *Martin Affonso de Sousa*, (by a Ship which went before) having had notice his Successour was near, provided to receive him with such Jollity as might shew the content he had, in welcoming his Guest, and leaving his Government; he went presently in a Rich Brigantine to meet him at Sea, whence he carry'd him to *Antoni Correa's* House of Pleasure, whilst the Solemnity of his reception was preparing; there he Feasted the Governour, Gentlemen, and Captains of the Fleet, with so much Exquisiteness in the manner, and aboundance in the meat, that it seem'd he was doing the last honour to his expiring charge. That night there were Balls and Dancing, Rejoycings which the simplicity of old *Portugall* carry'd to the *East*. Here the Governour staid two days, attended by all the Gentlemen of the place, who forsook *Martin Affonso de Sonsa*, even those who were his Favourites, and he had rais'd from nothing, discipplin'd in the Oriental ingratitude of the *Indians*, who cast stones at the setting Sun, and adore him rising.

His arrival, and reception.

40. When the Entry was to be, the two Governours were in a Faluque with gilded Oars, and an awning of divers-colour'd Silks; the Castles and Ships entertain'd 'em with the horrour of reiterated shootings, the Vivas and expectation of the common people did without any cunning flatter the new Government; they came to Land at a great place where the Common-Councel in a body expected them, and when they were plac'd with all the Ceremony vanity for that purpose hath invented, one of the Magistrates made an Elaborate speech, in which the State expected a great deal of happiness

in

in the new Minister: after the Governour had heard the publick Flatteries, he listned to the private ones of a great many, who with them made way for their particular Interest.

41. When the Solemnity was ended, and *Don John* possest of the Government of *India*, *Martin Affonso* went to *Cochim*, to provide for his return into the Kingdome; the Governour immediately was engag'd in the care of quieting the People, who were all in an Uproar for the alteration of the Money, which the King's Officers had rais'd, to the prejudice of the Subjects, and the scandal of the Neighbouring Pagans; I'le tell the occasion begun it.

What condition he found his Government in

42. There is current in *India* a low sort of Money, which they call *Bazaruccos*, which amongst *Christians*, *Moors*, and *Pagans*, had always the same Valew; this being of Copper, (which then came from *Portugall* and bore no price) the Officers thought fit for the King's profit to raise the price, the alteration of the Money was solemnly Proclaim'd, and it began to pass at the new Rate; but, as this Legal worth was not intrinsical, (the Valew coming from the Law, not from the weight) the *Pagans* (not subject to strangers Laws) brought not in the usual Provision, and the people seem'd to suffer by their own orders; the Chief Officers back'd it as the King's cause, standing for the King's profit, in the Peoples destruction; the whole City cry'd out, that the Kings of *Portugall* never encreast their Treasuries by their miseries, nor us'd to Drink in Gold plate their Subjects tears; that the *Pagans* and *Moors* made their Braggs that not being able by the Sword to ruine the *Portuguese*, by their own Laws they Destroy'd 'em, arming against 'em the ambition of their Governours. The hunger and liberty of the Petitioners grew high, justify'd by a good cause, and the Conformity of the common oppression; with these grievances the Magistrates of the City, with the poor, Women, and Children, (some full of Complaints, the other

by the Alteration of the *Bazaruccos*.

He hears the City and People.

other of Arguments) went to the Governour, who Commanding the people to be quiet, heard, as a Judge the Magistracy, as a Father the rest, and hunger admitting of no long Cures, ordered the next day for determining the business; thus he sent them away satisfy'd, some believing that (as was the custom of *India*) it being his predecessors Act, it would by him be counted unjust. The same evening he sent for the King's Officers, and after hearing what they had to say for themselves, referr'd the matter to the ablest Lawyers, and those best skill'd in the policy of that State, who unanimously agreed the decree to be Cruel, and very contrary to the Pious intentions of our Princes; this opinion too was countenanc'd by Custom, and the Peoples privileges, besides other Legalties, which (not to make our History tedious) we lay aside. This Law being revok'd by the Governour, Provisions began to come in from the Inland-Country, and the people made him a present of those Lives he had by the indulgent remitting the Tax redeem'd.

His resolution about it.

43. This business made an end of with so much repute to the King's Clemency, Embassadours came to him from *Hidalcaon*, who (after the Customary salutes and giving him joy of his Office) desir'd the Delivery of a Prisoner on the terms agreed on with his Predecessor, and this business coming to that height as to engage the State in an open Warr, we will not leave its beginning unrelated.

Hidalcaon's first Embassy.

44. *Bazarb* Prince of *Balagate* Dying, when *Nuno de Cunha* was Governour, *Meale*, though in his Cradle, was Heir apparent to the Crown, then was *Hidalcaon* the second Person in the Kingdome in Power, and the first in Courage, having in the late Warr with the Neighbour Princes given a large testimony of his Actions; *Hidalcaon* (as amongst this so Barbarous a people Men reign oftner by making use of their Opportunities, than by observing what's Right) seeing his own strength, and the Heirs incapacity, pave his ambitions way

Meale's is the better cause.

way to the Crown, began to try the hearts of the great Ones, before whom with a great deal of Artifice he deplor'd the miseries of the Kingdome, in so Infant a successour, under whom they must obey or endure, as so many Kings all those he fancy'd; that the Princes with whom they had now Warrs would not let slip this occasion of ruining 'em, when they saw him who should defend 'em in the Cradle; that where, there were so many, they ought to find out one to save their Country; that he would be the first should obey him, because the Government of the Kingdome could not wait those slow motions, by which Nature gives a little one first Strength, then Understanding; that if with unprofitable obedience they should adore *Meale* in his Nurses arms, he did not doubt but by keeping their King, they would lose their Kingdome. He was affable to the People, liberal to the Souldiers, as if he desir'd to Reign not for himself, but for them: Ambitiously making use of, the whole Chain of Vertues, not as necessary for Living, but Reigning. The great Ones at last offered him the Crown, believing, he would always remember he was his Subjects Creature, and retain constantly in his Memory so signal a grace.

45. *Hidalcaon* was Liberal and Stout, and without doubt would have been a great Prince, had he kept the Kingdome by the same Vertues he put on to atchieve it; but seeing himself obey'd, those affected Artifices not having any natural motion, were at an end, and broke out into ambition and pride, the Vices of his Person; He did not then speak of killing *Meale*, either out of a counterfeit Clemency, or an unheard of Cruelty, intending perhaps that the poor Prince should by a servile obedience confirm the Scepter he had usurp'd from him. The Nobility of the Kingdome (repenting when 'twas too late, and seeing they now could not without danger, be either Traitors or Loyal) consulted how *Meale* might secure himself from the Tyranny of *Hidalcaon*, as if the unfortunate Prince had had more

right to his Life then his Kingdome ; some years past in these contrivances, in which *Meale* arriv'd at Age to apprehend his danger, and considering that his presence reproach'd the Tyrants guilty Conscience, (who plotted with his blood to quiet the memory of his usurping the Crown,) by the Counsel of those who took the Kingdome from him, He went to *Cambaya*, where he was well receiv'd, both King and People shewing, how much they resented the miseries of the Blood-Royal; but, as such favours have more ambition in them, then charity, they lasted not long, for, only the first days they treated him as a King, the rest as one Persequuted, but *Meale* still continu'd in *Cambaya*, counting more tolerable, the sleights of a Stranger, then the injuries of a Tyrant.

46. In the mean time, *Hidalcaon's* great design was, to destroy those who gave him the Crown, whom, for all they had a just title to his favour by being complices in his Treason, he hated, because they put him in mind, either of his Obligation, or faults, and being now jealous of his own Actions, he found that Cruelty would root him faster then Clemency, so that his own Vice, and necessity together made him doubly so; upon pretence of correcting faults, either imputed, or forgot, (covering his Tyranny with a veil of Justice) he inchroach'd upon the Estates of the great Ones, to Level 'em with the common people, Confident, by pulling down the Nobility, to get into the poorer sort, who (out of a natural dislike of their own Fortune) do always delight in the fall of those above them; and they (seeing their patience work'd not their quiet) consulted how they might restore *Meale*, some were for Revenge, others for Calling him in; they had their private meetings, where they took divers Resolutions, which fear, or the difficulty of the business, (harder to execute then design) every day altered; their forc'd obedience being at last wrack'd to the utmost stretch by new oppressions, they endeavour'd by *Hidalcaon's*

Death

Death to redreſs their Error, and hide the ſhame of their former Treaſon; the Deſperate, not the Bold were of this opinion, becauſe now *Hidalcaon* liv'd with the ſtrength of a King, and the circumſpection of a Tyrant; He was aſſiſted by the people, who hating the King, lov'd the Cruelties he us'd againſt the Gentry, who, for the diſproportion of theirs, and the others Fortunes are always obnoxious. The Plotters fearfull of themſelves, and that their hatred would cool by delay, their baſe ſervitude too, turn Cuſtomary, ſeeing their own Force not equal for the enterprize, laid out for aſſiſtance from abroad; they bethought themſelves of imparting the buſineſs to *Martin Affonſo de Souſa*, (then Governour of the State of *India*) deſiring him to ſend for *Meale* from *Cambaya*, and let him be at *Goa*; that though he refus'd the glory of reſtoring him, he thereby would keep *Hidalcaon* in awe, and inclinable to ſerve the States occaſions.

47. *Martin Affonſo* being perſwaded, that 'twas more convenient to increaſe then extinguiſh this Flame which begun to burſt out, 'twixt *Hidalcaon* and his Subjects, and that the weakning of a Warlike and Powerfull neighbour would turn to the States advantage; (Cloaking theſe conveniences with more plauſible pretences, as the ſheltering under our Arms a diſpoſſeſt and perſecuted Prince, an Action glorious abroad and profitable at home) reſolv'd to find out *Meale* at *Cambaya*, giving him notice of his Subjects inclinations for his Reſtauration, who would be more eager when they ſaw the State protected both his Cauſe and Perſon. The *Moor* upon the receit of ſo unlook'd for a meſſage, (counting the pity, of men not only different but contrary in Religion, extraordinary) betook himſelf to the faith and favour of the State, and with his poor Family embarking himſelf, arriv'd at *Goa*, where he was by the Governour receiv'd, with honours more befitting his Blood then Fortune, by ſome conſtrued to be done him, more for effronting the Neighbour then reſpecting

See *John de Barro's* Hiſt. of *India*, Dec. 5. Lib. 10. Cap. 11.

specting the Guest. *Meale's* arrival (who begun now to Reign in the hearts of a great many) being voic'd all along that Coast, his party began to be stronger among the Plotters, who now saw, his cause sheltered under the protection of our Arms, and his name sounding better in the peoples Ears.

Hidalcaon's Embassage.

48. *Hidalcaon* upon consideration, that the State (whose victorious Arms were the more dreadfull by their nearness) did not send for *Meale* only to secure his Person, but defend his Cause, dispatch'd Embassadours to *Martin Affonso de Sousa*, giving him notice that he understood *Meale* was in his power, whom, he thought Fortune preserv'd, to disturb the peace of the *East*; that he knew what Tirle some Seditious spirits gave him, who being weary of Obeying, strove to set up new Lords whom they might Command; that *Hidalcaon* would not tell what mov'd him to seize on the Crown, because if Princes were bound to give account of their Pretensions, there were no difference 'twixt King and People; that the right of Princes was to be judged of God, not of Men; that 'twas the Worlds opinion now that there was no difference in Princes titles, but only in their Persons; that he deny'd not, that Contemptible and Cowardly *Meale* was of the Royal blood, but, that, the fault Nature committed, Fortune would correct by giving the Kingdome to him who was Daring and Stout; that nature to Lyons only gave a Crown by their Birth, Men she let winn it and wear it; that many things appear'd injust to the World, because besides Custom; that for a man who was worthy of it, to possess himself of a Kingdome, would at first be look'd upon as a Scandal, afterwards as a Law; that *Meale* was the basest Fellow ever Born in his Kingdome, and he the most Fortunate, and naturally all men hated natures Monsters, and lov'd Fortunes prodigies: that we should examine our selves, how we came to Lord it in *Asia*? what Kin we vvere to *Sabayo*, that he shoulo leave us *Goa*? how near vve vvere *Sultan Badour* to

Inherit

Inherit *Dio* from him? whether *Achem* left us *Malaxa* by his Will? and all the places which pay us Tribute all over the *East*? that he desir'd us not to quarrel at that Title in him, that made us absolute Lords of the World; that, we should let God alone with the Government of the World, and being Born farthest *West*, not busie our selves to compose the Disorders of *Asia*; that he would have us know; he had in his Kingdome Mines of different Metals, that some furnish'd him with Gold for his Friends, others with Iron for his Enemies; that in the last place, he desir'd the Governour to deliver him up *Meale*, that, by the mercy he should use him withall, the World might see how worthy he was to Reign, who so treated his greatest Enemy; that, his Embassadours had order to settle all that concern'd the State.

49. *Martin Affonso* having receiv'd the Letters, and given Audience to *Hidalcaon's* Embassadours, understood by 'em, that they proffer'd for *Meales* person an hundred and fifty thousand *Pardaos*, and the main Land of *Bordez* and *Salsete*, very considerable to the State for its Revenue and Nearness to *Goa*. *Martin Affonso* look'd upon the business, as very weighty, and either Face promising great advantages; the restoring of a Prince, and pulling down a Tyrant, was a design worthy the Arms of Christians, by which the State would purchase no ordinary reputation, letti g the World see, that our Banners were not displaid in *Asia*, either to usurp Kingdoms, or get Riches, since their employment was that the *Pagans* and *Moors* of the *East*, should keep the true Faith towards God, and Justice amongst themselves: On the other side 'twas said, that if *Meale* after a long Warr should come to Reign, he could not give the State more, then now without it *Hidalcaon* offer'd, and that the *Moors* by their hatred and Religion being Enemies, the World would laugh to see us with our own Blood, destroy one Infidel and set up an other; when too our happiness depended on both their ruines,

besides that our Arms came not to *India* to defend the Enemies of the Faith, but to destroy 'em; that if *Meale* found no Protection from the King of *Cambaya*, his near Kinsman, why should he look for't from the *Portuguese* to whom he was an Enemy? that when he found himself restor'd, and strong, the first Lance that was hurl'd against the State would be his, because the Neighbourhood of so brave men who made him King would be suspicious to him, and the Memory of so great a good turn was enough to make him Hate us.

50. *Martin Affonso*, on grounds not throughly weigh'd, resolv'd at last to deliver up *Meale*, dispach'd the Embassadours; and with them *Galvaon Viegas* an Honourable Gentleman, with full Power, to settle the Contract, in the manner it hath been related, sending with the consent of the Embassadours to take immediate possession of the main Land, in virtue of *Hidalcaon*'s profer.

51. In this condition did *Dom John de Castro* find the affairs of *Meale*, and was sued to by a new Embassy from *Hidalcaon*, in confidence of the Capitulation made with his Predecessor; but *Dom John* with different maturity answered *Hidalcaon*, that the *Portuguese* were faithfull to their Enemies, much more to their Guest; that the propositions of his Predecessor, were more for a right understanding of the cause, then to determine it; that the main Land belong'd to the State by more antient Grants, and that it was just out of its Revenue to maintain *Meale*, in gratitude to the Kings his Predecessors, who annex'd it to the State, that he should suffer him quietly to enjoy this little memory of his Right; that the States securing his Person, was not yet Protection but Charity; that he should not with over-hasty Arms disturb the Peace, for then he would make sure what he fear'd, provoking the State to take in hand the revenging of both; and because his Embassadours had hinted that, the denying *Meale* would necessarily make a Breach, He put 'em in mind that most

The Governours answer.

See *John de Barro's* History of *India*. Dec. 6. Lib. 1. Cap. 2.

most of the Fortresses we had made in *India*, were founded on the ashes of destroy'd Kingdoms; that the *Portuguese* were like the Sea, which raiseth it self and grows greater in Storms; that for his part as he sought not a Warr, so he could not deny one.

52. With this answer the Governour dismist the Embassadours, who, by his firmness in delivering it, understood that neither fear or advantage would bend him to give up *Meale*; Immediately he put himself in readiness to make or expect a Warr, which coming from a neighbour Prince we might sooner feel the Blow, then see the Sword. He gave orders for the raising of Horse, which were to be about two hundred, and to serve under the same Colours, a more stout, then orderly Militia: He entrusted the Guard of the City with the Train-bands, and had Souldiers in pay ready for any suddain invasion of the Enemies. He set upon the making ready the Fleet out of hand, which by the Voyages and Warrs of his Predecessor, and the poverty of the State, he found all in pieces, and the strength of the Navy, being what is most considerable, here he wholly laid himself out; He new fitted the Vessels which lay in the River, made three Galleys, and six Round-bottom'd Ships with wonderfull speed, not failing the Officers in their pay, or his thanks; by which means the work went on, diligence over-coming time; He nam'd Captains of those Galleys and Ships, who intended the work as their own business, an expedient, which did a great deal towards the quickness of the dispatch, the goodness and plenty of Ammunion and Provision, with which (in an opportune and short time) the Fleet was ready, with this he so bridled the Neighbour Princes, as he hindred 'em from joyning with *Hidalcaon*, who had already sollicited them to shake off the yoak, as an advantage to the common Liberty.

53. *Hidalcaon*, having notice of the Governours resolution, appeal'd to the Justice of his Sword, endeavouring to carry the Warr from home, before *Meale's* *Hidalcaon's* first motion.

presence

presence rais'd the people, who by their commands, and advantages in the Warr, would make the cause their own; He presently on severe penalties forbid the Victuallers carrying the ordinary Provision, to *Goa*, which, having it all from the Inland, was not furnish'd to endure so suddain a Warr; after this he sent *Acedecaon* a stout *Turk* with ten thousand men, to take in, that part of the main Land, which Liv'd under our Obedience.

The Governour goes in Person.

54. But *Dom John de Castro* knowing, that first successes give reputation to a Warr, went out with two thousand Foot, and the Horse of the place to resist the Enemy; and being perswaded by a great many Gentlemen, that he should not engage his Person in so unequal a party; that it was not for the honour of a Governour of *India* to put on his Sword against one of *Hidalcaon's* Captains, nor to let the World know he look'd so much upon this Warr, especially having Gentlemen who deserv'd the honour and danger of the Action; it was not possible to disswade him from his first resolution, saying with more confidence then his Forces would bear, that he went out to Chastise, not to Overcome, and marching two Leagues from *Goa* he came in sight of the Enemy, who, lodg'd at the foot of a Hill with a River in their front, (which was to them instead of a Ditch and Trench) with the advantages of their numbers, and Encamping, expected ours, who though wearied with their March, re-inforcing themselves by the presence of the Governour, or sight of the Enemy, begun to pass the River with more Resolution, then Discipline, the Commanders could not stay, or order them, the most daring cast themselves into the River, and the more cautious were by this put upon a necessity; as to most of 'em to follow their Comrades example, past for Discipline.

55. The Governour with admirable prudence commanded those who staid behind to go over the River, knowing, that what was in the beginning a fault, was

now

now the Cure; and because that day he had not room enough to Order as a Commander, he Fought as a private Souldier. Our men run upon the *Moors* so furiously, that discouraged, with the first Onset, they gave ground, and their Ranks, being confus'd and broken by themselves, were disordered and overcome; Our men (which seldome happens) seeing an Army routed without loss. The *Moors* loss was great in their Flight, none at all in their Resistance; Ours were two Leagues executing the Liberty, and cruelty of Victory, gathering up the Arms those poor men flung away, as a burden, not a defence. The pursute lasted as long as the Day, the horrour of the Night freeing the Enemies from that of the Victory; Our Souldiers retreated, full of Blood, Honour, and Booty; the Governour kept the Field till the next day, without censuring the Souldiers for that Disorder which gave them the Victory, following the course of human judgements, which never speak well of Losses, or blame Victories.

He fights and routs the Enemy.

56. The Governour, at his Entry into *Goa*, was receiv'd with an extraordinary applause, from that people, so us'd to see, and slight Victories; and because, in this and many other Fights which *Dom John* wonn, he call'd upon the name of St. *Thomas*, the Apostle of the *Indies*, we believe they were got by the favour of so great a *Padrone*, who, to recompence the piety, and honour the memory of *Dom John de Castro*, was pleas'd, in the days of his Government, to discover that miraculous Cross, found at *Meliapor* on the Coast of *Choromandell*; the wonderfull Cross and the Body of the Saint being as it were cover'd with the same Earth, and as *Dom John de Castro* worshipp'd this sign of our Redemption, with a due, but a strange Reverence, (lighting always from his *Palanquim* or Horse when he met the Cross, and putting himself on his Knees) this discovery will not seem to have been by chance, since the mercies of Heaven come not by accident. We will give you the relation of the Mystery, because it carries

He returns to *Goa*.

His veneration to the Cross.

A kind of Sedan in the *Indies*, carry'd on mens Shoulders.

with it a successive miracle in testimony of the faith of the *East*, cultivated in those Countries with the Blood and Doctrine of our *Portuguese*.

The finding St. *Thomas's* Cross.

57. After the wonderfull finding the Body of this holy Apostle in the City, or rather ruins of *Meliapor*, (then call'd *Calamina*) the Kings, *Dom Manoel*, and *Dom John*, being with a pious Zeal inflam'd to revive those dead Ashes, which had been there from the first planting Christianity by the Apostle, (though now corrupted by the Doctrine of the *Armenian* and *Chaldean* Priests; who separated from the *Roman*-Catholick Church, did make those well-meaning Christians swallow dangerous Opinions, which by the pains of our Missionaries have in part been reform'd) set upon Building a Church in the same place where the Venerable Body of the Apostle was found, and opening the Foundations for the Fabrick, found a Cross (wrought in a Marble Pedestall) of four Spans long and three broad, besprinkled with dropps of Blood; which might be thought to be newly done, (the Cross was like that of the Knights of *Avizi*;) on the bottom of the Pedestall were lesser Crosses of the same fashion with the biggest, sprinkled with the same spots of Blood; on the top of the great Cross was a hovering Pidgeon, there was Old writing about it, which, (being in an unknown Tongue, and not in one continued sence) the Natives understood not; the oldest and most knowing Antiquaries in different Languages were consulted with, but none could make out the Character or meaning of the Writing, till a while after was brought a *Bramene* from *Narzinga*, who expounded it in current Sence, and said thus;

Thirty years after the Law of the Christians came into the World, on the 21th. *of* December, *the Apostle Saint* Thomas *Dy'd in* Meliapor, *where was the knowledge of God, change of Laws, and the destruction of the Devil; This God taught twelve Apostles, one of whom, with a staff in his hand, came to* Meliapor *where he Built a Temple, and the*

the Kings of Malabar, Choromandell, *and* Pandi, *with others of different Nations and Sects freely submitted themselves to Saint* Thomas's *Law; time was when the Saint was put to Death by a* Bramene, *and with his Blood made this Cross.*

This Exposition, being an hir'd Interpreters, in a matter of so great moment, our Nation did not too confidenly believe, but sent for an other *Pagan* Learn'd in all the Oriental Languages, who, knowing nothing of the other Exposition, decypher'd the Letters in the same manner, without any difference, the Copy of the Print (as you see it here) was brought to the King *Dom Sebastian* in the Year 1562.

Our Nation (with the greater expence in reverence to that place, which had been the Depository of so Sacred a pledge) went on in Building the Church, the Piety and Conflux of the people of *Malabar* was great too, at the sight of so notable a Testimony of their Faith. The Church was in a short time perfected, the Cross engrav'd on Marble (as we have said) serv'd in place of an Altar-piece. Divine Service began to be said there, with the Decency so remote a place would permit; and on the 18. of *December*, (the day of our * Ladies expectation) as Mass was saying in a full Congregation, when the Priest began the Gospel, the Holy Cross too began to be cover'd with a great Sweat, letting fall no little drops on the Altar. That the signs of the Miracle might be more Visible, the Priest stop't in the Sacrifice, wip't off the Humidity the Cross breath'd with the Corporalls, which (before a great many there present immediately seem'd dip't in Blood); the Holy Cross began presently to change its Alablaster to a paler Colour, which turn'd to an obscure Black, that too chang'd to an unusual bright *Azure*, which lasted as long as Mass, when that was done it came to the natural Colour of which 'twas found.

* A peculiar Feast in *Spain* and *Portugall*, when the B. Virgin look't to be brought to Bed.

A famous Miracle of the same Cross.

58. The same Miracle hath successively for many years been seen on the same day, and we know by good Authors and faithfull Relations that it yet happens sometimes, by which means, those Christians with a stronger Faith receive our Doctrine. This Miracle, after much arguing on both sides, was clear'd before the Bishop of *Cochim* in open Court, the proceedings came to this Kingdome, in the time of the King *Dom Henry*, the Cardinal, who, by the consent of Pope *Gregory* 13th. confirm'd the Miracle, which is now divulg'd in our own Chronicles and forein Authors. *Dom John de Castro* receiv'd the news of this Miracle with no ordinary shew of Piety, protecting Saint *Thomas's* Christians, opprest with the slavery of *Pagan* Princes, who had taken from 'em certain Grants and Priviledges, which by the intercession

How the Governour was affected with the News.

cession of the Holy Apostle had by the Kings their Predecessors been indulg'd 'em, but, by the hatred of the Infidels, and corruption of the times were only remembred.

59. *Hidalcaon* gave not over infesting us on the main Land with his usual incursions, which kept us on continual Duty, and hindered the Husbandmen from Tilling; upon which the Governour resolv'd to strike where the Blow might be most felt; He presently Commanded his Son *Dom Alvaro* to go out with the Fleet, he had provided, with Orders, to do all the hurt he could in *Hidalcaon's* Ports, giving the Souldiers all free Pillage, that the hopes of Plunder might make 'em not mention some Arrerages the State ow'd 'em; and put by others from playing the Merchants, a Corruption which stole upon a great many by the foul example of their Superiours.

He sends his Son *Dom Alvaro* against *Hidalcaon*.

60. *Dom Alvaro* put to Sea with 900. *Portuguese* and 400. *Indians* on six Ships and some long Boats with Oars, and after a few days Sailing spy'd four of *Hidalcaon's* Ships going with Stuffs and other Commodities to *Cambaya*. *Dom Alvaro* presently commanded his Captains to come on Head him, and the Boats to keep close to the shore, for fear the Enemy should out of Desperatness run a ground; the Ships were Merchant men, and but few Souldiers in 'em, who, seeing they could neither fly, nor defend themselves, sent aboard the Admiral two *Moor* Merchants, who, with reasons and tears, shew'd themselves not concern'd in the difference 'twixt *Hidalcaon* and the State, and profer'd a reasonable present toward the expence of the Fleet; but neither the covetousness of the Souldiers, or the policy of Warr would let them be heard, but the Ships were Boarded and sent to *Goa*, that the Prize might be divided according to the Governours Proclamation. Upon the arrival of those Ships at *Goa*, the people was strangely transported, seeing Victories so got one upon the neck of an other; in the first they prais'd the Cou-

He goes out with six Ships.

His prize.

rage

rage of the Father, in the second the Fortune of the Son.

61. *Dom Alvaro*, seeing opportunity and weather on his side, and that the Souldiers were contented because they had in hand the fruit of their late Enterprize, commanded his Pilot to steer to the Port of *Cambre*, where, since the breaking out of the Warr, *Hidalcaon* kept double Garrison; there were two Forts with Ordinance planted at the entrance of the Barr, and the Chanel was so narrow that without eminent danger our Ships could neither pass through, or ride there. The General *Dom Alvaro*, put to the Captains of the Fleet the apparent difficulties, which every one concluded of moment enough to be considered of; alleging that voluntary undertakings ought not to be set upon with so certain danger; that they should more to purpose carry on the Warr against *Hidalcaon*, by Lording it in his Seas, and in his sight, taking away his commerce; that there was more hazard then profit in what could be done by Land; that (as they saw) the Chanel was so begirt with those Forts, our Ships must pass by the mouth of the Canon; that the first Ship they should shatter, would hinder the rest from passing. But *Dom Alvaro* urging, that he was resolv'd to execute his Orders, which were, to get on shore and burn the Enemies Ports; the Councel replied by proposing, that he as General should stay to Command at Sea, and that most of the Commanders of the Ships would strive to pass the Barr, because if any thing should happen amiss to the Admiral of that Fleet, Son and Heir to the Governour of *India*, what greater Dammage could the State receive, then the necessity of engaging in so just a Vengeance? On which *Dom Alvaro* in a great deal of passion brake off the consult, saying, that he car'd for no Victories where his danger was not as great as the least common Souldiers; that, out of obedience he was their General, and in danger their Companion; that, he had instructions from the Governour, to venture his own Person

Dom Alvaro proposeth the Entry into Cambre

He resolves to invest.

Person on every occasion, his Souldiers but upon necessity; that he look'd upon the Dangers they represented to be less then those he came in chase of; because Honour was not to be purchas'd without hazarding; that he came from *Portugall* to find out this Day, which he hop't would be glorious for them all, and that in this Resolution he ask't not their advice; only that they would consult about the manner of the falling on. The Generals Gallantry, and Youth, did then excuse his Rashness, afterwards the Success; 'twas agreed that the men should go into the long Boats, and that at the beginning of the Dawning when Day-light was not well broke, and so the Enemy not sure of his aim, they should get on shore; they all that Night provided themselves, seeing in the Generals looks hopes of Victory. The General (having left sufficient Guard on the Ships) got on shore, with 800. Choise men, and with Fortune so declaring for him, that of a great many Shot that lighted on the Boats, not one either kill'd or wounded a Souldier, this accident being a Disposition to, or beginning of the Victory.

He gets on shore.

62. The City (which ran along a great Plain) contain'd five thousand Families, the Houses by themselves, and not leaning on one an other, without any other policy, union, or share of ground, then what every one took for his pleasure or ability; and yet the Turrets and Balconies of every House, did altogether present a rude Stateliness, as if Built with more Pride then Art; it had on the North-side a little Mountain, whence ran some small Rivulets, with no name, which, contributed both to the pleasantness and fertility of the Soil. The City was antiently Inhabited by the *Bramenes*, now by Merchant *Moors*, a place amongst the *Eastern* people always famous, then for Superstition, now for Wealth; it was not defended by either Walls or Works, the Inhabitants being secure by the Power of their Lords, or the Peace they preserv'd with the Neighbouring Princes; but at present, the Warr we had with *Hidalcaon* beginning

The largeness and strength of the place.

ning Victoriously, the *Moors*, saw the danger they were in, by example, and had drawn two thousand paid Souldiers to Guard the City, who with the standing Militia, were (according to their computation) sufficient for their Defence.

63. These came, with their Colours flying, and with so much resolution to hinder our men from Landing, as for a good while they retarded us, obliging us to Fight at a stand, and so close as our Souldiers could not make use of their Musquets, whose first charge only, they receiv'd with notorious resolution. Here *Dom Alvaro* notably shew'd his Valour and Conduct, encouraging his men to Fight, sometimes by Speeches, sometimes by the Example of his own Actions. Ours at last saw themselves so streightned as they fought more for Life then Victory. The success, for an hour hung doubtfull, till a great many of the Inhabitants, wounded with their own fear, and our Swords, quitted the Field, shewing in the first encounter, Valour, above Men, in the second, below Women, a thing very ordinary in raw Souldiers, where the greatest fear follows the greatest daring; the rest by this example were getting off, in fear and disorder; here the *Moors* receiv'd great loss, falling with little or no Resistance, those who drop't too were so many as they hindred the rest from Flying. The Enemies resistance.

64. Ours entred the City mingled with the *Moors*, where the poor men stop't, o'recome with the fondness and tears of Wives, and Children, who then with useless compassion bore 'em company, rather Witnesses, then Defenders of their Lives; some there were, who embracing their Husbands let themselves be run through with our Lances, inventing fresh sadness by a new remedy; Of our Souldiers, some Robb'd 'em, some Defended 'em, some following the disposition of the Season, others of their Nature; Out of desperate Love some of those Women ran amongst our arm'd Squadrons to seek their Dead, seeming not to valew their Ours enter,

Lives; full of tenderness for others Wounds, without any for their own; at last we gain'd the City with less loss, then danger, because resolving to enter under the Enemies Canon, *Dom Alvaro* was more lead on by Courage, then Discipline; the greater part of the *Moors* was Destroy'd, some in the Fight, most in the Flight; the VVomen shew'd more Courage, then their Husbands; These lost their Lives, they could not defend, the others despis'd theirs they might have sav'd; of ours there Dy'd twenty two, the VVounded were more, of whose number was the General hurt by an Arrow. 'Twas necessary to end one Cruelty to begin an other, their Anger ceast, and their Covetousness began; *Dom Alvaro* gave order to Plunder the City, where the Booty was as great as the Victory, because, either out of Confidence or Carelesness the *Moors* had sav'd nothing, and kept in the City those who were useless for the Defence of it, out of contempt of our Forces, or not to dishearten their own. In fine, the Prize was so great, that it could not all be carry'd aboard, the Souldiers took the best, leaving the rest as Fuel for that Fire which was to Consume the City, by *Dom Alvaro* given up to the mercilesss Flames; which did not a little strike the Neighbouring Colonies, that place being the Richest and most Tenable of all the Coast, once, as it were, the Bulwark of the rest, now their Lamentable example.

and gain the City.

The Destroying and Plundring of it.

Dom Alvaro returns to Goa.

65. The General with all the Fleet weigh'd Anchor, and steer'd for *Goa* to unlade the Ships, (put out of their trim, by too great a Burden;) resolving to leave there the Sick and VVounded, and return to carry on the VVarr, which the Souldiers, content with the Liberality, and Fortune of their new General, very much desir'd. The news arriv'd at *Goa* before the Ships, the Governour very much valued the Victory, the people the Plunder; not long after came intelligence, that those who had scap'd the Rout had been to acquaint *Hidalcaon* with the lamentable Destruction of their

City,

City, who, while they vented their first grief for their Children and Kindred, could not keep in the second calamity of their Goods and Houses, where the devouring Fire had so mingled the Ashes, they could not with peculiar tears, weep over their Dead; they told *Hidalcaon*, that if he resolv'd to continue the Warr with such a people, they would go and Inhabit the Deserts, where they should be out of sight of those *Western* Beasts, Born for the reproach and ruine of *Asia*, they told and curs'd our Victories one after the other, which look't bigger in their Fears, then our Books.

66. *Hidalcaon*, considering the fortune of our Arms, the complaints, and calamities of the Inhabitants, and many disaffected to his Service, whom the Warr, and those Successes would more embolden, was inclinable to Peace, thereby to remedy the Dissentions and Seditions at home, which might grow stronger by the liberty of men in Arms; and communicating to his Councel the present condition of things, all were of opinion, they ought by a feignd peace to cloak their grievances, expecting till time offered 'em a fairer opportunity to set upon the State, joyning their Forces with other Kings who were offended. And the *Moors* fighting more for their conveniency then quarrel, *Hidalcaon* sent Embassadours to the Governour, frivolously excusing the Warr he made, and minding him of the benefit the State might receive by his Friendship.

Hidalcaon profers Peace.

67. The Governour, in publick and in great State, gave audience to the Embassadours, answering them, that as he sought not for Warr, so he could not deny it; that the felicity of the State consisted in having many Enemies, because with Spoils and Victories it grew always greater; but, that he never deny'd Peace to any one, who by his Actions, and faithfull Friendship deserv'd it; that he would deprive his Souldiers of the conveniences they look't for from that Warr; but *Hidalcaon* must know the first day he was to pass for a King,

The Governour accepts it.

King, was that in which he treated Peace with the *Portugueſe*. Thus did he diſpatch the Embaſſadours, aw'd with ſo great a Courage; with the ſame neglect did he always manage the Warrs in the *Eaſt*, in which his Valour was equal to his Fortune.

He looks to the affairs of the State,

68. He preſently betook himſelf to the diſpatching particular buſineſs, rewarding the Souldiers who had ſerv'd him, whom he parted with as well ſatisfy'd with the rewards he gave them, as his acceptance of their Service; He put Commanders into the void Forts, which were unprovided by the King; making ſo juſt an eſtimate of Deſerts, that he was Debtor neither to conveniency, or the State, a virtue hardly arriv'd at by Princes, and very rare in their Miniſters.

and matters of Religion.

69. He was not leſs fir'd with zeal for the honour of God, then for that of the State, in the confuſion of Warr, and the noiſe of Arms, applying himſelf to matters of Religion, as if he had been only ſent to ſtickle for them. And the King *Dom John*, knowing his Piety, as well as his Valour, commended to him the propagation of the Faith, and Divine worſhip. Out of a Letter, which on this Subject the King writ him, is well gathered, how both King and Miniſter were inflam'd in God's cauſe, of which we will here give a Copy, that the World may ſee our Arms in the *Eaſt*, brought more Sons to the Church then Vaſſals to the State.

The King's Letter to Dom John de Caſtro.

Friend and Governour. The great Concernment, which lies upon Chriſtian Princes to look to matters of Faith, and employ their Forces for its Preſervation, makes me adviſe you how ſenſible I am, that not only, in many parts of India *under our Subjection, but even in our City of* Goa, *Idols are Worſhipp't, places in which our Faith might more reaſonably*

nably be expected to Flourish; and being as well inform'd with how much liberty they celebrate Heathenish festivals, we command you, to discover by diligent Officers all the Idols, and to demolish and break 'em in pieces where ere they are found; Proclaiming severe punishments against any one who shall dare, to Work, Cast, make in Sculpture, Engrave, Paint, or bring to light, any Figure of an Idol, in Metall, Brass, Wood, Plaister, or any other matter, or bring them from other places; and against those, who publickly, or privately, Celebrate any of their sports, keep by them any Heathenish Frankincense, or assist and hide the Bramenes, *the sworn Enemies of Christian Profession; whosoever of the fore-nam'd shall run into the like Crimes, 'tis our pleasure you Punish 'em, with that severity the Law in that case, or our Prolamation requires, without admitting any appeal or dispensation in the least. And that the* Pagans *may submit themselves to the yoak of the Gospel, not only out of Conviction of the purity of its Faith, and fed with the hopes of Eternal Life, but be advantag'd too, by some temporal favour shew'd 'em, (which doth very much work upon Subjects hearts) you are with all Diligence to see that the new Christians, may henceforward have and enjoy all the Exemptions and Liberties from Taxes, enjoying those Privileges, and places of Honour, which the* Pagans *did hitherto use to do. We have too been inform'd, that many* Indians *are forc't to go in our Fleet, and are for that at charges against their wills, desiring that so great Exorbitancy should be remedy'd, we order that the* Christians *be exempt from that Oppression, and in case the necessity be very pressing, you shall if they go, (with that trust we look for, from your care, and diligence) provide, that they be every day satisfy'd for their Labour; Having known too, from grave and credible Persons, (and what we particularly resented) that some* Portuguese *buy Slaves for little, that selling them to the* Moors *and other Infidel Merchants, they may get by 'em, which is done to the great Dammage of their Souls, they being easily to be Converted to the Faith, we command you to employ all your power for the preventing so great an evil, by hindring such Sales, for the great service which by it is done to God, and you will do to us, if with the rigor the case requires, you remedy a thing which appears so foul to us. You are to take care for the curbing the excessive liberty of some Usurers, who as we are inform'd, are amongst you under the protection of an old Law of* Goa, *which we do at this present, and you are also to revoke, taking it away from the Body of the rest, as contrary to Christian Religion; you are to give order for the speedy Building a Church in* Bacaim, *which is to be Dedicated to St.* Joseph, *and upon our account to assign it rent for a Rector, some Beneficiaries, and Chaplains who may officiate there; and because the Preachers, and Ministers of our Faith, by going about to Convert the* Pagans, *are in Necessity, we think it fitting, and 'tis our will to give 'em something towards defraying their Charges, and only for that you are to lay a yearly Tax of three thousand Pardaos on all the Mosques the* Moors *have in our Territories. You shall too out of our Customs and Rights for ever give three hundred Bushels of Rice for the maintenance of those whom the Vicar* Miguel Vaz *either hath or shall Convert about* Chaul, *which quantity we order to be put into the Bishops hands, that he (as he sees necessity) may distribute it. We have too been inform'd that about* Cochim, *Saint* Thomas's *Christians are cheated in their weights and measures by our Merchants who sell Pepper there, and that they take from 'em the Surplusage they (according to an old Custom) ought to have over and above the just weight, and measure, whom for many respects, 'twere better to favour then oppress; for that end you are to give order, they may enjoy their old Customs; you are also to treat with the King of* Cochim, *that he cause to be tane away certain* Pagan *Rites and Superstitions which his South-sayers use to practice in the sale of Pepper, his advantage by 'em being very little, and the Scandal to the* Christians *who contract there very great; and because we have been advis'd of the Cruelty* that *King useth against those* Indians *who receive our Faith, by seising on their Estates, you must zealously endeavour the said Kings (to whom we have writ about it) leaving that so Barbarous*

cruelty,

cruelty, which so much injures the Souls and Bodies of his Subjects, which, being our Friend, he will do; you on your part employing that care we charge you with. For that, which by your Letters and Advises we have, concerning the delivering the people of Socotora *from the miserable Slavery in which they Live, we are of opinion so to remedy it, that the* Turk *(whose Subjects they are) shall not with his Fleets infest those Seas, you are to look how that is most conveniently to be done by the advice of the Vicar* Miguel Vaz, *whose Experience, both in that and all other business of moment that shall occurr, will very much help you. We know that those who Fish for Pearl, besides other wrongs and oppressions they lye under, suffer in their Estates; our Sea-Captains out of their little fear to God, forcing 'em on very hard terms, only to Fish for them, upon which, (desiring that none of our Subjects should suffer any Violence or Oppression) we order you to see that those people be not so hardly us'd, and that our Captains usurp not so unjust a Power; and further, for the avoiding the like grievances and cruelties you are to look if those Coasts be sufficiently Guarded, and, if 'tis possible for us to recover our Dues without having a Fleet there: and finding it Feasible, you are to withdraw thence our Captains, commanding none to Sail along those Coasts, by that means the Natives may enjoy their Estates, and Cruelties and Extorsions be prevented; above all we recommend to you the consulting with the Father* Francisco Xaverius *in what ever occurs, chiefly what is to be done for the encrease of Christianity on the Fishing Coast, that those who are newly Converted may not be employed in the Fishing, if they be, it may be upon knowledge that with their new Religion they have got new Manners, and the great abuses they use in it may be Curb'd. We have been likewise inform'd, that those who from* Paganism *are Converted to our holy Faith, are ill us'd and despis'd by their Kindred and Friends, who, with so great Outrage and so high an Hand banish 'em their Houses, and seize on their Estates, that they are forc'd to Live miserably in great want and necessity; that such things may be redress'd, you are (with the Counsel*

of

of the Vicar Miguel Vaz *) to see they be reliev'd at our Charge, putting, what is to be given 'em, in the hands of the Rector who hath care of 'em, that he may every year distribute it as is most convenient. We know too that from* Ceilaon, *there came a youth to* Goa, *flying the fury and anger of his Kindred, and being (as he is) of the Royal Family, that he ought to succeed in the Kingdome, upon which, (for the encouragement of those already, and those yet to be Converted) we have thought good that you accommodate him (now he's a Christian) in Saint* Pauls *Colledge in the City, where, at our Charge, such Lodgings, and necessaries may be provided him, as are fit, not only for his maintenance, but pleasure, that our Grandeur with Persons of his quality may be seen; besides, you are to endeavour to clear his claim to the Kingdome; and what you find in the business, send us with the proofs, that we may according to conveniency provide; in the mean time 'tis our pleasure, that with all imaginable severity you call the Tyrant to account for his Cruelties against those who are Converted to our holy Faith; obliging him to give satisfaction for so great insolence, that all the Princes of* India *may see our love to Justice, and how we put upon our own score the protecting those who cannot help themselves. And because, 'tis not fit* Pagan *Artificers should (as hitherto hath been allow'd 'em) Cast, Paint, or Work any Images or Figures of our Lord Christ, or his Saints, to sell 'em; we command you to use all diligence, for the hindring it, laying Penalties, that he, who shall be prov'd to make any of the fore-mention'd Images, shall (besides the having two hundred Drubbs) lose his Estate, because without doubt it looks not well that Images representing so holy Mysteries should pass through the hands of* Pagan *Idolaters. We have it from the same hand, that the Churches newly begun to be Built at* Cochim, *and* Coulaon, *want finishing, being uncover'd and expos'd to all the injuries of the Weather; which is not only an ill sight, but prejudices the Building; you shall therefore give Order, that (without sticking at the charge) they may be gone on with, till Finish'd, by the work and design of the best Architects and Overseers; you are too,*

too, to cause a Church to be Built in Naraon, *in Honour of, and with the Dedication to, the Apostle Saint* Thomas, *and to look to the finishing of that already begun in* Calapor, *by the name of the holy Cross; you are too, to make another in the Neighbouring Island of* Coraon, *for design and stateliness as you shall think convenient, there being nothing, which, in the* Pagans *will more stirr up Devotion for the matters of our holy Faith, then the affection they see on our part. Besides which, we do more straightly charge you with the founding Schools and Houses of Devotion, in all places fit for't; whether, on certain Days, not only the* Christians, *but* Pagans *may resort to Sermons, and Spiritual exercises, that so they may come to the Love of our holy Faith, and the Knowledge of the errors in which they Live, being illuminate with the Light of the Gospel; for which you are to choose Ministers with those parts such a Ministry requires. And above all, earnestly desiring that the Name of God may be known and worship't, and his holy Faith receiv'd in our State, we will, and 'tis our pleasure, that in the Territories of* Salsete *and* Bardez *all the Idols, and infernal Worship, which hath hitherto been practis'd there, be utterly rooted out; and that it may be done with the less difficulty, and without the necessity of using any force or violence, we command the Preachers in their Sermons and Disputations, to manage the hearts of the* Pagans *with such prudence and zeal, that (by God's blessing) they may be sensible of the good intended them, by bringing 'em to the knowledge of their Errors, and delivering 'em from the miserable servitude of the Devil in which they are, out of which, they only are to be freed by closing with our holy Faith, the sole way to know that blindness in which Satan leads 'em, not to consider how much the Salvation of their Souls concerns 'em; and because it very much imports this business, that the undertakers of it be Men of a good Life and Conversation, and able Scholars, you are to pick out such, from whom we may expect the Effect we desire, and to recommend to 'em the care and diligence requisite on their part; and on yours, you are to endeavour the drawing of, and favouring all men, especially*

cially

cially the Nobility and Great ones, (whose example the multitude follows) and who being once reconcil'd to our holy Faith, the difficulty will be but little to Convert the common people, who will immediately be doing, what they see done by the Grandees. Let them who turn, be well us'd, (that more may be wonn) having favour shew'd 'em, not only in the general, but in their particulars, be they never so poor and miserable. Of all this, we thought fit to inform you, that, for the confidence we have of your care and diligence, you might remedy all, from which, great Glory will result to our Lord God; and we will reckon it to you as a peculiar service. Dated at Almeirim *the eight of* March *in the year of our Lord Jesus Christ* 1546.

By the KING.

70. *Dom John* put as much of this Letter in Execution, as his being always in Arms would permit him; for the time of his Government was one continued Battail, and the Souldiers, by the Licence of VVarr, were readier to ruine the Laws, then reform their Manners; yet will the History shew us no slight Arguments of his Zeal, recompens't extraordinarily by Heaven with signs and miracles, one of 'em, which hapned in the *Molucca's*, (annex'd to his Government,) I'le relate with my Customary brevity.

71. The light of the Gospel had shin'd in those Islands; (Saint *Francisco Xaverio* as a faithfull Labourer in the Lord's Vineyard, having in a great part clear'd those places of the Thistles and Briars of Infidelity) though we owe the first Cultivating to that great *Portuguese Antonio Galvaon*, the most Couragious Governour and Zealous Apostle of those *Pagans*, whose Prowess was answered by its Fruits in the wonderfull Conversion of Souls, who with their Baptism receiv'd the easie Yoak of Christ, the Princes and great Ones, as well as the People, being all Tunable to the Obedience

Obedience of the Gospel. The Devil perceiving that, in that Cessation of *Paganism*, a Light appear'd from Heaven discovering the ways of Life, arm'd against the innocent *Christians* a *Pagan* thereabouts call'd *Tolon*, who had usurp't the Island of *Moro*. He with infernal Zeal began to persecute the new Converts, forcing them by new Torments to turn *Renegados* from that Faith they had profest; for which, many chose to shed their Blood in a happy Martyrdome, others of weaker Faith yielded to the Torments. The Tyrants boldness encreasing to the Affronting of our Arms, oblig'd 'em out of obedience to the Faith, and for the service of the State, to Chastise that Idolater. The persecuted, and fearfull, came with complaints to the *Portuguese*, in *Ternate*, who resolving to bring down the Infidel, with more zeal then strength went to find him out at his own Home. Their motion could not be so secret, but the Tyrant had notice of it; who, by fortifying the entrance of the Island with Trenches and strong Barricados, provided for his Defence; and in case our men should get those, he had strew'd Splinters and long poyson'd Crows-feet in all the Avenues which led to the City, o're which, whilst ours in the heat of Anger, and Victory, past, they must necessarily lose themselves. It hapned, that after winning the first Stacade, (which the Infidels probably quitted without any hot dispute, in confidence of their second Stratagem) whilst ours, baited with the flight of the Enemy, were incautelously passing on, there fell on a suddain, (a thing miraculous) such a quantity of Ashes from the Sky as made ours stop, till, after the Air was clear'd, they pursu'd their Victory over the Crows-feet, where the Ashes had made the way hard and sure; so the astonish't Infidels afterwards related it, making use of the Miracle, for an argument of the truth of that Doctrine they persecuted.

A miraculous success in the *Moluccas*.

72. Thus did *Asia* yield to the Faith and the State in the time of *Dom John de Castro*, who had in one hand the

the Gospel, in the other a Sword, and fill'd the *East* with the discourse of so great an Action, as was, the Voluntary undergoing a Warr for the defence of *Meale*, a persecuted *Moor*, whose Subjects had refus'd him their Obedience, and the Princes his Allies their Protection.

73. *Asia* gave him but little time of rest in the Triumphs of his Victories, *Cambaya* beginning immediately to rouse him with the Alarums of a new Warr; the noise of it was already in the States intelligence; but being the most notable piece of our History, we will relate it in a Book apart.

THE

THE LIFE OF
DOM JOHN DE CASTRO.

The Second Book.

1. THE *Portuguese* were more fear'd, then lov'd by the Princes of *Asia*, on the Death of *Sultan Badur* King of *Cambaya*, whose private Faults and publick Punishments got him (by the Prerogative of the Blood-Royal) the peoples affection, either out of the natural Commiseration to Sufferers, or reverence of Majesty, and hatred of our Government, not less abhorr'd as Forein, then Powerfull.

2. *Mahumud* King of *Cambaya*, Heir to the Crown and wrongs of *Badur*, (who Dy'd in the Government of the great *Nunho de Cunha*) equally fir'd with glory, and revenge, did (as our Chronicles relate) design to take *Dio* from the *Portuguese*; and (by the Confederacy of other Princes) to drive 'em out of *India*; an undertaking, (as some of his own were of opinion) not very difficult; their Arguments were, that the State was a monstrous Body, whose Head being in the *West*, fed the Members so infinitely distant from it, by the interposition of so much Sea, and Land; that *Cambaya*'s strength was so great, that as well by its Ruine, as Victories, it could crush the State, already weakned

The King of *Cambaya* consults how he may take *Dio*.

weakned with so many accidents. The great Ones, and Nobility of the Kingdome, were divided in their Opinions; some, arguing from the first Siege, (their VVounds at it, and Memory of it, being yet fresh) thought the *Portuguese*s Arms fatal to *Cambaya*, and though they took to heart the Death of *Badur*, yet by others patience in taking Affronts, did they excuse their own; they tax'd those, who were the first Authors of making peace with the State, and those who now would have it broken; the last, because they kept not their Faith; the first, because they were not sensible enough of injuries. Others, (as when things are uncertain, it frequently falls out) discours'd to the contrary; and found as many arguments for Warr, as Victory.

Is perswaded by *Coge-Sofar*.

3. Amongst all the rest, *Coge-Sofar*, the most Powerfull and Obnoxious man of *Cambaya*, and who had got the best share in the King's favour, with a great deal of Caution spurr'd on the Warr, believing, the Heart-burnings which were against his Fortune, and the Envy of the great Ones, would, being the fruits of Peace, cease in the common danger; and by his Command and Power in the Warr, he should preferr others, who being his own Creatures would be true to him; I'l give a short relation of the man, because his name will often occurr in this History.

What *Coge-Sofar* was.

4. *Coge-Sofar* was by Nation an *Albanese*, and the Child of *Catholick* Parents, though the Fruit degenerated from the Stock. He had serv'd some time in the Warrs of *Italy*, more taken notice of for a brave, then a Souldier; in all Mutinies and Tumults, pick't out as the worst; for some years he led this loose Life, without, either reward, or punishment; untill, like a restless man, who had rather seek then expect his Fortune, he chang'd his Profession; of a Souldier becoming a Merchant, for being Cunning and Covetous, this was the nearest and surest way to what he aim'd. He begun in a little time, (knowing the opportunity and seasons of Commerce) to grow great by his business, being at

once Liberal, and Covetous, for his own ends cunningly making use of both Vice and Vertue. His Stock and Credit was at last so considerable, as Trading up and down the *Streights*, with three small Vessels of his own, of different Lading, he was met with by *Rox Solyman*, Admiral for the *Soldan* of *Cairo*, who Boarded him, made him yield, and took what he had. The Prize was greater then the Victory, and *Solyman* for the credit of his own reputation, treated him Honourably, presenting him to the *Soldan* as a Prisoner of Quality, valuing more his Person then his Booty. *Coge-Sofar* began to be as content with his misfortune, as if it had been of his own seeking; He was experienc't Souldier enough by his Service in the Armies in *Italy* and *Flanders*; He spoke of the Forces of the *Christians* with malice and undervaluing, as if intending to teach the *Soldan* to know his own strength. The *Soldan* was by these Artifices brought to look on the Slave as capable of great things, and begun first out of curiosity to listen to him; afterwards out of affection. *Coge-Sofar* with so sly a flattery commended what ere he did, well, or ill, as it past but fot freedome, because making a shew to be only zealous, not acceptable, he kept to himself, the *Soldan*'s favour, and avoided all publick honours more out of cautiousness then modesty. He came to be Treasurer of *Cairo*, a place of very great trust, which he manag'd with prudence, and fidelity, Vertues so pris'd by the *Soldan*, as if not till then known amongst the Infidels. At the Councels of Warr his Vote weigh'd most, sometimes for his experience, sometimes for the reason of it; in all designs against the *Christians*, particularly in those which were to be carry'd on by others, He declar'd his sence with a great deal of confidence, and by this means grew so great that he could not bear his own Fortune, till, not minding the preserving himself by the same Arts he was advanc't, his Ambition and Pride burst forth; He possest what places he could, and more sollicitously look't after Preferments then Friends, whose

whose help or company he now Valew'd not, he desir'd to be known, only for the *Soldan's* Slave, and for Master of the rest. He plotted the Destruction of the great Ones on publick pretensions, as if he aim'd that two only were to Govern, till the *Moors*, wearied of so base a patience, began publickly to complain and disturb the *Soldan's* inclinations to favour *Coge-Sofar*, they very feelingly acquainted him with their grievances, saying, they might now be very well excus'd from setting out Galleys against the *Christians*, if their Slaves were to be made their Masters, when *Turks* of the best quality were by the *Christians* so cruelly us'd, as to go up and down *Italy* and *Spain* dragging their Chains after 'em, and had their Faces stigmatis'd with infamous Letters, in token of their Captivity, that 'twas not to be born for so many great Bashaws to receive Laws from a despicable Slave; that, though every day they with their eyes saw their own Outrages, they could not disgest those which were offered to their Prophet, by a vile, irreverent and haughty *Christian*, not so much as going into their Mosques; that now nothing more was to be done then the setting up Crosses in the streets of *Cairo*, and commanding 'em to be ador'd.

5. These things were said with so much freedome, as they look't more like conspiracy then complaint, and with particular grievances involving the cause of Religion, (which ordinarily carries with it, its own Justification, and the affections of the People) were willingly listned to by the *Soldan*, who put *Coge Sofar* out of his Office, with command to change his Religion; so frail do even the greatest Favourites find their Princes favour.

6. *Coge-Sofar* seeing himself falln, put on again his first Humility, and those Artifices the necessity of the times taught him, and having now only the name and memory of a Christian, easily chang'd, for the Poyson of the *Alcoran*, Evangelical Salvation, quitting the name given him in Baptism for that of *Coge-Sofar*, by which

we before hand call'd him, not knowing the first he had. *Coge-Sofar* being a *Mahomitan*, began to winn upon the *Moors* in their confidence in him; healing by gifts the hatred of those who envy'd him; by his new Apostacy, (by which he Cancel'd the suspition of his fidelity) the malice of the people; carrying on his designs with a more sly ambition, which made him more affable to his Enemies then to Strangers; but knowing the *Soldan*'s Ficklenesss, fearing too a second complaint, not reckoning on reconcil'd favour as secure, He treacherously one night Kill'd his mortal enemy *Rox Solyman* and his Son, and putting together all the Jewels and Money he could, went away secretly for the Service of the King of *Cambaya*, of whose Grandeur and Liberality he had had full information, and how he valew'd Strangers, those especially who had any experience in the Warrs and Policy of *Europe*; the succefs answered his fore-cast, for in a little time, either by his Fortune or Indu-dustry, he came almost to engross *Badur*'s favour, being his Companion in his Victories and Losses, being in the last which befell him at his Death. So that now grown by the King's bounty, to be in Power and Authority the greatest Subject, holding also with *Mahumed* Heir of the Crown the same repute, for the reasons we have already related, and to deserve the favour of the new Prince, by the love and fidelity he shew'd to the Ashes of him who was Dead, he urg'd him to revenge *Badur*'s Death; 'tis reported, that he spoke to this purpose be-fore the King and Nobility of *Cambaya*.

How he came to *Cambaya*.

7. "The favours which for ten years I receiv'd of "*Sultan Badur* (for which those abroad admired his "Grandeur, those at home envy'd my Fortune) are "known to every one. He cast his Eyes upon me, and "like a Vapour rais'd me from the ground, preferring "me, a Stranger, and a Vagabond, before those who "were born in his Palace; of a Subject he treated me "like a Friend, and lov'd me as a Son. From this most "Gracious Prince, (whose Ashes I reverence as my Lords,

"and weep o're as my Fathers) have the *Portuguese* "under the sacred shew of peace ta'ne away his Life, "to the great Scandal of all other Kings, and no less "Outrage of his Subjects, unworthy to have been so, "to so mighty a Prince, since we so insensibly and un-"gratefully behave our selves; Feeding at our own "home the Murderers of our Monarck, who enjoy, as "Inheritance, a place, which by so hainous an offence "they made their own, lately Strangers, now Patrons. "You! Oh Prince, Heir and Lord of this Empire, see "your Subjects every day receive Laws from these In-"sulters, 'tis for you to decide, whôm we are first to "Obey, our King, or our Enemies; their boldness will "grow greater by our patience, after committing the "foulest fault, what will they count little? where no "Vengeance is ta'ne on injuries, who will stick to be "the Offendor? Lets at last awake out of this so mor-"tal a Lethargy. Lets put our Arms up to the Elbows "in the Blood of these so unhuman Usurpers. Lets "bathe our Semitars in this Poison, that with their "Lives they may lose the glory of their so great boast-"ings. The *Portugall* Arms by the Blood of *Badur*, "receiv'd the greatest repute, by the foulest crime, and "we suffer that Sword in their hands still, which cut off "our King, that with the same, they may usurp his "Kingdme; Lets cast from amongst us those Vipers "bred furthest *West* for the infecting all *Asia*, as will "be evident by running over their Outrages, by them "calld Victories. And to begin with the first of "them, [a] *Gama*, (to whom, for the disturbing the

[a] The *Portuguese*, having, with infinite danger, difficulty and expence employ'd 75 years in discovering the *Western* Coast of *Africa*, *Bartholomew Diaz* in the year 1486. and in the Reign of King *John* the second, discovered the Cape of Good Hope, (so call'd by the King after the return of the Fleet, from the hopes he had after that to discover the *Indies* so long design'd; but by *Diaz* at first nam'd *Capo Tormentoso*, from the Storms and foul Weather he met with there) K. *Emanuel* (who succeeded King *John*) in the year 1497. sent *Vasco de Gama* with a Fleet to the *Indies*, who past the Cape, and Sailing by the Island of *Mocambique*, the Kingdome of *Quiloa*, *Mombaca*, and *Melinde*, doubling the Cape *Guardafu*, (at the mouth of the *Red-Sea*, and Cape *Rasalgate*, at the *Persian* Gulf) arriv'd at *Calecut* the chief City of *Malabar*. *Camoens*, Cant. 1. St. 12. of his *Lusiade*, says of him,

Douvos tambem aquelle illustre Gama
Que para sy de Eneas toma a fama.
The Illustrious *Gama* in the rear I name,
Who robb'd the wandring *Trojan* of his Fame.

So rendred by the Right Honourable Sir *Richard Fanshaw*, (Embassadour to *Portugall*) in his excellent Translation of that Poem.

"peace

" peace of the *East*, the Seas gave so fatal a passage)
" the *Samorim* of *Calecut* was the first his Sword cut off;
" the Fleet of *Meca*, which under the protection of our
" Prophet, and the peace they enjoy'd by Sea, Sail'd
" securely, was by this successfull Rover set upon, and
" made to yield, who for so many years like a Sea-Mon-
" ster had for his House the Waters, and for his shelter
" the Winds, and Tempests. After him came [*b*] *Dom*
" *Francisco de Almeyda*, who, in one day, and with the
" same stroke shatter'd the Fleets of *Egypt* and *Cambaya*,
" who so behav'd himself, as if in [*c*] Vengeance of his
" Son's Death, he would have drunk up the Blood of
" the whole *East*; if [*d*] *Albuquerque* who succeeded

[*b*] *Dom Francisco de Almeyda* went (with a great Fleet, and the first Title of Vice-Roy,) to the *Indies* in the year 1505. *April 6.* His Son *Dom Lourenco D' Almeyda* obtain'd against the *Samorim* of *Calecut* in sight of *Cananor* an eminent Victory on the 26. of *March* 1506. The King of *Calecut's Armado* consisted of 208 Sail, 84 great Ships, and 124 others Vessels (by 'em call'd *Paraos*) on which were vast numbers of *Moors* and *Naires*; The *Portuguese* had but eleven Sail, and on 'em 800 men, with whom they Destroyed the whole Fleet, which was well furnisht with Artillery. See the relation of this Fight, History of *India*, Dec. 1. Lib. 19. Cap. 4.

The *Samorim* to reverge this loss, sent to the *Soldan* of *Egypt*, and the King of *Cambaya* to assist him against the *Portuguese*, and joyn'd with their Fleets, set upon *Dom Lourenco's* in the River of *Chaul*, who (after his Ships striking and springing a Leak) was Kill'd by a Canon shot, History of *India*, Dec. 2. Cap. 8. *Camoens* Can. 10. St. 29, 30.

[*c*] *Eys vem ò pay com Animo estupendo*
Trazendo fúria, & magoa per antolhos.
Com que ò paterno amor lhe està movendo
Fogo no coracaon, aqua nos olhos
A nobre ira lhe vinha promettendo
Que o sanque fará dar pelos giolhos
Nas inimigas naos: Sentiloha ò Nilo
Podelo ha ò Indo ver, & ò Gange ouvilo. Camo. Can. 10. St. 33.

Behold! the Father comes a Mad man like,
In whom for Mastry, grief with fury strives,
Whilst at one time paternal Love doth strike
Fire on his heart, pumps water from his Eyes.
A noble anger whispers him, his Pike
Shall blood his Foes so that the Tide shall rise
In their drown'd Decks Knee-deep; *Nilus* shall bear,
Indus shall see his blows, and *Ganges* hear.

Sir *Richard Fanshaw's* Translation.

[*d*] *Dom Affonso D' Albuquerque* went from *Lisbone* for the *Indies*, was Commander of a Squadron design'd for the Coast of *Arabia*. See his taking *Malaca*, History of *India*, Dec. 2. Lib. 5. Cap. 9. His reducing *Ormus*, see History of *India*, Dec. 2. Lib. 10. Cap. 3. How he got *Goa*, see History of *India*, Dec. 2. Lib. 5. Cap. 3.

See *Camoens* Can. 10. Sta. 40, 41, 42, 43.

See *John de Barro's* Dec. 2. Lib. 6. Cap. 5.

" him in his Cruelty, and Government, had not tane " the Sword out of his Hands; this Man was Born to " affront all our Monarchies, for by Conquering *Malaca* " he Curb'd all the *South*-Seas; he reduc't *Ormus* the " Mart of all the Riches of the World; took *Goa* from " the *Sabayo* to make that the seat of his usurpt Em- " pire, and without the Armies of *Xerxes* or *Darius*, " made Tributary more Kingdoms then he had Soul- " diers; He was puft up with the thoughts of taking " the Body of our Prophet from *Meca*, debated the " changing the course of *Nilus* to drown *Egypt*, un- " dertaking out of his ambition the doing two such " notorious Outrages, one against Heaven, the other " against Nature. I will not go about to relate the " ambition of so many, as by our wrongs have grown " famous, because I fear neither my time or memory " will allow it, do but look with your sight or judg- " ment on the remotest parts of the *East*, and you'l see " so inconsiderable a Power giving Laws to the greatest " part of the World; they Sail'd from that part of " *Africa* which runs along from the Cape of Good Hope " to the *Streights* mouth of the *Red-Sea*, possessing on " that shore *Mocambique, Sofala, Quiloa*, and *Mombaca*, " and passing the Cape of *Guardafu*, looking into the " mouth of the *Red-Sea*, go in sight of *Adem*, *Xael*, " *Herit, Caxem*. The Cities of *Dofar* and *Norbete* on " the Cape of *Fartaque*, first dreaded their Fleets, after- " wards, *Curia, Muria, Rozalgate*; here lies the City of " *Ormus*, not farr off the Island of *Quexiome, Cûriate,* " *Calayate, Mascate, Orfacaon*, and *Lima*; then they " come to the Capes of *Mocandaon*, and *Iasque*, which " form the mouth of the *Persian* Gulph, which reach- " eth to the River *Indus*; next pass by the Cape of *Gu-* " *zarate*, and *Cinde*, in our *Cambaya*, whence as farr as " Cape *Comori* their Fleets sail all along *India*, for the " space of three hundred Leagues, beginning from our " City of *Cambaya*, they rove by *Madigaon, Gandar,* " *Baroche, Surrat, Reyner, Moscarin, Damaon, Taraper,*

"*Bacaim*, *Chaul*, *Bandor*, *Cifardaon*, *Galauci*, *Dabul*, *Cor*-"*tapor*, *Corepataon*, *Tamega*, *Banda*, *Chapora*; they first "got *Goa* the residence of their Governours, now they "have the Coast of *Canara*, with *Onor*, *Baticala*, *Bra*-"*calor*, *Bracano*, and *Mangalor*; then got they that "Chief part of *Malabar*, which their Fleets allarm, "where is the Kingdome of *Cananor*, and in that *Cate*-"*coulaon*, *Marabia*, *Tramapataon*, *Maim*, *Parepataon*; "with no less insulting they keep in awe the Empire of "*Calecut*, with its Havens of *Pandarane*, *Coulate*, *Chare*, "*Capocate*, *Parangale*, *Tanor*, *Panane*, *Balcancor*, and "*Chatua*. In the Kingdoms of *Cananor*, and *Cochim*, they "Domineer without Controul, in *Porca*, *Coulaon*, *Cale*-"*coulaon*, *Dotora*, *Birinjaon*, *Travancor*. The dread of "their Arms reacheth as farr as the famous Cape *Comori*, "before which lies the renown'd Island of *Ceilaon*, "where they lade their Ships with sundry sorts of "Druggs. The Bay of *Bengala*, or Mouth of the "*Ganges*, doth not scape them, where they are in sight "of *Tacancuri*, *Manapar*, *Vaipar*, *Calegrande*, *Chercapale*, "*Tutucuri*, *Calecarem*, *Beadala*, *Canhamorra*; they o're "run *Negapataon*, *Nahor*, *Triminipataon*, *Tragumbar*, *Co*-"*loraon*, *Calapate*, *Sadrapataon*; They scare with the "quantity and bigness of their Vessels *Biznaga*, and "the stormy Coast of *Orixa*, and all that distance "which lies from *Segopora*, to *Oristaon*, and the mouth "of *Ganges*; they Sail by the Cape of *Negraes*, *Arra*-"*caon*, and *Pegu*, with those so many and so famous I-"slands; they go along by *Vagatu*, *Martavaon*, *Tagala*, "and *Favay*, *Tanacari*, *Lungur*, *Tairaon*; *Queda*, *Solungor*, "going as farr as their *Malaca*, which commands all that "*Archipelago*, after that, doubling the Cape of *Sinca*-"*pura*, they come to an Anchor in the Ports of the "Kingdoms of *Syaon*, *Camboya*, *Champa*, and *Cochin*-"*china*, and going as farr as the Kingdoms of *China*, "venture to look upon that so reserv'd Empire, which "never admitted of a Trade with Strangers; there "they Built the famous City of *Macao*, whence they in-

"ſtill the Myſteries of their Faith into the *Chineſe*, "making their Trade a ſtep to their Religion; from "hence they Rove amongſt the numberleſs Iſlands of "*Iapaon*, viſiting *Tava*, *Timor*, *Borneo*, *Banda*, *Maluco*, "and *Lequios*, ſo as the *Portugueſe* Ships with a reſt- "leſs Sailing Coaſt the greateſt part of the World for "the ſpace of more then nine thouſand Leagues, to ſo "difficult a Voyage animated by their Ambition, and "guided by their Fortune. I have tediouſly run o're "all the Coaſt of *Aſia*, where by the influence of "Power or Trade the *Portugueſe* Arms have made them- "ſelves known, becauſe the World doth, from ſuch "ſcattered Conqueſts, falſly conclude their Power, and "I their Weakneſs; for *Portugall*, being a ſmall King- "dome furtheſt *Weſt*, and in continual Warr with their "Neighbour *Africa*, where they conſume themſelves "both by what they Winn or Loſe, their Fights, and "Garriſons being always an expence of men, not being "able to ſtay where they were Born, in hatred of the "Soil and Clime which gave them a beeing, they go "Roving up and down the World, as if Men, Land "and Winds were theirs; I now leave it to the judge- "ment of the moſt ordinary underſtanding, how little "ſo divided a ſtrength is to be fear'd, which in their "Proſperity will be ſpent by their Victories; what "cauſe have we to dread the Government of theſe Mad "men, who with one Arm in *Aſia*, and the other in the "*Weſt*, ſtrive to graſp the World? they have in *India* "many Princes under 'em, but not one Friend, they all "adore and hate their Rulers, becauſe the *Portugueſe* "made peace with none but after Victories, and Out- "rages, ſo as not their affections, but their wrongs "unite 'em, and they all do Homage while they can- "not offend. But what will it be when they ſhall ſee "*Soltan Mahamud* take the Field with an Army? what "doubt is there but that all the Injur'd will be our "Souldiers? by force of Arms they have made many "Kings Tributary, and ſuppoſing they now are Pro-

"tected by them, a good turn is sooner forgot then an "injury. The Grand *Signor Selim*, sees the Wounds "his *Janizaries* receiv'd at *Dio*, yet gaping, and one so "little us'd to receive affronts will not let slip the op- "portunity of revenging the first, by beginning the "Warr, or seconding you in it, who is ambitious also "of having the greatest part of the World under his "Empire. The *Samorim* hath not one Port, which since "the *Portuguese* came into the *East*, hath not been the "Theatre of their Victories, and scarce hath he one "Subject who hath not been wounded by their Swords. "*Hidalcaon* sees every day his Territories of *Bardez* and "*Salsete* running with Blood, and when the Governour "made an unjust Warr against him, he brought *Meale* "to *Goa* to countenance, by his pretended justice to an "another, the ruining him; all the other Princes will "take Arms against the common Enemy, that they "may enjoy the antient Liberty they liv'd in. For my "part I offer my Children, my Estate, and my Person "towards this VVarr; if I fall in it, *Badur* by my Blood "shall see my Loyalty, and be the success good or "bad, I shall not count Death less Honourable, then "Victory.

The *Soldan* approves them, and commits the design to him.

8. *Coge-Sofar*'s Arguments were, for the Odiousness of the cause, and the Authority of his Person, well ap-prov'd of; The King, after magnifying his Loyalty, commits to him (as to one who out-went all the rest in his Zeal, and Conduct) the design: He immediately quickens the preparations by diverse messages to the Neighbouring Kings, putting them in mind of the Af-frons had been put upon 'em, and offering them his Princes arms in favour of their grievances. He dispach't Embassadours to *Constantinople*, inviting the *Turk* to redeem the credit of his Arms by beating the *Portuguese* out of *India*, a thing which as much concern'd their Religion, as Policy; He made way for the Succour he ask't of him, with a present of so great Value, as'twas more likely to stirr up the *Turks* ambition against his Riches,

Riches, then that he should send him Auxiliary Forces to maintain 'em.

Dom John Mascarenhas Commander in Dio.

9. *Dom John Mascarenhas* was then Commander in chief in *Dio*, great by his Birth in *Portugall*, by his Virtue, in the *East*, a man who deserv'd as well from his Fame, as Fortune; He, by private intelligence knowing *Coge-Sofar*'s designs, and that all his preparations threatned that Fortress, writ what advise he had to *Dom John de Castro*, and that he wanted Men, Ammunition, and other necessaries; neglects which so many years Peace wink't at; or, 'twas perhaps, that our men thought themselves secure, by the reputation of the former Victory; he added too, that the *Soldan*s Levies were very forward, and the Enemy near, and that Winter would shortly come, which would shut out all Relief.

He adviseth the Governour,

History of India, Dec 6. Lib. 1. Cap. 6.

10. When *Dom John de Castro* receiv'd this advise, he had already sent two hundred Souldiers to the Fortress, under the Commands of *Dom John*, and *Dom Pedro de Almeyda*, Sons to *Dom Lopo de Almeyda*; the other Commanders were *Gil Coutinho*, and *Luis de Sousa* Son to the High Chancellor of the Kingdome. And that he might know the condition of the Enemy, He dispatch't two Envoys, (experienc't in the Coast and In-land of *Cambaya*) with Letters to *Soldan Mahamud*, in which he told him the advice he had, of the Levies, and preparations he had made, of which, he hop't, for an account from him, because like a Friend he would accompany him in his design, which he could at present very easily do, having ready at Sea a very strong Fleet, and in the Fortress of *Dio* stout Souldiers with an Overplus of Provision, who had much rather enrich themselves with the spoils of VVarr, then be at the pittance of an idle Peace; He charg'd too those he sent cunningly to observe the Enemies Forces, what Auxiliaries he had, and what the people said, that so by that, they might Dive into the bottom of the design. But whilst our Envoys are setting Sail, we will forbear speaking

Who writes to the *Soldan*.

about

about the business of *Cambaya*, to make room for the successes in the *Molucco's*, which depend on this Government.

11. The *Molucco's* were many years under the obedience of our Laws, Discovered and Conquer'd by the Arms of this Crown, which were the first of *Europe* came to those Islands, assign'd to us by the partition the Pope made 'twixt the Kings of *Portugall* and *Castile*; the King *Dom Manoel*, had on his side the right of Arms and Laws; these Islands not coming to *Portugall* by Conquest only, but by Inheritance. In the time of the King *Dom Manoel*, the last and first of the Name, the Church and State equally flourish't in those Islands, the light of the Gospel, in the ecclipse of *Paganism*, shining there through his Zeal; many Kingdoms receiv'd from this so happy Prince their Religion and Government. This King *Dom Manoel*, (Baptiz'd in *Goa*) was amongst others King and Lord of the chief Islands of the *Molucco's*, who well grounded in the Mysteries of our Faith, returning to Govern and Instruct his people, Dy'd without any Heir, in *Molucco*; and out of Gratitude, for the benefits receiv'd of this Crown, left, by Solemn will, (Confirm'd by all the Formalities of the Law) the King *Dom John* the third, Heir of the Kingdoms of the *Molucco's*, to be successively annex't to the Crown of *Portugall*. These Islands first discovered with Pains, defended with our Blood, and possest with so much Right, have we seen parted with (against the opinion of the best Lawyers and Geographers) to *Castile*.

The Kings of *Portugall's* right over the *Molucco's*.

History of *India*, Dec. 5. Cap. 10. Lib. 10.

12. The Governour *Dom John de Castro* found in *Goa* *Cachil de Aeyro*, one of great Power in the *Molucco's*; who had for his Service deserv'd well of the State, and was the nearest Ally'd to the Royal blood of the last Prince *Dom Manoel*, but, by many accidents so poor, as he came to *India* to recommend himself to our Charity. The Governour, thinking his misfortunes not deserv'd by his Blood, (believing too that the memory

The Governour gives 'em to *Cachil Aeyro*.

History of *India*, Dec. 6. Lib. 1. Cap. 4.

of our Kings would be more honour'd by giving away, then receiving a Kingdome) invested him in the Crown of the *Molucco*'s, with this caution, that in him, and his Posterity, the exercise of the Regality should depend on *Portugall*. Amongst the Kings of *India*, some, made so great a gift a piece of Prodigality, others of Pride, but all stood amaz'd that we should take so much pains for what we gave away so easily.

The *Castilians* come thither.

13. Whilst this was doing, things in the *Molucco*'s; were not a little disturb'd, by the arrival of three *Castilian* Ships, which, falling from their intended course, got sight of those Islands, and, (to refresh themselves after a Storm at Sea, and carry their Prince more certainty of their discovery) Landed in the Island *Tidore*; I will not relate the Resistance our men made 'em, because that hapned under an other Government, and is Written by a better Pen; I'le but just tell what fell out in *Dom John de Castro*'s time, who sent *Fernaon de Sousa de Tavora* to the *Molucco*'s to dislodge the *Castilians*, who, invited by the Plenty and Richness of the Soil, had a mind to enjoy the Fruits of other mens Labours, and disturb the Peace, and Trade of those Islands, to which, by Conquest and Inheritance, we had a double Title. *Ruy Lopez de Villalobos*, a man more wary then Valiant was Commander of the *Castilians*, he had proudly boasted of the strength of the Emperour Charls the Fifth his Master, and, of the advantage, which from his Friendship those *Pagan* Kings might receive in their Warrs and Trade, had too handled the report of us with a great deal of Disparagement; and, (things hop't for, being in the opinion of men, greater then those at present;) some of the Islands listned to the *Castilian*, pleading for it, either sleight or forgotten Grievances.

Who was their Commander.

Fernaon de Sousa arrives at *Molucco*.

14. *Fernaon de Sousa*, sent by the Governour, arriv'd about this time at *Molucco*, who upon information, how things stood, by *Jurdaon de Freitas*, (Commander in chief of the Fortress) perceiv'd the *Castilians* party grew greater,

greater, in hopes of Succour and Money promis'd from *Spain*; As soon as *Ruy Lopez* had notice of *Fernaon de Sousa*'s coming, and of the business he came about (desiring artificially to excuse or delay breaking with us, till the assistance he hop't for, came from *Spain*) he sent to Visit him, and by a plausible Letter, minded him, that they were amongst *Pagans*, who, that they might be their own Masters, Coveted our falling out; that we already had Warrs, and Enemies enough in *India*; that we were very few to plant so great a World; that he profer'd us his Sword, with that to keep the *Pagans* more in awe; that, as *Spaniards* they were good Souldiers, and as *Catholicks* they were better Friends; that he was to consider, Peace with the Emperour more concern'd *Portugall* then the Cloves of the *Malucco*; that those differences betwixt the Subjects, might prove like Mines, which often play a great way off the place they were Sprung at.

The *Castilian* goes about to amuse him.

15. To this Letter, compos'd of *Rodomontados* and Flatteries, *Fernaon de Sousa*'s answer was, that he was but a little man, but as short in his Resolution as his Stature; that those Islands were his Masters the King of *Portugall*; that he was able with the same Sword which got 'em to defend 'em; that he very well knew him to be a *Spaniard*, and a *Catholick*, but that being so, did not warrant him to take away his Cloak; that the Emperour would not make Warr with *Portugall* before first reading in the Chronicles of *Castile*, how it far'd with his Predecessors; that what he was to do, was, either to embarque for *India*, or put himself with his men into the Fort; thence he would provide him with safe Shipping for *Spain*.

Fernaon de Sousa's answer.

16. The *Castilian*, by this so peremptory Letter, saw that *Fernaon de Sousa* would not by slow-working Physick Cure the distemper, and, neither able to resist him, nor willing to obey him, writ to him the second time, for a suspension of Arms; that they might advise their Princes how things stood, and they make an accom-

The *Castilian* continues his first motion.

modement

modement of this affair; for, if before employing that diligence there should be any Blood shed, it would lye upon both the Kings to revenge their Subjects injuries; that there were betwixt *Portugall* and *Castile* many pretences and grievances which Peace cover'd; that he was not desirous to revive that Fire which was Buried in the Ashes of a long *Amnesty*; that if the *Castilians* went away with complaints in their Mouths, their own injuries might easily bring them back again; that, though broken with the Sea, and their Sufferings, if oblig'd to unreasonable conditions, their own Gallantry would inspirit 'em, with more vigor then their present necessity.

17. *Fernaon de Sousa*, by the intrigues of this Letter, and other intelligence, knowing, that the *Castilians* aim'd at doing their business by delays; answer'd, that leaving off Arguments he should prepare to defend his right by the Sword.

The Captains see one the other.

18. *Ruy Lopez de Villalobos*, by this answer finding himself, either detected or scorn'd, chose rather to be overcome by reason, then force, and immediately writ to *Fernaon de Sousa* that the next day, only with three Companions they might meet at Sea, to conclude on the terms of Passage and Shipping he had proffer'd, which was accordingly done, *Fernaon de Sousa* coming from the Fort in a Boat very richly adorn'd, and steering to the *Castilians*, who staid for him, they spent a great deal of time in the tedious Ceremonies of concluding who was to go into the others Boat; the *Castilian* went into *Fernaon de Sousa*'s, where their Salutes and Civilities made way for the business in hand.

Their agreement.

See the Copy of this agreement, History of *India*, Dec. 4. Cap. 1. Lib. 7.

19. *Fernaon de Sousa* with a great deal of moderation insisted on the reasons of his pretensions, which were engrost and allow'd of, by the Kings of *Portugall* and *Castile*, and which *Ruy Lopez de Villalobos* was glad to see, our right being his discharge; they concluded, that within three days the *Castilians* should come into our Fortress of *Ternate*, where passage should be provided

'em

'em for *India*, with liberty to carry away the Goods, Commodities, and Arms they had, and that the King of *Tidore*, of their Faction, should continue as before in our favour; the Solemnities which ended this agreement were a great Banquet, and merrily Drinking their Kings healths, a civility they often afforded 'em; *Fernaon de Sousa* (as the custom is in *India*) added presents to the entertainment, giving Jewels to the Captain and his Companions, so leaving 'em more satisfy'd with their Merchandize, then dispatch, for the pleasantness of the Cloves made up the Disgusts of their reception.

20 *Fernaon de Sousa*, having sent away the Captains, return'd to the Fort, very well satisfy'd that he had so much, to the advantage of his own Honour, and the State, 'plaind so perplext a business; on the third day, (the day appointed for the *Castilians* to come to our Fort) *Fernaon de Sousa* made all the Pompous preparations he could, to shew the Pleasure with which he expected his Guests, whom he went out to Sea to seek, which when *Ruy Lopez* was advis'd of; he sent off a Boat from shore, desiring him to put off the business till the next day, for he was then encountring with some difficulties, which from him he should be acquainted with. *Fernaon de Sousa*, taking this delay to be design, and that the *Castilian* kept not touch with him, and receiving the message at Sea, commanded his men to Row, and with more passion then prudence went alone amongst the *Castilians*; *Ruy de Lopez* saw it, and with a Guard of fourscore Musquetiers came to wait for him at the Sea-side, whence carrying him to his Lodgings, told him what a Tumult had hapned amongst his men, for *Dom Alonso Henriquez*, Captain of a Ship, cloaking his own interest with the zeal of serving his Prince, refus'd to stand to the agreement, and had about him (who upheld his party) his Friends and some mutinous Persons, possessing the King of *Tidore* and others with extravagant Jealousies, thereby to encrease his

The *Castilian* keeps not his promise,

What *Fernaon de Sousa* doth in the business.

Faction, calling his Sedition, Zeal, and the Generals moderation, Cowardise, for delivering up the Arms and Banners of *Spain*, which with his Life he had sworn to Defend, and depriving the Emperour of the Command of such plentifull Islands, and the poor Souldiers of the fruit and reward of so dangerous a Voyage; that the *Portuguese*, a proud Nation, and always Cross to theirs, would Laugh at our so tame a surrender: But that he knew all that bravery to be falsly grounded, for 'twas neither the service of *Cesar*, nor the love of Honour, which mov'd 'em, but the desire of the Cloves, of which they had gather'd great quantities, and could not trust us, that we would let 'em carry to *Spain* the news of that Commodity, whose worth would pay 'em for all the dangers and troubles they had run through; *Fernaon de Sousa* and the rest, (who said as he did) hearing this, as to that particular, took off their fears, and (the *Castilians* gallantry only covering their interest) the next day they rendred themselves at the Fort, forgetting the high words in which they had Ranted.

Coge-Sofar's proposition to the Captain of *Dio*.

21. But the noise of *Cambaya's* Arms allows not a Digression for less concernments. *Coge-Sofar* did absolutely superintend this Warr, the good Event of which he laid partly in his Forces, partly in his Stratagems. Whilst he brought together his Baggage and supplies, (which for their greatness required several opportunities) he writ to *Dom John Mascarenhas*, that he was desirous to take away that Scandal which disquieted the Peace made betwixt the *Soltan* and the State, that with mutual Friendship they might enjoy the Fruits of so just an agreement; that we had, by the Articles, agreed a Wall should be made 'twixt the Fortress and the City, which was then not done, not to shew any Jealousie in so young a friendship, but now, when so many years Peace had carry'd away any unjust affection, 'twas fit to satisfie the people who desir'd that separation, as a mark of the Liberty they liv'd in; that when on that side we sleighted the Wall of the City,

History of *India*, Dec. 6. Lib. 1. Cap. 2.

'twas

'twas out of Anger, and the liberty of Victory, and the Inhabitants could not endure to be every day minded of their Ignominy by so scornfull a Memorial; that when no Symptoms of hatred were in their minds, 'twas not well to preserve them in scattered stones; that we being but strangers in *Dio*, 'twas not for us to give Laws like Masters; that the *Citizens* would take it very ill that what their Kings allow'd 'em, their Neighbours should take away; that we ought from others Subjects to seek for Friendship, not Obedience; that the *Sultan* had given him that City, which he resolv'd to enlarge with new Inhabitants, who should see that Fortress was not a Bridle, but a Defence to those who Liv'd there; that 'twas but fit the *Portuguese* should give the people all possible satisfaction to secure a Peace founded on oppression.

22. *Dom John Mascarenhas* by this Letter perceiv'd that *Coge-Sofar* sought for pretences to break, for, to permit the Building of the Wall, help't his design; to deny it, justify'd the Warr; whereupon he answered him, that in so well grounded a Peace as was 'twixt *Mahumud* and the State, 'twould be more secure to throw down, then go about to build up Walls; that the Wall would neither endanger us nor secure them; that 'twixt the Fortress and the City there was an other manner of defence which Guarded it, which was the Loyalty of the *Portuguese*; that he gave him joy of his new Seigniory, that he might reckon on the *Portuguese* as of his other Subjects; that what he propos'd was to be referr'd to the Governour of *India*, who was setting out a Fleet to come and Visit the Fortress; that upon his arrival he would acquaint him with his proposition; and immediately advis'd the Governour how things stood, who by the Envoys he sent to *Cambaya* had already a more perfect knowledge of the intended Siege, receiving but a dubious answer from the *Soldan*, who neither own'd, nor deny'd the Action, unseasonably repeating past offences, as if (with-

The Captains answer,

and advice to the Governour,

(without disturbing the Peace) he would commence a Warr.

Who succours *Dio* with Men and Ammunition.

23. The Governour, giving himself wholly up to this business, and considering the importance of the place, resolv'd for its defence to engage all the strength of the State, without sparing expence, danger, or diligence. He very feelingly recommended the succour of *Dio* to the Cities of *Bacaim* and *Chaul*, which were the nearest to him, putting them in mind of their Honour, Reward, and Duty; in *Goa* he ordered the providing a great Carvel with Ammunition and Provision, and two hundred and fifty Souldiers, who finding the Seas high, with a great deal of difficulty recovered *Bacaim*, and striving to cross over to *Dio*, were by strong and contrary Winds shattered and forc't back.

The Trechery *Coge-Sofar* set upon.

History of *India*, Cap. 6. Lib. 1. Dec. 6.

24. *Coge-Sofar* not having his Forces together, set upon us by other ways. With large gifts, and greater promises, he bought out the fidelity of one of our Souldiers, that in the dead of the Night he should either fire the Powder, or poyson the Cistern, or if he could not compass either of those designs, he should endeavour, through the House in which he Liv'd (fit for that mischief by its joyning to the VVall) to let the *Moors* into the Fort. The Souldier being timorous, or irresolv'd, acquainted an intimate of his (a *Moor*) with the business, who (the reward for discovering Treasons being surer then for Executing 'em) told it to the Commander in chief, he having, by two other hands had it, and considering how foul the fault was for the example of it, and not sufficiently prov'd for the punishing it, that the Offence deserv'd not pardon, nor the Conjuncture allow'd not the punishment, sent away the Souldier with Letters to the Governour, acquainting him with what proofs he had of the suspected Treason.

What preventions *Dom John Mascarenhas* made.

25. *Dom John Mascarenhas* making sure of a Warr, gave order (whilst a pretended Peace gave Colour to a Trade) to buy up what Provisions were in the City, a

a care which for some time kept off, or reliev'd their Starving; for the security of commerce was soon altered, by a Captains coming into the City with five hundred *Turks*, more to dispose, then make a Warr. He brought fresh Letters for the Commander from *Coge-Sofar*, in which both warily and earnestly, he prest the making up of the Wall; *Dom John Mascarenhas* would not now return any answer to 'em, telling the *Turk*, the *Portuguese* granted no Petitions, which were writ by men with Musquets on their Shoulders. That day was not the first of Warr, being the last of Peace; for on the next *Coge-Sofar* entred with eight thousand men to begin the Siege, cutting off from us all succour by Land; what was to be expected by Sea, the storms of Winter began now to hinder; the worst Enemy the Fortress had. * This being the place where the *Portuguese* acted so great wonders, we will in short inform you of its situation.

* *Illustre em Ce.cos & batalhas.* Fam'd for Sieges and Pitch't fields, *Cam.* Can to. Sta. 35.

The description of *Dio.*

26. The Island of *Dio*, renown'd for the Richness of its commerce, deplorable for the ruine of its Inhabitants, famous for the report of our Victories, lies in a Bay, and on a Point, which bounds the Kingdome of *Cambaya*, in the heighth of twenty two degrees Northward. The *Natives* do fabulously speak of the antiquity of its Foundation, allowing it a more noble, then certain beginning; keeping the Records in their Traditions for want of writing: The Port was always the chief Scale of the Bay, frequented by Ships which went to *Mecca*, which Voyage, Religion and Trade make very gratefull to the *Moors*. The City, is by a Channel which goes about it, divided from the main Land; 'tis by situation strong, and by helping out nature with art, is made more tenable. The Channel which surrounds it, hath two Outlets, one toward the *North*, which shallow, and full of Sands is of no use; the other toward the *South* inconvenient too for the Cragginess of the Rocks which form it; it hath on the fore-part of the Isle an other Channel where Ships may Anchor, and

by this is the best passage to the City. 'Tis not of that figure, *John de Barros* describes it of, having been altered by the differency of *Moors* who have possest it, each of them Fortifying it a new way, as they were taught by their judgment or the variety of Times.

The famous *Portuguese* Historian who hath writ their Voyages to, and Conquests, in the *Indies*; often quoted in this Translation.

27. *Coge-Sofar* came into the Town with eight thousand men, (many of 'em *Turks* who serv'd him for Pay) sixty great Pieces, ('mongst which were eighteen Basilisks) Ammunition and Provision for his men, as fore-seeing the length of the Siege; He had too in his Camp a thousand *Janizaries*, who had more then ordinary Pay; who, out of their Habituated insolence slighted the design, condemning *Coge's* fear for bringing Forces together, and disturbing the Grand *Signior's* Arms against four pitifull *Christians*, defended by a rotten Wall, against whom, neither Honour was to be gain'd by Fighting, or Plunder by Conquering. *Coge-Sofar* neither commended, or condemn'd the *Turks* courage; but (better taught by his fear, or experience) look't upon the Victory as not so sure; in opening his Trenches, planting his Batteries, forming his Squadrons, he shew'd himself a Souldier; and when he was laid down before the Fortress made this short Speech to the *Turks*.

Great Canon so call'd.

Coge-Sofar Speech to his men.

28. "Friends, and Companions, 'tis not my design "to teach you, either, to fear or despise those few *Portuguese*, whom you see besieg'd within those Walls; "for though Souldiers, yet are they not more then men. "Fortune hath hitherto, bore 'em company, or serv'd "'em all over the *East*; and the Fame of their first "Victories hath help't 'em to the rest. VVith a few "men they make VVarr upon the whole VVorld; and "by the course of things, an Empire (kept up only in "the Opinion, or by the weakness of the Conquer'd) "cannot last, without Forces; they have scarce five "hundred men in the Fortress, most of whom are Garrison Souldiers, who of custom use to be the poorest, "or most useless; by Land they can have no relief,

"what

"what is to be had by Sea, the Winter cuts off: they "want, by the security of their Peace, or Pride, (out "of which they despis'd every thing) Ammunition and "Provisions: being but few, the same men must always "be upon that Wall, not having one Souldier in re-"serve, to supply an others place; they have not "Pioneers to repair the Breaches of our Batteries, and "their Duty amongst so few must necessarily make 'em "yield; they are insolent upon the Dammage they did "the Grand *Signior's* Galleys at the siege of the same "Fortress; it concerns so many honourable *Turks*, and "Valiant *Janizaries* as are here to go on, for the ho-"nour of your Nation and Empire, as the most justi-"fiable cause of this Warr; for though *Cambaya* hath "Armies and Souldiers, 'tis not for the Grand *Signior's* "repute, with Forein force, to revenge his injuries. I "therefore put you upon this design, that none else "might Rob you of the glory of so just vengeance; "this same Ground you now tread upon, covers the "Bones of your Comrades, Kindred, and Friends, who "(me-thinks call upon every one of us by Name) tel-"ling us the Deaths and Wounds, they from these "Murtherers receiv'd, hoping by your Prowess to rest "reveng'd. These are those who kill'd *Badur*, ingrate-"full for benefits, presuming too farr on the Majesty "of so great a Prince; the revenging of whom, will be "acceptable to all Kings, necessary to us who are his "Subjects.

29. Having made an end of his Speech, either desiring, more to justifie the Warr, or gain time for the expectance of supplies, he try'd *Dom John Mascarenhas* with harder terms, resolutely insisting on the Building up the Wall, and demanding that the Ships of the *Soltan*, (his Master) might Sail freely up and down without passes from our Generals, an affront, which, the *Sultan* bore as a Friend, but could not endure as a Prince: He further requir'd that the Merchants Ships might not be oblig'd to put in at that Port; which was

He sends again to the Captain of *Dio*.

History of *India*, Dec. 6. Cap. 7. Lib. 1.

The Captains anſwer.

a Liberty he ought to grant for the benefit of Trade. *Dom John Maſcarenhas* return'd anſwer, that, friendly Treaties were not to be made amidſt Drums and Guns; that, 'twas the Cuſtom of that Fort to give Laws to every one, not to receive 'em from any; that he hop't ſhortly to Baniſh him for a breaker of the Peace, when to his grief, he ſhould accept of worſe Conditions which ſhould be writ with the very Blood of his *Janizaries*.

The Governour ſends his Son *Dom Fernando* to *Dio*.

30. The Governour, by this time, had, with ſtrange Expedition, made ready nine Veſſels, telling the Souldiers who went on 'em, that in ſo Honourable a deſign, only his Favourites were to be truſted; that he would now change the Confinement of his Place, for the liberty of any Souldier; that, though he was reſolv'd in Perſon to go raiſe the ſiege of *Dio*, he could not diſſemble the Envy he had to thoſe who were firſt to Grapple with the *Turks*, and preſently calling for his Son, [*a*] *Dom Fernando*, told him in the publick Hall; "I ſend you Son with this relief to *Dio*, which (as "I'me inform'd, is now beſieg'd by a great Army "of *Turks*;) for what concerns your own Perſon "take no care, for, for every ſtone of that Fortreſs "would I venture a Son. I charge you to remember

[*a*] *Baſiliſcos medonhos, & lioens*
Trabucos feros, minas encubertas,
Suſtenta Maſcarenhas *con baroens*
Que taon ledos as mortes tem por certas
Ate que nas mayores oppreſſoens
Caſtro *libertador, fazendo offertas*
Das vidas de ſeus filhos, quer que fiquem
Com fama eterna, e a Deos ſe ſacrifiquem.

Drakes, horrid Baſiliſks, Engines of Wood
As bad as either, ſecret Mines and Plots,
Hath *Maſcarenhas* with his men withſtood
Meeting their certain Deaths with willing Throats,
When in the utmoſt ſtreſs of Fleſh and Blood
Caſtro their freer his two Sons devotes,
That everlaſting honour they may gain,
And ſacrifices to their God be ſlain.

Camo. Can. 10. St. 69.

"from

"from whom you come, who are by Kindred your Ancestors, by their Exploits your Example; strive to "deserve the Name you Inherit, considering that by "Birth all are equal, and men only differenc't by their "Actions, and that I tell you, he who returns most "Honourable shall be my Son; That's the blessing our "Fore-fathers left us, to Dye gloriously for our Laws, "for our King, and for our Country. I put you in the "way of honour, 'tis in you now to winn it. With that he gave him his blessing, and recommended him to *Diogo de Reynoso*, one of the bravest Cavalliers who came for *India*; In this relief was *Sebastion de Sa*, Son to *John Rodriguez de Sa*, who, in this occasion, and others gave remarkable proofs of his Courage, there went too with him, *Dom Francisco de Almeyda*, Son to *Dom Lopo*, to be a Companion to two Brothers he had in *Dio*; there were in the same relief, *Antonio da Cunha, Pero Lopez de Sousa, Diogo da Sylva, Iorge Mascarenhas, Antonio de Mello*, and many other Gentlemen, who then pursu'd dangers as if they fled from 'em.

31. The Governour writ a very civil Letter to *Dom John Mascarenhas*, telling him how much greater it was on this occasion to be Commander of *Dio* then Governour of *India*; that he had in that relief sent him his Son *Dom Fernando*, that if ever he return'd into the Kingdome, he might amongst the Vanities of his Old age tell of his being a Souldier under him; that he might be confident, all the strength the State could make should be ingag'd in the Defence of that Fortress; that there were on those Ships many young Gentlemen, whose forwardness it behoov'd him to temper, because men Besieg'd were only to stand upon their Defence; that he had there sent him, as much Ammunition as would expect a second Relief, two Engineers, and a great many ordinary Work-men (with Instruments and Materials for that purpose) to make up the Breaches of the Enemies batteries: In which *Dom John de Castro* shew'd not only the zeal of a pub-

lick Minister, but the experience of a Souldier, by fore-seeing their extremities and preventing 'em.

The Captain of Dio disposeth of the Commands of the Fort,

32. *Dom John Mascarenhas* had Commanded a Bridge (which went from Saint *James*'s work for the convenience of the Garrison over to the other side) to be broken down, and the making of a Draw-bridge in stead of it. Saint *James* his Tower he committed to the charge of *Alonso de Bonifacio* Clerk of the Custom-house, Saint *Thomas*'s work to *Luis de Sousa*, St. *John*'s to *Gil Coutinho*, that which was over the Gate to *Antonio Freire*, and another work of Saint *James*'s which commanded the River to *Dom John de Almeyda* and his Brother *Dom Pedro de Almeyda*, Saint *George*'s to *Antonio Pecanna*, the Fause-bray to *John de Venezeanos*, and the Curtain to *Antonio Rodriguez*; amongst those Officers he divided one hundred and seventy Souldiers, He and thirty more were Supernumerary to help upon occasions. *Dom John* with so few men expected so great an Army as came against him; providing with so much security for his Defence, as if the danger was neither fear'd or unexpected. He ordered the Ammunition and Provision to be kept very strictly, because the hindrance of the Weather, and the Enemy, made the receipt of any more uncertain. He set the Slaves and those who were not fit to bear Arms, to bring Lances, Powder, Stones, and Provision to the Works, that the Souldiers might not be taken up in any thing but Fighting; in this Work he employ'd too the Children, the Old men, and the Women, so that there was not in the Fortress Person, or Sex idle or unserviceable, and calling them together upon the Parade of the Fortress, he smilingly spake to 'em;

History of *India*, Dec. 6. Cap. 7. Lib. 1.

and speaks to his Souldiers.

33. "Those *Turks*, and *Janizaries* you see from "hence, are come to winn of us the Honour they lost "in the first Siege, yet are they not more considerable "then those who were beaten, nor we less then those "who overcame; I confess to you I envy the meanest "Souldier who kept this place, because the memory of "his

"his Valour doth yet honour his Posterity, whom we "know not so well by their Name, Country, or Birth, "as by being the Sons, or Grand-children of those who "so gloriously fell, or triumph'd in *Dio:* The greatest "honour'd their Families, the meanest begun theirs. "Fortune hath brought us upon such an other action; "those stout *Portuguese* had not Buried with 'em all "the glory of Fighting, they have left us what will "make us famous. Let not the inequality of our Forces "fright us, for Renown is not to be purchas'd by ordi-"nary dangers; we have Sail'd five thousand Leagues "only to find out this Day, and in it to gain that ho-"nour neither Kings or Countries can give us; for "Kings give Rewards, not Deserts; we want not Pro-"vision or Ammunition to hold out the Siege till Re-"lief arrives, and though in this Season the Seas are "high, yet have we a *John de Castro* (who with his "Sword in his mouth will come under the Waves to "help us) and so many other Gentlemen and Persons "of Quality who will think themselves injur'd if with-"out them we gain the honour which is before us; "after which we are not to look for any thing more "from Fortune, being to be put on their List who "have memorably serv'd their King and Country, for "the keeping up of whose Honour we are come from "farthest West-ward thus remote, and (what's above "all) we Fight against the Enemies of our Faith, and "in so just a cause cannot want owning, since we serve "the God of Victories.

34. When the Speech was ended, there was In the *Turks* Camp heard a great Shooting, by which *Coge-Sofar* welcom'd a Relief of two thousand Foot, which were come to him from *Cambaya*, all old Souldiers, who made the succour more considerable by its quality, then number; there came with these two of the *Mogull's* Commanders, Persons very much Cry'd up by their own men. The same day there came in a great part of the Nobility from the Court, which at some distance

There comes in more Relief to the Enemies.

distance from the Leaguere, Lodg'd themselves in Rich Tents, with such Order, as wanted nothing of the Discipline of *Europe*; Our men, by not valuing their Lives, put off the Terrour of such great preparations, encouraging one the other by Discourses suitable to the occasion, taking Counsel of their necessity how to behave themselves.

They begin to batter the Fort.

35. The next day (which was Maunday Thursday in the year 1546.) there appear'd betimes in the Morning near our Fortress a solid work of Earth, with its Skit-gates, and in them some great Pieces, and on top of the work a great many Sacks of Cotton, cover'd with Raw hides to resist the Fire, a thing, which for the little noise and time it was contriv'd in, much startled our men, and did not look like the design of a Confus'd and Barbarous multitude, who, whilst the Siege lasted, shew'd as much Valour, as Discipline; they presently began, with a great deal of success, to batter our Fort, dismounting four of our Gunns, which did the greatest Dammage to their Battery.

A Stratagem of the Enemies in a Ship.

36. That days good fortune Counsell'd 'em for the rest, making in five Nights as many Forts, at a proportionable distance, to give by the several Breaches a general assault, which so few Defendants so divided would not be able to withstand; the success might have answer'd the design, had not our Fort which lay on the Sea, and commanded theirs, done 'em so much harm, that they thought fit to look to their own Reparations before our Offence; the great Gunns were silent for two days, in which they contriv'd a second Fabrick to secure their first. They put to Sea a Tall Ship, full of Powder, Stone-pitch, and other Combustible matter, this they laid on the first Deck, as a Stratagem prepar'd for a second design, over this they made a false Deck, capable of two hundred Fighting men, as if with them designing to Scale: The Ship so lay, as to command that part of the Fort, whether, they concluded, our men upon their advantage of place to Fight on, and numbers,

History of *India*, Dec. 6. Lib. 1. Cap. 8.

numbers, would probably come, when in the heat of the Conflict, quitting the Ship, they would set her on Fire, which lighting on the Fort, might burn it without any Dammage or Danger to their own men; and that presently entring on the ruins the Fire had left, they would on them cast up an other, whence they might batter our Fortress, and by this new work secure their former, and so their Gunns play securely. A Stratagem grounded on Soldier-like conclusions.

37. *Dom John Mascarenhas* had (by some Spies he had in the Camp) notice of the *Machine* and design, and calling to him *Jacome Leyte*, Commander at Sea, a Souldier of great trust, told him he would not Rob him of the honour belong'd to his employment; that he thought the first Atchievement of this Siege ought to be his, and acquainting him with the advice he had, gave him Orders to be ready in the second VVatch. *Jacome Leyte* put to Sea at the hour appointed in two Boats with thirty Souldiers, and Rowing quietly till he came up with the Ship, began to cast in her a great many Pots of Powder. The *Moors* at once saw their danger, and the Fire burning 'em, and running to their Arms, distracted by fear and sleep, did faintly and confusedly defend themselves, hindring one an other by the Noise and Tumult so unexpected an Onset had caus'd: some began to throw themselves into the Sea, who shew'd the way and example to the rest; at last, with Complaints and Clamors they left the Ship, giving the Alarum to the whole Camp. *Jacome Leyte* had time enough to make fast a Cable to the Ship, and tow her after his; The Captain receiv'd him with Praises and Embraces, making more of this success, because it so happily began the Warr. The *Moors*, though with eminent danger, continued their Battering, for every stone they unloosned of the Fortress, paying Souldiers, and Canoneers, their Battery did no considerable harm; only Saint *James*'s Bastion, being the weakest or the most Batter'd, was open in two places, and the Breaches

Set on Fire by our men,

And brought to the Fort.

 wide

wide enough to enter upon assault; though those within defended themselves with Retrenchments, and by Night stole Earth to make up the Breaches.

38. The Battery continued not without Execution, the Wall being in many places open, every where shattered, and not a Souldier could peep through the Battlements, who was not peirc't with the Enemies Arrows, or wounded with their Shot, which was so thick as it appear'd to be a continual Discharging, *Coge-Sofar* little valuing the spending Ammunition, or venturing Soldiers, as being sufficiently furnish't and stock't with both; He was too, answered by our Gunns from the Fortress, and with more Dammage, for the *Moors* being in multitudes, not a Bullet was spent in vain.

39. The *Turks* were earnest to go on upon the Assault, because in many places the Battery had done Dammage enough to scale the Wall, yet did *Coge-Sofar* keep them off, expecting more Force, or willing by continual Duty and Wounds to abate the height of our men, whose eagerness he hop't by slow Fighting to tame, and waste the Forces, Ammunitions, and Patience of the Besieged; an Argument not altogether out of the way, for the Winter, which had begun furiously, took away the possibility of that succour which was necessary, and wanted from the first day, for the carelesness of Peace and suddain invasion of the Enemy had made ours unprovided to endure the weight of that Warr, their confidence in that kind being so extravagant, that since the siege *Antonio da Sylveira* held out, the place was only kept by the repute of that Victory; and *Dom John Mascarenhas* had no more then forty Barrils of Powder for Canon, and twenty for Musquets, scarcity of Provisions, as well as of Men, who saw the VVarr before they expected it, the Defendants were but two hundred, most of them Garrison-Souldiers, who were to have their first credit by that Siege.

40. The Captain was not a little troubled at the State of things, and the uncertainty of relief, which, it

concern'd

concern'd him as cautiously to keep from his own as the Enemy, neither would he in the beginning of the Siege stint the Provision, and Ammunition, seeing, one way, the ill consequence, the other, the necessity of doing it; when the VVatch came to tell him there appear'd nine Sail, which seem'd by their Built to be Ours, the transport of this News brought all the Souldiers on the VVall. The distance, and closeness of the VVeather made them of different Opinions, but within an hour they made the Colours of the Squadron, and presently after the Admiral with the King's Arms, which by contrary VVinds was working it up towards our Fortress; they all had their Pendants flying, and Flaggs of defiance in the main top; they immediately saluted the Towers, who return'd them the same Sea-civility. The *Moors* from the Shore made many a Shot at them whilst they cast Anchor; They first unladed the Ammunition and Provision, afterwards the Souldiers, and last of all *Dom Fernando* went on shore, which was either the Fathers advice, or the Sons gallantry.

Dom Fernando arrives at *Dio*.

History of *India*, Dec. 6. Cap. 9 Lib. 1.

41. The Commander in chief, having receiv'd those Gentlemen as Companions of his Fortune, knowing of *Dom Fernando*'s coming, went to seek him on Board, and met him on the steps of the Fortress as he was coming up, he took him in his Arms, and spake to him as time and place requir'd, offering him his own Lodging, which *Dom Fernando* would not accept, desiring him to reserve that honour till they had Peace; that for the present, that part of the works where was the greatest danger should be his Chamber; that his Sleep would do him no good; one step from the Wall; *Dom John Mascarenhas* again embrac't him, wondring, in so Green years, to meet so Manly a temper.

Dom John Mascarenhas receives him.

42. There came in the Ships good store of Powder, Arms, and Provision, with which they might hold out the Siege till fresh Relief; neither did the Governour forget to send Physick and Regallos for the Sick and Wounded. The Commander shew'd the Souldiers the Gover-

Governours Letter, in which (as we said) he secur'd him of his coming, for which he was providing with the greatest diligence and strength the State was capable of, which put new hearts into the Besieged, and made them look with an other Face upon the exigencies and preparations of the Warr, which was like to continue. *Coge-Sofar* receiving every day supplies, and laying new designs, for which he had from diverse places brought Engineers, who were, by ambition and reward, put upon new inventions, which made our men more sollicitous for the danger they saw not, then for that before 'em.

The Governour proclaims Warr against *Cambaya*.

43. The Governour, after having dispatch't his Son *Dom Fernando*, gave Order for Proclaiming a Warr at Fire and Sword against the King of *Cambaya*, as one who was perjur'd, and had broke the Peace betwixt him and the State: this he did with Warlike and Legal solemnities, thereby to publish, and justifie the motives of a Warr, which kept in suspence the judgments of the whole *East*. He writ to the Inhabitants of *Bacaim*, minding them, that as nearest, they were oblig'd to succour *Dio*, that other places help't in the States danger, they in their own, the Gunns which battered *Dio*, shaking the Houses of *Bacaim*; that he was providing to go raise the Siege, and use all imaginable Hostility against *Cambaya*, because the State never had a defensive VVarr with the Kings of the *East*; that he desir'd 'em to be ready to accompany him with Ships and Men, as was to be expected from so many Honourable *Citizens*, and Loyal *Portuguese*; that he left it to themselves what they would do for the Service, looking that every one out of Loyalty and Love to his King, should out-go his possibility.

44. He writ in the same manner to all those places from which he could receive any help, finding them dispos'd to the Service, and for that to the spending their Estates: an happiness which we must reckon upon as peculiar in his Government, as on diverse occasions the

the History will shew. He fell upon providing the Fleet with a great deal of earnestness, and finding the State too poor for such an expence, ask't great summs of the Merchants upon his word (which was the Gold and Diamonds he only laid up) a Pawn on which all men of Trading offer'd him what they had; I know not if now amongst men of Power Estates of that nature go currant for so much. He ordered publick and private Prayers to be made, beseeching God, since t'was his own, to protect the cause of the Faithfull, relying more upon Sacrifice, then Arms; his ordinary discourse was with Experienc't men about the business of *Dio*, and was more inclin'd by the reason, then the authority of the Votes.

He borrows of the Merchants.

He goes to God by publick Prayers

45. Our Arms in *Dio* did not grow rusty. The Commander having advice that there was expected to be put into the Army a great Caravan of Provisions, which were to be Laden on the Coast betwixt *Balsar* and *Damaon*, upon it sent forth the Sea-Commander *Jacome Leyte* with three Ships, to lye about the Island *Dos Mortos*, who by Night getting over the Barr and Sailing along the Shore, took by it a great many Vessels which came to furnish the Army, he put the *Moors* to the Sword except some he kept to hang at the Yards Arms when he came over the Barr; which he did, presenting the Army with a Lamentable sight, who had too the Confirmation of what had past by the Fire they saw burning the Vessels, the Provisions were brought into the Fortress, which were what they then most wanted.

They take a great deal of Provisions from the Enemy.

46. *Coge-Sofar* had already lost a great many men, without seeing the Fortress or minds of the Besieged shaken to flatter his hopes of getting it. Our men walk't upon the VVall with wanton Ornaments and Feathers, to shew their pleasure in, or contempt of the VVarr they were engag'd in. *Coge-Sofar*, seeing us with so inconsiderable a strength Masters at Sea, and that the Provisions his Army had came by stealth or in

danger, ordered the setting out a Fleet from *Surrate*, which met with three Ships of ours coming from *Bacaim* and *Chaul* to furnish the Fortress; the *Portuguese* fought very desperately, but by the Odds of their strength, most of them Dy'd, who sold their Life at such a rate, that the *Moors* had no cause to rejoyce in either the Prize or Victory. *Dom Fernando de Castro* ask't leave of the Commander in Chief to go with some Ships to their help, which he did not grant, knowing 'twould be labour lost, for the Enemy stole out and presently retir'd.

The Captain sends News over Land to the King.

47. *Dom John Mascarenhas* thought of advising the King by Land how things were with him; there was fit for that purpose an *Armenian*, skill'd in the Language and Customs of the *Moors*; he was sent away in a light *Brigantine*, which was to set him on shore on the Coast of *Por*, thence in a *Jogues* cloaths (which is amongst them a Religious and poor Habit) he was to go to *Cinde*, and from thence to *Ormus* with Letters to the Captain; He travell'd in the company of some *Basora* Merchants, who by the River *Euphrates* carry'd him to *Babylon*, where he was to stay for the *Caravans* to go over the deserts of *Arabia*.

48. *Coge-Sofar* carry'd on his works with no less danger then toil, and with so Cruel and Barbarous a resoluteness, that he us'd the Bodies of those Pioneers our men Kill'd, for filling up the Ditch; using so inhuman a Discipline, to cover perhaps the loss which novv began to be knovvn in the Army, though made up by daily Reliefs vvhich continually fill'd the Camp. *Coge-Sofar*, vvhere the advantage vvas most, planted sixty great Pieces, of which there vvere *Basilisks*, *Salvages*, *Eagles* and *Camells*, besides less Gunns vvhich exceeded that number; He secur'd the five vvorks he had rais'd vvith nevv VValls, and covered the Pioneers vvith crooked Traveses of so many vvindings that our Guns could not come at 'em; The *Moors* by this means commanded the Fossee of the Fort, vvhere they had planted

Names of Canon.

The Enemies command the Fossee.

planted eighteeen *Basilisks*, which plaid for a fortnight together, with so much Dammage, as our men for their last remedy defended themselves with the very ruins, making Forts retrenchments and reparations of the stones which had been thrown down.

49. We had now lost fourscore men, and had more then an hundred VVounded, besides the scarcity and badness of the Provisions had made many sick; most of the Ammunition was spent, and by it our men brought into a great deal of danger, which *Coge-Sofar* having notice of by some Slaves who run away from the Fortress, ordered the Batteries should be re-inforc't, believing the hearts of such shattered Forces could not hold out; and as one, who would divide with his Prince the smiles of Fortune, sent to the *Sultan*, who was at *Champanel*, to come to the Camp, to put the Fortress on the first assault into his hands; upon the credit of that promise the *Sultan* came with ten thousand Horse, and most of his Court, he was receiv'd with a Vollee Royal, seconded with diverse Instruments of Warr and Mirth, Musick which ours heard, as abating their Courage, and grating their Ears.

History of *India*, Dec. 6. Lib. 2. Cap. 1.

The *Sultan* comes with a great Army.

50. Our men believ'd that the Mirth in the Camp, so Solemniz'd with repeated Vollees, was to welcome those *Turks* they look't for; *Dom John Mascarenhas* presently commanded *Fernaon Cavalho* Commander of the Fort next the Sea, to set out a little Boat to know what past amongst the Enemy, (the Spies he had in the Camp, being either Treacherous, or Discovered) which was done that very Night, and a *Moor* brought us, who told us of the *Sultan*s coming, *Coge-Sofar*'s promises, and the confidence they had of their design. The Commander freed the *Moor*, and bid him from him desire the King of *Cambaya* to stay in the Army, for he hop't to come and Visit him in his quarters. The *Moor* rejoyc't at his Liberty, and wondred at the Captains answer; being brought before *Mahumud*, and repeating the Captains words, he told him, the *Portuguese*

tuguese had their Fort thrown down, and their Hearts whole.

51. *Coge-Sofar* commanded they should continue Battering, and bid *Simaon Feo* (one of ours whom he had against the Law of Arms detain'd Prisoner) tell *Dom John Mascarenhas*, that he wondred to see him so pent up, without Sallying out to Fight in the Field, as did the brave Cavallier *Antonio da Sylveira*, that his actions very much disagreed with his words; our men answered the message with Bullets from the Wall; the Battery lasted five hours, not without doing a great deal of Dammage to the Buildings, which were tottering before; yet our Shot return'd it with more loss, and better fortune, for a Bullet at randome kill'd a *Moor* in the *Sultan*'s Tent, as he was discoursing with him; and the Eastern *Moors* credulously addicted to *Omens*; the King looking upon what had hapned, as a warning of some mischief which was coming (perhaps dissembling his fear by his Superstition) immediately went out of the Field, leaving behind him *Juzarcaon*, a stout *Abessine*, who in the *Mogull*'s Warrs serv'd against *Sultan Mahumed*, and now as a Souldier of fortune, was by some advantages perswaded to take pay in this Warr.

He retires and leaves *Juzarcaon* in his place.

52. The King, having left the Tents, stouter in Peace then Fight, and retiring to his pleasure House of *Melique* on the same Island, did hasten relief, which daily recruited the Camp. *Dom John Mascarenhas*, who in so close Siege knew no certainty of the Enemies designs, was talking vvith the Cavalliers and Gentlemen how much it concern'd 'em to get some advice. *Diogo de Anaya Coutinho*, (a Gentleman vvho Liv'd upon his Pay, yet of bravery becoming his Birth) hearing this discourse, offer'd himself to the Captain, and let down by a Cord from the top of the Wall, protected by the darkness of the Night, went to the Enemies quarters, he had not gone farr, but he spy'd two *Moors* talking hard by him, he scrupled to set upon 'em, because to carry off two was impossible, to fight with 'em inconvenient,

A famous action of *Diogo de Anaya*.

venient, but advising with the occasion, he Knock't down one of 'em with his Lance, and closing with the other (who by Crying out biting and strugling defended himself) carry'd him to the Gates of the Fortress, where he found the Corps of Guard, who with Praises and Envy, brought him and his Prisoner to the Captain. I will now relate a Circumstance greater then the action, *Diogo de Anaya* had borrow'd a Head-piece of a Souldier, and missing it when he was in the Fortress, thinking he had lost it in striving and closing with the *Moor*, went by the same Cord down the VVall, and looking it in the sight of an incenst Army, found it, and brought it back, not less rash then fortunate.

History of *India*, Dec. 6. Lib. 1. Cap. 9.

53. By the News the *Moor* brought, the Captain knew, that *Coge-Sofar* and *Juzarcaon*, this stout, the other desperate, had both mutually Vow'd to *Mahomet* to take *Dio*, or perish in the design; that, if they could not brook us when vve vvere Friends, they should not endure us when Conquerours. By their continual Battering many of their great Guns burst, instead of which they fitted others, shooting impetuously against Saint *Johns*, Saint *Thomas*, and Saint *James*'s Bastions, Commanded by *Dom John de Almeyda*, *Lovis de Sousa*, and *Gil Coutinho*, who slept always in their Armour; in danger constant, unwearied in duty.

54. Saint *James*'s Bastion was the weakest and most battered, and the *Turks* in that fought with our men upon very little disadvantage. There was not in the Fortress Parapet or Battlement which was not thrown down, and from Saint *Johns* to Saint *James*'s Bastion all the Curtain was open, which made the duty of the Day be seconded by the labour of the Night, it being not possible, yet necessary for so few Defendants, so broken, to repair in a few hours the ruins of a Fortress so every where Battered, yet did they unanimously betake themselves to that Labour, they could neither master or excuse.

55. The Women of the Fortress help't to bring Ma-

 terials

The courage of the Women of *Dio*.

terials for the making up the Breaches, going without any fear upon the Wall, stumbling at Lances, Swords, and Bullets, mastring their Nature and Sex, as if they wore men's hearts in a disguise: some there were who put on Arms and brav'd the Enemy, running from their Needle to a Lance, from their Couch to the VVall; of all the rest *Isabell Fernandez* deserv'd the greatest glory, whom (instead of Praises to honour her Memory) our VVriters call the Old woman of *Dio*, famous by this name in the Annals and Memorials of the *East*. This great Matron spent part of her Estate in Junkets and Regallos, with vvhich in the heat of the dispute she fed the Souldiers, animating 'em (with Arguments above the courage and judgment of a VVoman) to defend themselves by Fighting. This diligence of the Matrons (which readily and seasonably put 'em upon any thing, were it servile, or hazardous) was in fine a lightning their Labour, and an example in Dangers.

History of *India*, Dec. 6. Lib. 2. Cap. 2.

56. *Coge-Sofar*, seeing that the mischief his Arms did by Day our industry repair'd by Night, contriv'd a design more subtil in the laying of it, then usefull by the success. Against Saint *Thomas's* work, (vvhich by its make and place lay most obnoxious) he resolv'd to cast up an other which should equal or command it, that by Battering it from above he might throw down the Battlements, so hindring the Defendants from Fighting, and from making up their Breaches by night, his Guns being so Levell'd by day as to be sure of their aim. He presently ordered vvhole mountains of Earth, and brush Fagotts to be brought to fill up the Ditch, and strengthned the Counterscarp vvith bodies of great Trees, to keep up the Earth. The multitude of Pioneers vvho vvere in the Camp made up an other Army, vvho without fear or time carry'd on the vvork. In the interim the Guns from our work plaid to the great loss of the Enemy, for the Work-men being so thick and expos'd, not one Shot from the Fortress was lost.

57. *Coge-*

57. *Coge-Sofar*, considering the greatness of the loss, gave order they should work by Night, when our shooting being without aim and at Rovers the Execution would be less, commanding them to make the most Noise, where they Work't least, that our Canoneers led by their Ear, might point their Ordnance as the Sounds and Ecchos reach't them. This was known to *Dom John Mascarenhas*, who fill'd the Fortress with Lights that the Pioneers who work't on the security of the Night, might be expos'd to the same danger as by day; but *Coge-Sofar* (who had learn't Experience in the Warrs of *Europe*) gave order for the making of crooked and cover'd Trenches, by which the *Moors* more securely went on with the raising their Fort, and we vainly to our loss spent store of our Bullets.

58. The Captain was not a little troubled at it, for if that work went forward there would not be any secure place in the Fortress, the Enemies Canon commanding our Fortifications; so that between the Besiegers and Besieg'd there would be no advantage of place, and that of numbers the *Moors* had eminently above us. Upon debate of the matter in Counsel every one knew the danger, none the remedy. Some, with more Courage then Prudence, were for our mens Sallying forth with apparent danger to interrupt their work, not considering the hazard they run upon, to be greater then that they freed themselves from; but few consented to this advice, yet none could give other. Some Sallies ours made but to little purpose, for the Numbers and Vigilancy of the Enemy secur'd with a great Guard the Posts of the Work-men. But in great Straights danger being usually the best Counsellour, *Dom John Mascarenhas* bethought himself of an eminency in the Fortress, which was higher then Saint *Thomas*'s Fort, from whence our Guns might play; here he made some Pieces be planted, which did so lucky Execution, as in a few days they beat down that Machine, which in its raising and falling cost the Blood of those who Built

Built it. But this *Hydra* being of so many Heads, with the same ruins *Coge-Sofar* set upon the filling up the Ditch, which was easier for him, being a Work that needed neither measure, design, or fore-cast.

59. Two thousand Pioneers began with the materials of the Fort, to fill up the Ditch, and whilst 'twas doing a great body from the Army with Darts, Arrows, and Musquet-shot, kept our men from coming to the Wall. The work increast as did the danger of the Besieged, for the Fortress being ruin'd above, the plain ground with but little raising would be equal to the Wall. The Captain laid about to frustrate his design, and being irresolv'd how, some Old men (brought up in the Fortress) told him that by their quarters there was a Sally-port in the VVall, which length of time had covered with loose Earth; that, by that, without any danger, and with a great deal of ease, might be stole away the Earth they brought to fill up the Ditch. The necessity demanded speedy Execution, the Captain commanded men to Digg, and found a Sally-port fit for his purpose. Our men Sallied out in the Night, and stole the Rubbish which was undermost, leaving a hollow superficies which covered the hollowness, solid in appearance to the Enemies, and as the ground was expos'd to the violence of the Weather it sunk of it self, with the fall of all that imaginary Superstructure in sight of the Enemy.

History of *India*, Dec. 6. Lib. 2. Cap. 3.

60. *Coge-Sofar* had presently intelligence of the way we took to delude that which cost him so much pains, and coming to that place (out of impatience to see all his designs Counterplotted) there came out of the Fortress a Bullet shot at randome which took off his Head, in the middle of a Squadron of *Turks*. There was in the Army a general resentment for the loss of so great a Souldier. Our men saw them with inarticulate Lamentations, and drag'd Colours bury the Body, with all the Military and Civil ceremony the vanity of VVarr could teach 'em: His Son *Rumecaon* swore presently by the

Coge-Sofar Dyes of a Shot.

the Blood of his Father, to be reveng'd of it, grief and anger being amongst them the last Sacrifice offer'd to their Dead.

61. *Rumecaon* succeeded his Father in his Enmity, and Charge, carrying on the Warr with the Obligation of a General, and Resentment of a Son, engag'd both by his grief and office. He commanded the filling up the Ditch should in six several places be gone on with, the Army being hourly furnish't with Pioneers, Provisions, Munition, and Souldiers, and the work every where rising, which *Rumecaon* hastned on, as a disposition to a general assault; by comparing designs, he too bethought himself to go on with contrivances that his Father had begun; He made six cover'd approaches, all which ended at the Sally-port of our Fortress, by which ours had tane away the Earth, these met upon a wooden Bridge, which we had made there, out of design under it to steal the Earth; upon this they were making the Fabrick we spake of, charging the Bridge with Stones and Timber, of such a bigness as the weight sunk it, and it presently fell to the ground with the loss of those who were at work under it. The Commander seeing this, ordered the shutting up of the Sally-port, the use of it being tane away, and to avoid any suddain invasion of the Enemy, who without any interruption work't on; while we were Hammering out, any Plot, or open Force to defeat so dangerous a Fabrick, on confidence of which, the *Moors* (by their Festivals and Shouting) seem'd already rather to enjoy then expect the Victory.

Rumecaon his Son succeeds him.

62. Those cares were seconded by others of no less weight, for there were not now in the Fortress two hundred Fighting men, some being wore out by Duty, others by Sickness, and Wounds, and had more need of recovering their strength, then exposing it in second dangers. Amongst the common Souldiers distrust made way for fear; Provision, and Ammunition were scarce; the stormy Seas and cruel VVinter cut off all hopes of

relief; for, either to send for't or receive it, the Season was not convenient.

The Vicar John Coelho goes to the Governour.

63. *John Coelho* was Vicar of the Fortress, who had besides the Virtues of Priesthood resolution enough to go upon any danger; He offered himself to the Commander, (which was very acceptable to him) in spight of storms to venture to Sea, and touching at *Bacaim*, or *Chaul*, as an Eye-witness to acquaint the Commanders how things stood, thence too, by *Corriers* over Land to give the Governour intelligence, promising on his Habit to return with the first news to *Dio* as a faithfull Companion of their Fortunes. The Commander presently provided him a Catch with twelve Mariners, where wee'l leave him wrastling with the Waves, till we are to give an account of the success of so stout and pious a Voyage.

64. The *Moors* by force work't in filling up the Ditch, imperious and cruel *Rumecaon* commanding them to Dye, or continue Working; for their reward, receiving in the very act, a miserable Grave. They at last came to lay the Ditch plain, and against *Gil Coutinho's* works where it could not be fill'd, they laid cross great Masts, with planks fastned to 'em, which they made use of for a Bridge, under that to ruine the VVall, which our Guns could not hinder 'em in, for they were cover'd.

65. *Dom John Mascarenhas* immediately ordered great Chains, to throw them from the VVall on the Bridge, there hung at 'em Sacks of threds dipt in Gunpowder, Salt-peter, and other Combustible matter, which being thrown, fir'd so violently on the Bridge, as presently to ruine it. *Rumecaon* came to make good the work with new Planks, more VVork-men, and Souldiers, these defended the place, the others continued Labouring; which our men endeavoured to interrupt by their Canon and Musquet shot, which did very much hurt the Enemy; but *Rumecaon* went on so obstinately, that he made fresh men pass over the Dead, who though

forc't

forc't upon't, overcome the danger by their Obedience. By so chargeable a way of working, he at last came to fill up the Ditch.

66. *Rumecaon*, by the few Defendants who supply'd the Posts, knowing how the case stood with us, had a mind to sound our Inclinations, believing in so dangerous a Conjuncture, Reason and Nature would teach us not to throw away our Lives. At the beginning of the Night, those on Saint *James*'s work heard one calling to the VVatch in *Portuguese*, saying, he was *Simaon Feo*, who upon some extraordinary business would speak with the Commander in chief. *Dom John Mascarenhas* had presently notice of it, and entring into discourse with the Souldier, he told him, that he was *Simaon Feo*, sent by *Rumecaon*, who had a mind, out of his affection to the Courage of so great Souldiers, to save their Lives, they now desperately defended; that they saw the Fortress every where Ruin'd, the greatest part of the Souldiers sick, or VVounded, without any hope of relief, in vvant of Provisions and Ammunition; that vve should not by perishing obstinately, discredit by the rashness of a few, the greatness of our Actions; that vve vvould give up our selves, he desiring for his own glory to keep alive so brave Enemies; that he vvould give us all Honourable terms, leaving us the disposal of our Estates, and Ships for our passage, vvhich if vve accepted not, vve vvere to look to endure the rigour of VVarr, and that Licentiousness vvhich in Onslaughts is Authoriz'd by Indignation and Victory. *Dom John Mascarenhas* answered him, that the Fortress the *Portuguese* kept needed no VValls; that in the open Field they vvould defend it against the strength of the vvhole VVorld; that on the first assault he should learn this truth, that he ought to bethink himself of sending to the *Sultan* for more men, and better Souldiers; that the *Portuguese* scorn'd such small Victories; that he hop't with Heads of *Turks* to make up the ruins of the Fortress; that if he vvanted Provisions, he vvould go look for

Propositions offered to our men by *Rumecaon*.

History of *India*, Dec. 6. Cap. 4. Lib. 2.

for 'em as Booty in his Camp; that as long as his Souldiers were Arm'd, they could want nothing in the possession of their Enemies; that he hop'd shortly through his arm'd Squadrons with Sword in hand to cut out the happy passage he offered him, he told *Simaon Feo*, that, though he was oblig'd to repeat an others words, he should not return with an other message, for he would make him be Shot from the Wall.

The Enemy assaults Saint *John*'s work. 67. *Rumecaon* seeing we fed upon Dangers, hard Duty, and Hunger, affronted too by so slight an answer, resolv'd to give the first assault; There broke upon us a Dismall day, (which was the nineteenth of *July* in the year 1546.) the Enemies Army at the Dawning, being seen round the Fortress. *Juzarcaon* with fifteen hundred choise men fell upon Saint *John*s work, Commanded by *Luis de Sousa*, with whom were *Dom Fernando de Castro*, *Sebastion de Sa*, *Diogo de Reynoso*, *Pero Lopez de Sousa*, *Diogo da Sylva*, *Antonio da Cunha*, and other Gentlemen and Souldiers not passing thirty; These with so much Bravery expected the first shock of the Enemy, that they beat back the first fourscore who began to Scale, who by their Out-crys, Blood, and Fall, shew'd the loss they had receiv'd; Others presently came after them, finding the dead Bodies had made their Scaling easier; *Juzarcaon* encouraged them, by minding 'em of their honour, their reward, and their vengeance. The striking on the Air by the Guns, and Clamours of men, made an hideous impression on the Walls of the Fortress. The Battery was continued against the other works, the assault against Saint *John*'s, and Saint *Thomas*'s; that those who in themselves were but few, might being divided, sooner yield.

And Saint *Thomas's*. 68. *Rumecaon* with his *Turks* assaulted Saint *Thomas's* work, kept by *Dom John de Almeyda*, and *Gil Coutinho*; his men pick't out for their Valour, and of a proud Nation fell on so furiously, as though run through with our Lances, they gave not over Scaling, seeking for Victory in their Death; they had the advantage of numbers,

numbers, we of place, and those who had bestrid the Wall, must either Fnter Victoriously or Dye wounded, Retiring being more dangerous, then Fighting. The Enemy with fresh men continually re-inforced the Assault; Ours, always the same, were too hard for the first Assailants, and match for the last. The Women came to their help with Arms, and Powder, putting on that Courage which was rather seasonable then natural; some of 'em with Regallos and Drinks put Life into the Souldiers, and not able to show their own strength, did encrease it in others; there were of them, who animated 'em with Speeches, deserving to have had in so great hearts the force of men; and amongst the actions of this Siege we shall relate theirs as most unusual, if not as the greatest. There was seen at the foot of the work a Mountain of Dead bodies, some with their Wounds bleeding, others burnt with the Fire; some at their last Gasp, 'twixt anger and grief, cry'd for Vengeance; sometimes too it hapned, that those who went to Vindicate 'em Dy'd first. Our men that day did wonders, which were more easily seen by their success, then they can be by Writing; for in particularizing accidents the truth is uncertain, most of all in the chances of Warr, where anger, fear, and other passions so captivate the judgment, that each particular man can hardly be a faithfull Historian of his own Actions.

69. *Dom Fernando de Castro* that day gave proof of a Courage befitting his Birth, and above his Years. *Sebastian de Sa* left us a famous memory of his Valour, till having his Knee shot through with a poyson'd Arrow, and falling down for Dead, not being able to maintain the Fight, he would not forsake it; He was at last by his Camrades, full of grief and envy, carry'd off, having before sufficiently reveng'd his Blood on the Enemy. Every one in fine behav'd himself so Stoutly, as that one day was enough to make 'em Souldiers. After Fighting two hours they seem'd but to begin the assault,

What resistance our men made.

History of *India*, Dec. 6. Cap. 4. Lib. 2.

Rumecaon carrying himself as if in one day he intended to make an end of the VVarr. He commanded every Nation to Fight by themselves, either the more to Spurr 'em on by Emulation, or that they might better observe Orders; he himself, Commanding and Fighting, by his Voice, and Example made 'em stand to't, and not glutted with the Blood he saw spilt, Prais'd the forwardest, and Vilify'd the backward'st, carrying out midst the horrour of Arms, his anger with prudence. *Dom John Mascarenhas* behav'd himself not only as a Commander, but a Companion where the greatest danger was, Fighting, and Commanding so prudently, that he came off owing nothing to Courage, less to Conduct.

The Enemy retires with loss.

70. *Rumecaon*, seeing the great numbers of Dead which were about the VVorks, and that his men kept back when commanded to come on, commanded the sounding of a Retreat, carrying off in great haste the Dead and VVounded, so to keep from his own their Loss, and from us our Victory; yet we had it from themselves, that they lost in this assault five hundred men, the VVounded were many more; there Dy'd of ours but one Souldier, the VVounded were less then twenty. By this disproportion 'tis seen that the Victory was not only obtain'd by Human force, but that God maintain'd the cause as his own; our Arms being the happy Instruments of his Power, of which the History will yet give us greater proofs.

71. Upon the Enemies retiring the Commander in Chief summon'd our men to a second Labour, which the Necessity, or Victory made them easily digest. The Breaches of the Fortress were of force to be made up; the Stones and Mortar, being the soft Beds which our Souldiers had to recover their so decaid strength with; they all went willingly and chearfully on the Service, led on by the example of the Commander, who after the Enemies, Conquer'd his own Nature. The Fortress in the morning appear'd in part repair'd, our men by their working recovering themselves, as if they had been

at rest; the weight of their Arms not permitting them to make any difference 'twixt Day and Night. The Enemy was by this assault so broken, as he durst not in many days come to Blows with us, his experience making him more Cautious or Cowardly; He now and then fac't the Fortress with some inconsiderable Piqueering, to shake us with continual Alarums, or by our taking our Posts, to observe the inclinations of our minds; yet did he not leave off Battering, intending by a long Siege to weaken us: but the Camp daily encreasing with new Recruits, and the ***Sultan*** declaring his concernment for this Warr, *Rumecaon* resolv'd to give the Fortress the second assault.

72. And considering the loss he had receiv'd, though Fighting with so much advantage of numbers, he look't upon the slaughter of his men as having higher Causes, for which 'twas fit to appease the Prophet. He immediately commanded the bringing forth of a Banner which had in it the Picture of *Mahomet*, and that the Army with that should go so many times in Procession about the Mosque, and with other barbarous and ridiculous Expiation should appease and reconcile *Mahomed*, whose displeasure retarded their Victory. *Fernaon Carvalho*, Commander of the work toward the Sea, saw the Army that night go in Procession with great store of Lights, and by times heard Noise and Clamours which presently ended in a suddain silence, again bursting forth into Groans of a confus'd multitude, their Sighs and Out-crys were seconded by Instruments of Warr, and in this Superstitious vanity were many hours of the Night entertained. *Fernaon Carvalho* was troubled at the strangeness, and could not guess for what it was; but acquainted *Dom John Mascarenhas* with what he saw, who guest it a preparation for an assault, abetted by some Barbarous ceremony and Superstitious rite, with which they hop't to reconcile the anger of their false Prophet.

Juzarcam falls to Superstition.

History of *India*, Dec. 6. Lib. 2. Cap. 5.

73. The Commander in Chief made ready for this second

second storm of the Enemy, finding in such shattered Forces, all his Souldiers heart-whole, the Wounded and Sick quitted their Beds and Cures, more eager to go upon Dangers then recover their Health. *Dom John Mascarenhas* with Courage and Judgment ordered and dispos'd what was necessary for their defence; Day-light was hardly broke when the Enemy appear'd before the Fortress with Clamours and dolefull Noises, which by the sounding of Warlike instruments were in the silence of the Night made more Dreadfull; The Army came up divided into three Squadrons, and had carry'd before 'em (amongst the rest) a Banner in which was the Image of their Prophet, that both Religion and their King's honont might animate them; at the same time they fell upon Saint *Johns* and Saint *Thomas*'s work, and *Antonio Pecanha*'s Guard with so much fury as they neither saw or fear'd danger, but were by ours so receiv'd, as they were with more haste forc't back, then they came in to the Onset, many falling down Dead, most of 'em Wounded, and others burnt by Fire. *Juzarcaon* and *Rumecaon* were heard to incite others to Scale the Works, who under shelter of the Vollees of Musquets, infinite Arrows, and other Shouting, did go on afresh. 'Twas here the assault was Kindled in a great deal of heat, the *Turks* earnest to recover their lost Credit, were by rage and shame put upon Fighting, obstinately getting up through Fire and Sword, like men who less valued their Lives then the Victory, so as they got to be on the same ground with ours, Fighting man to man upon the Work.

An other assault.

74. *Louis de Sousa, Dom Fernando de Castro*, with the other Gentlemen and Souldiers of their Company did that day give new repute to our Arms, so behaving themselves as *Rumecaon* represented 'em to his men, sometimes for their example, others as their shame; the *Turks* were continually reliev'd, Ours, always the same, shew'd themselves as stout against the last as first; the Fight grew hot every where, of the Enemies a great many

many were Kill'd and VVounded, yet did their rage or anger, either hide or flight the loss; for, on the Body of him who fell did an other plant himself, to fling his Lance, or Fight more firmly, the heat and impatience of Victory inventing new Subtilties or never heard of Cruelties.

75. They at last entred Saint *Thomas's* work, which for a good while they kept, as some fell others coming in their place. 'Twas here the fury of the Enemy was great, as well as their Slaughter. *Dom Francisco*, and *Dom Pedro de Almeydo* shew'd themselves Brothers as well by their Soutness as Blood, withstanding the shock of so many Enemies all the time of the assault. The *Turks* enter Saint *Thomas's* work.

76. The *Turks* of *Rumecaon's* Division fought with ours Body to Body, upon equality of ground, and advantage of numbers, the danger heightning our Courage. Few of those who entred the work got off Alive, but having this Door open towards Victory they endeavour'd though with eminent danger to keep it so. This being the first honour the chance of Arms had in the Warr conferr'd on *Rumecan*, he with praises and promises rais'd the pride of the *Turks*. 'Twas nois'd amongst ours the work was lost, which Alarum, whether 'twas craft, or chance, might have lost the Fortress; for those who fought in other places almost all forsook their Posts to relieve the work they gave for gone; those chiefly who Guarded the Houses toward the Rock, came so furiously to the Relief, as the rest had time to Breathe, who by their Duty and VVounds were now wearied and broken.

77. *Dom John Mascarenhas* went about the Posts, assuring them all, that the work was yet ours, and how Couragiously 'twas maintain'd; that *Rumecaon* stood looking on the Slaughter of his men, who cast themselves weltring in their Blood from the VVall, and by their fall made sure of their Deaths. The Storming continu'd, and on both sides Death and Wounds seem'd to add to their Courage and Bravery, which *Juzarcaon*

 observing,

observing, and believing those few Defendants the Fortress had, were employ'd in those Bastions vvhich vvere attaqu'd, leaving the Battail, vvith some Souldiers surrounded the Wall, and coming to the Fause-bray, vvhich vvithout art Nature had made defensable by the height and cragginess of the Rock on vvhich too the Sea beat, seeing it unguarded, vvithout either Souldiers or Watch, guest that the situation made us secure of it, and sending for a Senjack with a hundred *Turks* and scaling Ladders they begun to Scale there without being either seen or resisted; for the Souldiers who had the Guard there, upon the news Saint *Thomas's* vvork vvas lost, quitting the Post they kept, vvith more Courage then Discipline vvent to relieve it.

Juzarcaon invests the Courtain.

78. The *Turks* boldly clim'd the Rock, making their way to some Houses, joyning to Saint *James's* Church, which gave them passage to a Gallery where they planted Ladders for others to come up by. *Juzarcaon* stood without encouraging 'em, believing he had stole both the Honour and Victory from *Rumecaon*. The *Turks* won those Houses, and were going down into the Fortress, and one of 'em more resolute, or diligent than the rest, went into a Marry'd womans House, and asking Money of her to save her Life, the poor Woman surpriz'd with fear, made as if she went forth to procure it, and going into her Neighbours told her in a fright, the danger they were in, this, startled at the News, acquainted an other, who with Manly prudence and courage took up a Sphear, and going to the House where the *Turks* where, saw one of 'em at Door watching how things went abroad, and coming up to him, laying on with her Sphear, forc't him to retire within the Doors, with so much Mastery of her judgment in the danger she was in, as she had the Caution to lock the Door, and the Courage to wait on the *Turks*, and hinder their coming forth, worthy certainly to have her memory Recorded amongst the most famous Champions.

History of *India*, Dec. 6. Cap. 6. Lib. 1.

The Courage of a *Portuguese* woman.

79. The

79. The women who Liv'd thereabouts being seiz'd with so just a fear, went to look out the Commander in Chief, crying, *Turks* in the Fortress; they found him with three Souldiers running about the Works; hearing womens Voices, not less Prudent then Couragious, He commanded them to be silent, and took them with him to shew him the House where the *Turks* were, dispatching one of the Souldiers with commands to draw off some from the Works, where the Enemy was less pressing, without saying any thing of the danger the Fortress was in to those who were Fighting; he likewise sent off an other Souldier to bring him all the scattering men he found from Duty; by the way he light upon *Andre Bayaon* with an other, and coming to the House where the *Turks* were, he saw the Woman, who kept 'em fast, and, with more then masculine Courage disputed their coming forth; so unfortunate as to have no reward in her Life, so no name in our History.

The Captain comes in to her help.

80. *Dom John Mascarenhas* looking on the so extraordinary Valour found in a VVoman, as an Omen of the Victory, having it from her, that the *Turks* were Lock't up in the House, sent a *Abessine* (who by chance was there) for a Pan of Powder, and because he mov'd slowly, shov'd him by the Arm, when at the same instant from the Leads of the Church, (where were gotten some *Turks*) came a Bullet, which Kill'd the *Abessine*, who kept it off from the Captain. There presently came a Souldier with Powder, which *Dom John Mascarenhas* taking out of his hands, forcing open the Doors, threw in amongst the *Turks*, the Fire burnt most of 'em, and the Bullets which with certain aim they Shot from within mist him, which was interpreted to be by chance, by some others, providence. Behaving himself that day like Commander and Souldier, cover'd with his Buckler, and having his Sword in his hand, with four more he set upon the *Turks*, and by dint of Sword drove 'em to the Gallery, where he so prest 'em, as to make 'em throw themselves down the Rock, with no

And drives out the Souldiers.

no less danger then that they fled from, most of them Kill'd or coming off Maim'd by their fall.

The *Turks* get upon the Church.

81. *Dom John Mascarenhas* had now News, that on the Leads of the Church there appear'd a great many *Turks* with two Banners planted, beginning to Shoot our men from above as they camo on; here 'twas the danger was great, for there being no other then Fire-arms, Fortune out-went Courage. VVe were less then sixty, the *Turks* more then an hundred. *Dom John Mascarenhas* seeing, that by keeping the place they encreas'd, sent for Scaling-Ladders, chance and necessity so ordering it, that in his own Fortress he was forc'd to become the Assailant. Our men fastned a little Ladder to the VVall, and the first Souldier who Ventur'd on it vvas by the Lances of the *Turks* immediately thrown down; they then brought bigger and clapping 'em to the VVall, the Commander in chief striving first to get up, vvas by the Souldiers just violence kept from passing. Our men got up by the VValls of the Apostle Saint *James*'s Church, confident by the place, of the Victory; the advantage of place made great Odds in their Fighting, the Enemy had firm footing, Ours by their hanging in the Air broke two Ladders, for their strife and heat vvho should first get up vvas an other VVarr. The Commander by his vvords and example animated the Souldiers, vvhich he did more out of his Duty then Necessity. The Conflict vvas obstinate and resolute, some of our men fell back Dead, none came off VVounded. The impatience of getting room to Climb vvork't more upon those vvho stood below, then the Wounds they saw their Camrades receive; for, though in so long and dangerous a Siege they had not too much of the Warr, they cut one an other vvith unheard of Cruelty.

82. *Juzarcaon* encourag'd and reliev'd his, vvith fresh men so, as in a little time he fill'd the place where they fought, (which was the Leads or Roof of the Church) with Souldiers. Ours at last, after a sharp

contest,

contest, at the price of their Blood got upon the Wall, showing in the inequality of place and numbers, a difference in Courage. Three long hours the dispute lasted, in which time the few who were there so behav'd themselves, as that one Action deserv'd a particular History, yet find we not their names Recorded, who by their Blood challeng'd so distinct a memory. The Turks were almost all Kill'd, some by their fall, others in the Fight, and suppos'd to be their best men, who were singled out for so great an Action. And retire.

83. The Commander hearing the assault lasted yet on the Works, carry'd off his men to refresh 'em in a second danger, and visiting the Posts, found our men so engag'd in keeping off the Enemy, that after four hours the assault seem'd but to begin; The Dead at the foot of the Works were so many as they wanted ground to lye upon, whose Bodies made the Scaling of the Wall easier. *Rumecaon* without, encourag'd, or reproach'd his men, as he saw the bravery or coldness of their Courage in Fighting; provoking 'em by Rewards, and Punishments; on all occasions of this Siege showing both Resolution and Discipline. *Dom John Mascarenhas* gave not over Ordering, and Providing what was necessary every where, so as the Souldiers in no danger found him wanting; On that day which was the Apostle Saint *James*'s, it appear'd the Saint would shew us the Victory was his, and that he was not now less Powerfull against the *Moors* in *Asia*, then he had been before in *Spain*.

84. The dispute continued hot and dreadfull on both sides, *Juzarcaon* (taking it to heart, not to compass the Scaling of the Fortress which had cost him so dear) came with those men under his Command, to put more Life into the assault, when by a Bullet from the Fortress, which hit him on the Breast, and past through him he fell down Dead; And being a Person of such Value, for his Courage, and the place he held, the News was immediately disperc't through the Army, *Juzarcaon*'s. Death.

 when

when it came to *Rumecaon's* Ears (was it Fear, or Compassion) he receiv'd it with no little Resentment, immediately Commanding the sounding a Retreat, to bring off *Juzarcaon's* body, a loss could not be conceal'd from his men, and being greater then any they had before sustain'd, they now thought the Victory not worth what it had already cost, and if they should atchieve it, doubted who would remain to enjoy it. That their Prophet apparently shew'd himself angry with them, since he could endure to see his Banner so ignominiously torn. To these Considerations they added others which spoke against their Generals fortune, and the cause of the Warr; laying to his charge that they had the worst of it. *Rumecaon* by diverse Artifices remedy'd these jealousies, Palliating his own loss, and Enhauncing ours, laying before 'em the *Sultan's* Favour, and their own Fame, as the most considerable part of that reward they were to look for. We lost in that assault seven Souldiers, and had thirty Wounded; on the *Moors* side the Dead were above one thousand, and the Wounded neer two.

And that of many *Turks*.

85. *Dom John Mascarenhas*, after ordering the Burial of the Dead, and the looking to the Wounded, (in which he spar'd no Care, and less his Estate, which he profusedly spent, without keeping account) did by a *Brigantine* send the Governour word how things stood, and of his want of Men, Ammunition, and Provisions. *Sebastion de Sa*, at the instance of the Commander in Chief, and Friends, went on the Vessel, though with these Words in his mouth, that only on the work where he was Wounded, could he recover his Health, which every one desir'd he should preserve, because his Actions in that Siege deserv'd no little Fame, and a much longer Life; He recovered *Bacaim* when his Vessel was almost sunk, was received and entertain'd by *Dom Jeronymo de Menezes*, Captain of the Fortress there, who presently dispatch't the Letters to the Governour, with what advice he had from *Dom John Mascarenhas*.

The Commander in Chief advises the Governour.

86. Dom

86. *Dom John de Castro* was at that time very Sollicitous how things went at *Dio*, because the Winter kept him from having any News, or sending any Relief; yet did he, without sparing Cost or Danger, even under the VVaves, succour it, (vvhen most streightned) vvith Men and Ammunition, as vvill be immediately seen by the History. He had (with an intention to go in Person to raise the Siege at *Dio*) made march the whole strength of *India*, and the success seem'd as it would answer the design, for the Kings of *India* made him very honourable Offers, and the Gentlemen and Souldiers presented themselves without Pay or Reward.

How the Governour was concern'd to releeve *Dio*.

87. About that time, vvhich vvas the beginning of *July*, arriv'd at the Barr of *Goa*, the Ship, Holy Ghost, Captain, *Diogo Rebello*, she had been of the Governours Conserve, and by bad vveather had VVintred in *Melinde*, and though she came vvith some of her men Sick, the Air of the Land, the Governours care, and the excess of joy for the business of *Dio*, made them in a little time recover their health; *Dom John de Castro* vvas glad of so seasonable a Relief to encrease the Fleet; yet came no News from the Fortress, vvhich the people construed to be an Argument of some ill success; when arriv'd the Letters sent by the Vicar, by vvhich the Governour understood, the straightness of the Siege, the strength of the Enemy, and the vvant Ours vvere in of Men and Provisions, and the time rather requiring Execution then Counsel, he resolv'd vvith part of the Fleet to send away his Son *Dom Alvaro de Castro*, against the opinion of the Mariners, vvho in the beginning of the VVinter counted the attempt too hazardous. Yet *Dom John de Castro* would not be Over-rul'd, by the love of a Son, or the apprehensions of the Season, but resolv'd upon sending Relief; vvhich being known by the Souldiers, and Gentlemen, they came to offer themselves, even those vvho by their Years and Command vvere exempted; of their number vvas *Dom Francisco de Menezes*, vvho, after having had great Commands, offered

History of *India*, Dec. 6. Cap. 7. Lib. 2.

The news of the Vicar comes.

He sends his Son *Dom Alvaro* with relief,

offered as a common Souldier, to go vvith the Relief, the Governour took him in his Arms desiring him to stay to go on the Fleet vvith him, but seeing him resolute to go in that Succour, gave him seven Ships, vvith them to try to make his passage; *Dom Francisco* put vvith them to Sea, and vvith him vvere a great many brave Souldiers, and some of his Kindred, vvho out of love to Honour bore him Company.

and first of all *Dom Francisco de Menezes* with seven Ships.

88. Three days after departed *Dom Alvaro*, reconcil'd to his Father, upon his complaint, that he had sent before him, his Brother *Dom Fernando*, as if by Birth-right he claim'd the first dangers. There Embark't on this Relief a great part of the Nobility, whom, the pleasure of the design, and the company of the General, made to undervalew the *Turks*, and Storms. The Governour gave his Son his blessing, and put him on Board, with great tenderness from the people, for offering up his Sons for his Country, toward vvhich, then toward his own Blood, he shew'd himself a more indulgent Father. The Governour having given his Son some private Instructions, commanded him (though by his General-ship otherwise dispens't) to obey *Dom John Mascarenhas*, and so writ him word; *Dom John de Castro* having always a true Value for other mens Merits. The Ships of the Fleet were Nineteen, whose Commanders were, *Dom Iorge de Menezes*, *Dom Duarte de Menezes*, Son to the Count of *Feira*, *Luis de Mello de Mendoca*, and his Brother *Iorge de Mendoca*; *Dom Antonio de Attayde*, *Garcia Rodriguez de Tavora*, *Lopo de Sousa*, *Nuno Pereira de Lacerda*, *Athanasio de Freire*, *Pero de Attayde de Inferno*, *Dom John de Attayde*, *Balthasar de Sylva*, *Dom Duarte Deca*, *Antonio de So*, *Belchior de Moniz*, *Lopo Voz Coutinho*, *Francisco Tavarez*, and *Francisco Guilherme*.

Dom Alvaro parts with Nineteen.

The Commanders who went with him.

89. The Governour having dispatch't this Fleet, was busie in preparing for that himself resolv'd to go upon, laying out for Provisions and Money, which he took up upon his Credit, the only Treasure he kept by him in

The Governours preparations.

India,

India, with which he Commanded the Hearts and Estates of all men, as we shall prove by the visible Arguments of example.

90. The Ladies and Maids of *Chaul*, possest by the same generous Spirit, contributed all the Jewels and Gold they wore, and with a Liberality above VVomen, without either obligation, or asking, sent 'em to the Governour, and with 'em word that they had less tenderness then envy for their Children and Husbands who went with him. We read not in the Annalls of the *Cesars*, a braver Action of the *Roman* Ladies.

The Women of *Chaul* present their Jewels.

91. When the present came, there was accidentally in *Goa* a Lady of *Chaul* (by name *Catherina de Sousa*) who putting all the Jewels she had in a little Box, with this "Letter sent 'em to the Governour. Sir, Knowing the "Women of *Chaul* have presented your Honour with "all their Jewels for the carrying on this Warr, though "I am now in *Goa*, I would not be without my share of "that honour, which belongs to me, as one of that "place. I send your Honour my Jewels by my Daughter "*Katherine*. Guess not by the smallness of their number, "how many may be in *Chaul*, for I assure you I am she "who have the fewest, having divided 'em amongst my "Daughters; and your Honour may believe, that the "Jewels of *Chaul* alone, without being Exhausted, are "sufficient for ten years to continue the Warr. The "favour I begg of your Honour is, presently to spend "mine in *Dom Alvaro*'s expedition, because I hope by "the intercession of our Lady he will get such signal "Victories as will excuse your Honour's Voyage and "Trouble: this I begg in my Prayers, and that our "Lady by Hers will so add to your Honour's Life, as "you may return into *Portugall* to the presence of "your Lady-wife and Daughters. Dated in *Goa*, at "my Daughter *Donna Maria*'s House, this Eleventh of "*July*. I would, (were there need of it) for your "Honour's Service, pawn my Daughter *Katherine*. I

The present and Letter of a Lady.

know not, whether their love to their Country, or their affection to the Governour produc't these extreams. We have seen as much necessity for it, but not so great Bravery as in *Dom John de Castro*'s time. Many Gentlemen, after having been Generals, and now Old men leaning upon Staffs, came and offer'd themselves for Souldiers, there not being any one grown stiff by his Years or Command.

History of *India*, Dec. 6. Cap. 7. Lib. 2.

92. After both Reliefs were gone, the Governour was uniting the strengths which remain'd, and disposing the Government of the City in his absence. All the Exigencies of the State found him ready with one hand in Peace, the other in Warr. And the Fortress wanting Ammunition, and Provision, (besides what was already sent) he Laded a great Carvell, which being a heavy Vessel would have much ado to endure the Sea. Some Souldiers had refus'd to go upon her, counting it danger without reputation to strive with the Elements. The importance of the business made him desire to entrust the Carvell with some Person of Quality, whose honour would lessen the danger. He imparted the business to *Manoel de Sousa de Sepulveda*, a Gentleman, for his Courage and Judgment, very much indear'd to him; who told him, *Antonio Moniz Baretto* had Gallantry and Industry enough for greater things; that though, for some sleight Quarrel against him as Governour, he would not sue for, yet would he not deny the King's Service in so great an urgency; that he would feel him, and bring the answer of his Resolution. So it was, that *Antonio Moniz*, understanding the Governours pleasure, and that he put him on a Voyage whose difficulty only made others refuse it, presently embrac't it. We will in its proper place tell the success and danger he met with.

Antonio Moniz accepts of a Voyage to *Dio*.

93. There was by the Vigilancy of the Governour entred some Relief into the Fortress, by which the Danger and Duty lay upon more Shoulders, yet were they not in any proportion to the Enemy, because the last

last Recruit which came to the Army, consisted of thirteen thousand Foot, under the Conduct of an other *Juzarcaon*, in Valour not Inferiour, nor in Fortune above the first. He brought express Orders from the *Sultan* to streighten the Siege, and Letters from him to *Rumecaon*, that he could not stand by and see four contemptible Fellows, from the Worlds end, affront the Kings of *Cambaya* at home; that they should all Dye in the design; that he had rather have a desolate then a subjected Empire; that half the *Portuguese* being already Buried in the ruins of the Fortress, if they could not force 'em to yield as Men, they should as Lyons kill 'em in their Dens. *Rumecaon* gave no other answer, then by shewing (sometimes for his glory, sometimes for his excuse) our Walls, and Works, every where thrown down, being very much transported that the *Sultan* was not satisfy'd with what he had done, and more provok't with despair, then reward, he promis'd to satisfie him by Death, or Victory; and being more obey'd for his Cruelty then Command, he ordered the making of a Bastion before Saint *James's* work, which was with incredible haste perform'd, and furnish't with Men and Ordnance; and commanding our Works, our men could not appear without being fech't off by the Enemies Bullets.

There comes an other *Juzarcaon* to continue the Siege.

The Enemy makes a Bastion.

94. The Commander in Chief was not a little troubled at it; for if *Rumecaon* should (as his design was) Storm on that side, our Defendants would not be able to resist him, without lying open to the Enemies shot. Resolv'd therefore to throw down the Work, he recommends the Execution of it to two Brothers, *Dom Pedro*, and *Dom John de Almeyda*, who Sallying out about Mid-night with an hundred Souldiers, found the *Moors*, some sleeping, others careless on confidence of the place and hour. Charging them on a suddain, in a little time they made a great Slaughter; for; forgetting themselves they run upon our Lances and Swords, not aware of Death or Enemy. Those who by flying could provide

Our men throw it down.

provide for themselves, with Groans and Crys gave the Allarum to the Camp, without being able to affirm any thing for certain. In the same confusion came the news to *Rumecaon*, who (as dangers by Night appear bigger) concluded this Exploit of ours was grounded on some great Recruit arriv'd by stealth, which escap'd his Sentinels. He call'd the Officers to Counsel whilst the Army betook themselves to their Arms, and resolv'd with all his strength to relieve the Bastion. He wasted the time of Action in Orders and Preparations, and coming to the place found the Work on the ground, the Guards kill'd, and our men Retir'd; an Action of no less fortune then concernment. There Dy'd of the Enemy three hundred, of ours not one.

95. *Rumecaon* presently ordered the raising thick Walls of Earth against Saint *John*'s work, to be Guarded by a Troop of *Moors*, who by turns took the Watch, and on the top of 'em he planted some Canon to Batter the VVork at a more convenient distance. *Dom John Mascarenhas*, Vigilant in preventing the designs of the Enemy, put out through a Skit-gate fourteen Souldiers, in a stormy and dark Night, who charging on a suddain the *Moors*, drove them from their Posts, whilst the Labourers with Pick-axes and other Instruments threw down the Work, which being told *Rumecaon*, he resolv'd with open force to storm the Fortress, ordering for the next day a general Assault, on which he made a Speech to his Souldiers, encouraging 'em, by the affronts they had receiv'd from so few Enemies, brought Low by Duty, Hunger, and VVounds, that those who fell there were more honourable then those who surviv'd, to be to the VVorld an infamous testimony of an ignominious VVarr; that it was in them, to save their King's Honour, to revenge their Companions and to leave a glorious Fame of themselves in the *East*; that they ought to be confident of the *Sultan*'s thanks, for he would not fail to reward 'em, and take a particular account of all their VVounds; that if any would venture

The Courage of fourteen Souldiers.

to govern the Generals staff, he promis'd as a private Souldier to be the first should Scale the Wall.

96. Thus he left 'em fir'd with glory and revenge. Next morning by break of Day, at the Noise of warlick Instruments, and with their Colours flying (the Displaying of which was observ'd by ours) the Army march't, and coming to the Walls began to plant Scaling Ladders round about the Fortress, with the advantage of innumerable and different Shots, of Arrows, Bullets, and other Arms, which came from the Body of the Army. The horrour too of the Fight was increas'd by confus'd and repeated Noises, which, Violently, raising their Spirits and confounding their Judgments, hindred both Command and Obedience. The *Moors* boldly Scal'd the Walls, as did the *Turks* on the other side, as if they envy'd each others danger, all strove to be the first at hazards, and blows. Ours, though but few (every one his own Commander, and encourager) so behav'd themselves as if each single man had been to answer for the reputation of all. The first who came to the top with their Blood and Lives paid for their daring, but were immediately with the same eagerness seconded by others, some prick't forward by their own Courage, others by the General, who from below as he discovered in 'em, heat, or fear, prais'd or reproach'd those who Scal'd.

A general assault.

97. The *Moors* cast Granados, Pots of Powder, and Balls of Wild-fire in such quantity into the Works, that our men Fought in the Flames, which catching their Cloaths burnt them alive. The Commander in chief strove to avoid this danger with some Barils of water, which did partly extinguish or mitigate the heat of the Fire; but the Enemy, knowing how much hurt it did, us'd in all their assaults the same artifice, against which ours found out a more easie then effectual remedy, many Cloathing themselves with Leather, which the Fire did not so soon seize upon. *Dom John Mascarenhas* with Hangings he had of gilt Leather (the

How our men kept off the Fire.

Walls being naked) help't to Clothe many of the Souldiers.

98. The Warr grew hot, and the Fortress (hid in Clouds of smoak) was hardly seen, 'twas only discoverable by a weak Light, the continual Flashing of Shooting, what was seen, and what was heard was full of horrour; there were at the Foot of the VVall innumerable Bodies, some Dead, others Gasping, and all that was before the sight, or judgment, was a foul Spectacle, of Deaths, horrour, and wounds. 'Twas in all the VVorks on both sides Fought with great Courage, though with disproportion of Numbers 'twixt the Besiegers and Besieg'd. The work *Luis de Sousa* defended, (where was *Dom Fernando de Castro*) was near lost, the assault taking it with the most Breaches, and being attaqued by the Choise men of the Army: Yet did the Defendants give glorious marks of their Valour, Fighting with such Courage in the Flames, as they shew'd themselves, besides Valiant, insensible. *Dom Fernando de Castro* did here render himself singular by Actions above his Years, proving Courage stays not for Age. The *Portuguese* did that day things worthy a better Pen, and larger History. The very *Turks* were testimony of their Prowess, saying, the *Franks* only deserv'd to wear Beards.

99. During the assault the Work toward the Sea shot often amongst the Enemy, who Fighting in Companies were more exposed, and receiv'd no little loss, which *Rumecaon* taking notice off, seeing his Colours torn, and his best men Dead, and that without the loss of a stone the *Portuguese* had maintain'd the Breaches of their Fortress, commanded the sounding a Retreat, less sensible of the loss, then shame. That day was at several times happy to our Arms; for the Enemy losing on the place three hundred, and carrying off two thousand VVounded, there was missing none of ours, though some lost much Blood. The Commander in chief immediately look't after the VVounded; the tenderness with

The Enemy retires,

With the Death of three hundred.

with which he us'd them, being the chief remedy; By helping the infirm, not only with Expence, but grief and Fellow-feeling; he shew'd himself in Peace their Father, in VVarr their Companion. Their danger was presently succeeded by their Labours; for by Night they all repair'd what the Batteries had thrown down by Day, and all with such Chearfulness undertook the Task, as if they came to rest themselves by carrying Stones, Earth, and Fagots.

History of *India*, Dec. 6. Cap. 2. Lib. 8.

Rum on goes about filling up the Ditch.

100. *Rumecaon* seeing the hazard and difficulty of taking the Fortress by Scaling, commanded the filling up of the Ditch from Saint *Johns* to Saint *James's* work, a thing he put the *Janizaries* upon, who proud of their Repute and Courage did ambitiously covet the most eminent dangers of the Siege. There were Dead already four hundred, leaving their name and grief for 'em great amongst the surviving, who carry'd on the VVork, which prov'd to 'em of little advantage and great danger; for our Guns took 'em off, and a great many of the VVork-men; whose Bodies by a Cruel and Barbarous discipline were thrown in to fill up the Ditch, the VVork being of Fagots and Earth, went on, Kneaded with the Blood of the poor men who Labour'd in it. They planted some Pieces with which they did harm to our works, chiefly Saint *Thomas's*, where they took from us the use of a great Gun, and the Battery look't dispos'd for greater Execution.

The Vicar returns to *Dio*.

101. About that time the Vicar *John Coelho*, with nine Souldiers in a little Boat arriv'd at the Fortress, for though he found the Seas high, and the VVinds contrary, pains and necessity over-came the danger; He reported the Governour was with all diligence preparing to come to raise the Siege; that he had already sent great Recruits; that there were five hundred men in *Bacaim*, who hop't with the first opportunity to cross the Gulf; that many not brooking any delay had already ventred to Sea. This news went about the Fortress, and was by the Souldiers entertain'd with Dancing and

and Musick; every one looking out to Sea took the Clouds for Ships, so credulous are men upon any glimpse of hopes. The *Moors* had the news of our Recruits, and before our men should grow in Numbers with the force they expected, a general assault was ordered, and they resolv'd to enter the Fortress, or by their Deaths, Blood, and Perishing, show the World and the *Sultan*, the fault was not theirs.

A fresh assault.

102. That day with three and twenty Canon, and some Basilisks they began to Batter, which they continued till Sun setting, and the next day till three in the afternoon. They threw down most of the Walls, so that Ours could not by any Reparations or Traveses shelter themselves from the continual discharging of the Enemies Musqueteers. The *Turks* by the ruins of the Battery got presently on Saint *Thomas*'s VVork, yet did the Captain *Luis de Sousa*, *Dom Fernando de Castro*, and *Dom Francisco de Almeyda*, with other stout Souldiers who kept it, receive them with such fury on their Lances, as they forc't them back, some Dead, others Maim'd. There presently follow'd fresh men, whom our Swords made company for the former. The like fortune had the Fight in the other VVorks, the *Moors* loss, and our mens courage being the same. The Battery had so raz'd our Fortress, that the *Moors* (as in a pitch't Field) fought with Ours upon the same advantage of ground, Levell'd by the ruins, but by their Numbers and Fireworks did out-do us. Ours that day deserv'd immortal memory for many hours enduring the weight of so unequal a Fight; for those of the Enemies, who were wearied or wounded, were relieved continually by fresh men; the *Portuguese* being always the same shew'd no difference of either Courage or Time.

How our men keep off the Enemy.

103. *Dom John Mascarenhas* went about all the Posts commanding, and Fighting, one while their Captain, another their Companion, and seeing St. *Thomas*'s work in the greatest danger, being most charg'd by the Enemy, sent for a great many Pots of Powder, by those

so

ſo honourable Matrons, who deſpiſing danger and labour, came ſeaſonably through Lances and Bullets, to their help, with unheard of example, and with encouragements to the Souldiers full of great judgment and courage, whilſt others animated them with Regallos and ſweet-meats as if they coveted or deſerv'd equal fame with them. We had the wind in our faces, which, raiſing clouds of Duſt from the looſe ground the Enemy ſtood upon, almoſt blinded our men, who only by that accident run the hazard of being loſt, yet Fighting with their Eyes ſhut they received the *Moors*, more intent upon offending the Enemy, then providing for themſelves. The Enemies fought deſperately, *Rumecaon* every moment minding them of their Kings and their own honour.

104. *Juzarcaon* with the Souldiers he commanded, with ſo great a reſolution fell upon St. *John*'s work that our men were in no little danger: for after throwing down the firſt who came up, others with ſo much fury got upon the Walls, that for many hours they maintain'd the Fight equal, till wounded with our Swords, ſome Dead, others faltring in their Courage, loſt the place and their Lives. Here was the reſiſtance and danger greateſt, for upon our men, whoſe force was already wearied and ſhaken, came other freſh *Moors*, yet, as if they had kept their ſtrength and courage for the greateſt pinch, they repuls't the laſt as the firſt.

Juzarcaon falls upon Saint *John*'s work.

105. In *Antonio Pecanha*'s Poſt the Fight was not leſs ſtout or fortunate, and without particularizing accidents, we may by the ſucceſs judge the fortune of the Day: for the Enemy left ſixteen hundred Dead, beſides the innumerable number of the VVounded: an incredible thing of a few more then two hundred Souldiers, as were ours: ſo we find it writ in the Relations and Hiſtories of that Siege, which being ours do with a more wary Pen write their own praiſes. VVe came off with the loſs of three Souldiers, and thirty Wounded.

The great loſs of the Enemy.

106. The Fortreſs by the Battery which preceded this aſſault was every where Ruin'd and Open, and we to repair it wanted Time, Materials, and Men; yet did Ours ſteal the hours of their reſt, working by Night, and throwing down the Houſes of the Fortreſs, made uſe of their Stones and Timber, making a kind of ſuddain and ſtoln Defence, more becoming the time then the neceſſity.

The ſtrengths of the Fortreſs.

107. Ammunition and Proviſion was wanting, there was no more Powder then what was every day made, a little, and ill Dry'd, a want which the *Moors* began to know, and had thereby the hearts to continue the Siege, they had likewiſe advice that the ſcarceneſs of other neceſſaries was anſwerable, for Wheat was at three Cruſades an *Alquiere*, and yet the want of it greater then the price; the Sick inſtead of Hens eat Crows, which coming to feed on the Dead bodies, the Souldiers kill'd, and at an exorbitant rate Sold, the Famine came at laſt to that height, as they ſpar'd not Doggs, Cats, and other ſuch Food, unwholſome and unclean. Yet did they with ſuch miſerable Dyet recover their ſtrength, undervaluing dangers, and duty, by the greatneſs of their minds over-coming the paſſions and affections of Nature.

About one third of a Buſhel.

How the want of Pots of Powder was ſupply'd.

108. Pans for Powder (which the Militia of *India* uſe by Sea and Land, and in this Siege were of no little Execution) were as well as other offenſive VVeapons wanting, which was ſupply'd by putting together two Gutter-tiles, the Concave inward, and Pitch't without, at which hung lighted match, and being thrown amongſt the Enemy, divers were burnt by 'em: by this eaſie invention did ours haſten the Victory.

109. The Commander in chief deſir'd to get ſome intelligence concerning the practices of the Enemy, who ſlye, and deſigning, did yet with ſtrange reſerv'dneſs keep from us his deſigns. Beſides it was advis'd from the Fort next the Sea, that moſt Nights ſome *Moors* came as farr as the Bridge of the Fortreſs, vvhere they ſtop't,

as

as men, who for some end came to survey, and be acquainted with the situation; their silence, the time of Night, and the continuance of it, evinc't their diligence not to be casual. Upon which, *Dom John Mascarenhas* perswaded *Martim Botelho* (a Souldier of trust) with ten Camerades to go one Night upon the Bridge, and endeavour by Force or Craft to bring off one of those *Moors*. *Martim Botelho*, with the others about Mid-night went out at the Skit-gates of the Courtain, carrying only Swords and Bucklers, and being arriv'd at the set place, (not to be discovered by the *Moors*) they lay vvith their Faces on the ground, and listning awhile, heard some coming toward the Bridge, rising, they suddainly set upon the *Moors*, vvho vvere eighteen, and seeing themselves so unawares attaqu'd, did at the first Onset turn their backs, leaving only on the place a *Nobite*, vvho vvith a Lance stoutly defended himself. *Martim Botelho* seeing it greater concernment to take, then to Kill him, put by vvith his Sword a thrust of his Lance, and closing vvith him brought him fast in his Arms to the Fortress, vvhere his Reception vvas vvith that honour the Action merited.

Nob a Town in *Palestine*.

Our men get intelligence,

110. The Commander by the Prisoner knew the Enemies intentions, and made use of the advice to prevent some Stratagems the *Turks* vvere contriving, besides he told him there vvere missing in the Army five thousand men cut off by us, not to name Officers of note; that the Souldiers of the greatest Authority despair'd of the design, hearing vve should as soon as the Sea vvas down be Reliev'd; but that *Rumecaon* vvas by the losses he had sustain'd more obstinate in carrying on the Siege, as one engag'd by his honour, and by his promise given to the *Sultan*; that by the advice of a *Turkish* Engineer of *Dalmatia*, he had commanded the undermining Saint *Thomas*'s work, (vvhere vvas *Dom Fernando*, with *Diogo de Reynoso*, and other Commanders and Cavalliers) vvhich vvas done in so great silence as our men could not make out the design, because perhaps

whit News of the Enemy.

Saint *Thomas*'s work mined.

History of *India*, Dec. 6. Cap. 9 Lib. 2.

perhaps they believ'd that Fire-works were not as much us'd in *Asia*, as *Europe*; but the Chief Officers of the Army being *Turks*, they brought as well Discipline as Courage.

111. Whilst they were working in the Mine, *Rumecaon* commanded 'em to seem to sap divers places of the Wall, that we being intent upon the common danger, might not guess at the secret one. And by an other Plot to divert our attention, he ordered the making some wooden Horses to be plac't before Saint *Thomas's* work, as if by them he intended to take it by Scaling, and resolving to fall on the tenth of *August*, on the Ninth he commanded the drawing off some Guns which he had Planted. And that we might not by wondring at that find him out, He endeavour'd by an other design to make us more secure. He that night sent an *Abessine* subtilly instructed to the Fortress, who coming to the Wall, counterfeiting a Panick fear, cry'd to the Watch to take him in, that he might discourse things of great concernment with the Commander; being let in, and listned to by *Dom John Mascarenhas*, he discreetly began his Speech, cursing the desperateness of his condition, that being Born of *Christian* Parents, he had like an abortive fruit of Catholick Plants abjur'd the Faith of his Fathers in which he was bred; that now with his Eyes opened he came to Knock at the Door of the Church, that the Latin Priests might bring back to the Sheep-fold of Christ, so lost a Sheep; that this was the miserable relation of an uncompos'd Life; that about the affairs of *Cambaya*, he could assure him the *Sultan* had news that the *Mogull* with a great Army was entred the Confines of his Kingdome, putting all to the Sword; that *Juzarcaon*, who had lately brought thirteen thousand Foot to the Camp, had orders to joyn with *Rumecaon*, and both together go against the Enemy; that with that resolution he commanded the drawing off the Canon, but that he should be provided the next day to look for a general

Rumecaon endeavours to keep it from us.

assault,

assault, because the *Turks* would not without some Noise end that Warr. *Dom John Mascarenhas* commended and confirm'd his resolutions of turning Catholick, besides the taking kindly his intelligence, and again let him down the Wall, to acquaint him with any new thing that hapned in the Camp.

112. The news of raising the Siege, with the certainty of the assault which was to be given, was Nois'd about the Fortress, and the Souldiers for joy put on that day their Bravery, some rejoycing at the approach of the Enemy, others at the end of the Warr. The Commander in chief found a great forwardness in all the Souldiers to expect the assault, for all thinking 'twould be the last of so long a Siege, every one coveted to give the latest memory of his Actions.

113. *Dom Fernando de Castro* kept his Bed of a Feaver, and hearing of the intended assault, rose, his Gallantry offering violence to Nature; *Dom John Mascarenhas*, sometimes as his Commander, others as his Friend went about to hinder it; but Disobedience here passing for Virtue, he rather offended against Health then against Honour, putting on his Armour and coming to the Works.

Dom Fernando came sick upon the Works.

114. The day of the glorious Saint *Laurence* broke, Dedicated by his happy Martyrdome to Fiery trials. The Gentlemen with so much transport of joy came to their Posts as if already in possession of Reward and Victory. They presently saw at a distance the Enemies Army marching Orderly, and dispersing it self round about the Fortress. Our Canon plaid with no little Execution, the Enemy, Souldier like, enduring the Charge, rather then discompose the Order he march't in, till he had gain'd his Post, and planted Ladders to begin the assault; they fell on the Works with great resolution, hoping by Fighting to amuse us, that the confusion of the Conflict might cover the Stratagem of the Fire they had laid. Our men, shew'd great Bravery, as if in haste to rest them-

The Enemy makes shew of an other assault.

themselves in Victory, promis'd in the issue of that Day.

115. The fury of the Sword, without any fear of that of the Fire, was kept off, in Saint *John's* Work; the Enemy fought carelesly, till the sign of springing the Mine arriving 'em they all at the same time retir'd; the same fear, equal and suddain in 'em all, discovered us the Plot. The Commander in chief cry'd out immediately for 'em to leave the Work; that the Mine, now known by the suddain retiring of the Enemy, might without any hurt take Fire. Every one by leaving his Post obey'd their Commander, only *Diogo de Reynoso* with disorderly Courage kept the place, calling them Cowards who quitted it. At those words all return'd to their Posts, rather following example then reason. The Mine immediately with a most hideous report took Fire, and those stout Defendants lay Dead in that place, they had kept alive. [*b*] Here Dy'd *Dom Fernando de Castro* at the age of Nineteen, rais'd from a sickness Nature might have past over, but Courage made it mortal. *Dom Francisco de Almeyda* lost his Life, keeping up the courage and misfortune of his Family. Here lay Buried *Gil Continho*, *Ruy de Sousa*, and *Diogo de Reynoso*, who with his Life paid for so many Deaths, he so generously, but fatally was instrumental to. *Dom Diogo de Sottomajor*, flying with a Lance in his hand, fell upon his Feet in the Fortress, without any hurt by the Fire, or his fall; some lighted in the Enemies Camp, about sixty men were lost by this mischance; thirteen who came off with their Lives, were

The Mine takes Fire.

[*b*] Fernando *hum delles, (ramo d' alta pranta*
Onde o violento fogo com ruido
Em pedaços o muro no ar levanta)
Será aly arrebatado, & ao Ceo subido.

Fernand (this lofty Cedars highest bough
Where with a hideous crack a close Mine sprung,
Th' unrooted Wall into the Air will blow)
Shall in a sheet of Fire to Heaven be flung.
Camoens Can. 10. St. 70.

wounded

wounded or deform'd by the Fire. Others more largely write the accidents of this Fire. We had rather, then grieve the attention of those who read the History, amongst the chances of this so famous Siege, silently pass over this unfortunate Day. Our men wondered to see the Execution of smothered Powder should be so great, that the stones of the Fortress blown up by the violence of the blow should Kill a great many in the Enemies Camp, the Fire rather following the impulse of Nature then the prescrib'd Limits of the Engineer.

116. After some time, when the Fortress was clear'd from smoak, *Rumecaon* commanded five hundred *Turks* to enter at the ruins of the fir'd Work, the rest of the Camp in whole Companies seconding 'em. Yet met they with five stout Souldiers who resisted 'em, for a good while sustaining the weight of so strange a Combate; so unheard of a truth, as there goes as much Courage to the Writing, as Action, though qualify'd by the confession of our Enemies themselves, and by the reverence of so many Years. *Dom John Mascarenhas* with fifteen more came to that quarter to their Relief, where he beheld two Spectacles, one challenging Compassion, the other Amasement, and relieving the five, all together made so stubborn a Resistance, as to stop the fury of a Victorious Army; such a thing as, related only with the bare truth, out-does all the *Greeks* or *Romans* have in their Histories or Fables.

The memorable Courage of five Souldiers.

History of *India*, Dec. 6. Lib. 2. Cap. 10.

117. 'Twas given out in the Fortress that the *Turks* were Masters of the fir'd Work, upon which, some Souldiers who fought in the other Posts came thither, as where the danger was greatest. The false report happily sav'd the Fortress, for they made a Body capable of resisting thirteen thousand Foot, so many (as our Histories reckon) were they, who went on upon the Min'd work. The Women, taught not to value their Lives, brought Lances, Bullets, and Pots of Powder, and the Magnanimous *Isabel Fernandez*, with only a Bill in

The Courage of *Isabel Fernandez* and other Women.

in her hand, did by her Actions animate the Souldiers, though much more by her example and words, crying aloud; Fight for your God, Fight for your King, Cavalliers of Christ, for he is on your side. The Enemies, by the success of the Mine, having so fair a Door open to Victory, resolv'd that day to conclude the business, encourag'd by their General, and the opportunity, now Fighting as own'd by fortune. Those who were on the Work, (out of ambition to be the first in so eminent an Action) behav'd themselves the more resolutely, and being *Janizaries* and *Turks*, would have for themselves only the honour of the Day. *Rumecaon* commanded the re-inforcing the assault in other places, that against so inconsiderable a strength, diversion might facilitate the Entry.

The Vicar encourageth the Souldiers.

118. The Fortress was often lost, the Enemy being numerous and fresh, Ours, besides their being but few, spent with the labour of so unequal resistance. The Vicar *John Coelho*, holding up a Crucifix, came to encourage 'em, saying, that God whose cause they maintain'd was the giver of Victories, at which sight those Loyal, and stout Champions, put in Breath again, seem'd more then men in their Courage, for not one had any weakness or sence for his Wounds, continuing the Fight with the same vigour, and boldness, as they begun it.

119. Now was the Day declining, and the *Turks* closely mingled with Ours, now mortally Burnt, out of the same Wounds each man pour'd his own, and anothers Blood; and by a whole Armies charging on so few Defendants, our Souldiers receiv'd many thrusts in the same place. What we relate with truth, may seem heightned. The great things the *Portuguese* did that day let the whole *East* speak, I believe, every Stone of famous *Dio* will be for 'em a silent Epitaph; Our Pen shall not be ungratefully silent of the Names of those five Cavalliers we spoke of, who were, *Sebastian de Sa*, *Antonio Pecanha*, *Bento Barbosa*, *Bertholomew Correa*, and

The names of the five Souldiers.

Mestre

Mestre John a Chirurgion. With the Fight ended the day. *Rumecaon* commanded the sounding a Retreat, after losing seven hundred men in the assault, the Wounded were without number, of whom very many Dy'd (for want of looking to) in their Cure; the multitude tyring out the Chirurgions and making scarce the remedies. *Mestre John* only Dy'd of those five Cavalliers who kept the VVork, torn in pieces by his many Wounds, which he sufficiently Reveng'd, unwilling to leave the Fight, or obey his Friends, who would have forc't him to retire, as one so considerable for his Profession, not less for his Courage. His Wife *Isabel Madeira* came to bind up his Wounds, and after Burying him with her own hands, with few tears, and great grief, went with the other Matrons to work in the Trenches; so great a Courage, as hath been but seldome seen in the most resolute.

The peculiar Courage of *Isabel Madeira*.

Ib.

120. Upon the Enemy's retiring, *Dom John Mascarenhas* gave order for the Burying the Dead, which were in the ruins of the Work, removing them from one Grave to an other; for the straightness of time and place they were Buried all together, so honourable Ashes being without Funeral honours, and Officious tears; yet rest they, in so poor a Grave, more mist by their Country, then those who in Alablaster urns have left of inglorious Lives an idle Memory. *Dom Fernando de Castro* was laid in a Depository by himself, that if the Governour his Father would carry his Bones to any other place, he might make him a more Stately, but not more glorious Monument. After the Commander in Chief had with pious Earth covered his Companions, he fell upon repairing the Breaches the assault had left in the Walls, help't in it by the VVomen, who had their share of labour and danger, not reserving time and place for the grief and tears of their Sons and Husbands, whom they had seen expiring before their Eyes, and had themselves Buried, by unheard of examples smothering the inclinations of Nature.

The Commanders resolution.

121. After repairing the works with Stones, yet warm with Blood and Fire, the Commander in Chief call'd to Councel those few Companions who had surviv'd the Storming, representing to them the compassionate condition they were in; the greatest part of the Defendants being Dead; those who remain'd, Sick or VVounded; the Arms all in pieces; the Provision stinking; the Ammunition consum'd; the Fortress thrown down; the Seas, by reason of the VVinter, more innavigable; the Enemy vigilant, and hourly Recruited, besides his knowledge of all these wants; all which considered, he begg'd of 'em, that, without any regard had to their own Lives, they would consult with him, how best to Salve their Kings, and their own Honour; that they would bethink themselves, how the VVorld stood looking on, and that the whole *East* had their Eyes upon 'em, as being in a condition to deserve the greatest Fame, or Infamy; that if 'twere not in their power to get the Victory, 'twas in it to deprive their Enemies of it, every one having the power of Dying bravely; that they would purchase greater honour, cut in pieces, then the *Moors* if Victorious; that he had call'd them together to impart to 'em his Resolution, hoping every one would approve it, which was, that, wasting that little Provision and Ammunition they had, burning what ere might be Pillage, breaking their Guns, with Swords in their hands they should Sally forth to find the Enemy, then could not that be call'd a Victory, where neither Plunder or Prisoners were to be had. There was not a Souldier, who, having heard *Dom John Mascarenhas*, thought it not long till so generous a resolution was effected. Let *Rome* say, if in her Annalls she finds Recorded so great an Action of her *Fabios*, *Scipios*, or *Marcellus's*.

Ib.

122. Whilst

122. Whilst this was in debate, [d] *Dom Alvaro de Castro* was strugling with the storms of Winter, for, it being then the four and twentieth of *June*, a Season when those Seas are not Navigable, He, sollicitous for the danger the Fortress was in, not valuing that of his Fleet, did by force of Oars sail even under the Waves; The Whirl-winds were so Tempestuous, and the Seas so High and Counter as they swallow'd up the Ships; some with the force of the Weather broke, others losing their Masts and Tackling, lay without Steerage at the mercy of the Sea, Shipping in water on both sides, without any Government of their Helm. *Dom Alvaro*, resolute in the relief of *Dio*, turn'd too and again, finding himself every moment so under water, as with the Ships rowling the Sea beat off her Rudder; yet by his impatience, with some Ships of his Convoy got shattered and torn into *Bacaim*, the rest recover'd different Ports, and Bays. Here *Dom Alvaro* found *Dom Francisco de Menezes* for't back again with the same VVeather, after several times venturing into the Gulf, which he found so High and Stormy, as for saving the Bottom he was forc't to cast Over-board all his Lading of Ammunition and Provision.

Dom Alvaro de Castro's Voyage.

History of India, Dec. 6. Lib. 3. Cap. 1.

[d] Alvaro *quando o inverno o mundo espanta*
E tem o caminho humido impedido
Abrindoo vence as ondas, & os perigos
Os ventos, & depois, os inimigos.

Camo. Can. 10. St. 70.

Alvar, when Winter swathes the Earth in Snow,
And hath on humid Gates cold Padlocks hung,
These burst, through dangers to seek dangers goes,
And fights the Elements to fight the Foes.

Sir *R. F.* Translation.

123. *Antonio Moniz Barretto* at that time came in with his great Carvel of Provisions, which (so general was the Storm) had been oft times lost, and on his arrival deliver'd her up to *Dom Alvaro*, with a resolution in a little Vessel he found, in despight of the Seas to go for *Dio*, so season'd with one danger, as to venture

Antonio Moniz arrives at Bacaim.

venture on an other. The storm that day encreasing, the Ship began to drive, and spent two Cabells; the Vessel being of such consequence, as having in her all sort of Provision for relieving the place, *Dom Alvaro* endeavoured to help her, but do the Mariners what they could, so great was the Storm they could not get to her, yet did *Antonio Moniz Barretto* put himself in a little Boat he by chance found on Shore, and, though those from the Land saw him a thousand times under water, the Vessel being light, and yielding to the Seas, Liv'd in 'em; at last he arriv'd, made fast a Cabell to the Carvel, and against every ones judgment, with more fortune then reason, tow'd her after him, and concluding that only such a Vessel, little and light, could make her way through so great Seas, on which the beating and shock of the VVaves would make a less impression, he privately bought it of a Merchant, and with some Mariners whom he paid what they ask't, embark't on her. There was casually standing on the shore *Garcia Rodriguez de Tavora*, who seeing *Antonio Moniz* resolution, desir'd him, to take him with him, *Moniz* excus'd it, saying, 'twas not convenient he should have so eminent a Person for his Companion, who would ecclipse him: that only for himself he would have that danger, without any other going in his Boat. *Garcia Rodriguez* assur'd him he would every where confess, 'twas he who carry'd him, and give it him under his hand; so scrupulously in those times did they manage points of honour. *Antonio Moniz*, satisfy'd with that modesty, permitted *Garcia Rodriguez* to come on Board. *Miguel de Arnide*, a Souldier of a Gigantick body, and not less in Gallantry then Stature, seeing them put out to Sea, cry'd to 'em from the shore, What Gentlemen do you go without me to *Dio*? here's no room for you, answer'd one of them, but the stout Souldier, with his Cloaths on, Leaping into the Sea with a Musquet in his mouth, swom toward the Boat, and *Antonio Moniz* seeing so great Bravery staid to take him in, saying in one

Saves the Ship of Provisions.

Ib.

Two Gentlemen go for *Dio*.

Ib:

so

so good a Companion he carry'd a good Recruit to *Dio*.

124. Those Gentlemen were at Sea in so bad VVeather, as all that day and night they Sail'd at the mercy of the VVinds, the Boat, with her Helm lach't, and keeping no course, obeying the Seas; the VVaves sometimes drove 'em on shore, at others made them lose what they had got, they were with a Bonnet brought to their main Yard, turning up and down as the Seas carry'd 'em, which fill'd them so full of water, as very hardly did they free her with Bucquets; in that perplexity and danger past they the Night, all worn out with their continual Labour, by the darkness of the Night and closeness of the VVeather not knowing where they were; The day broke, but with little difference from the Night, and they were still striving with the VVaves, till about Evening they came in sight of the Fortress, so Battered, as, for the ruins, they hardly made it; they came at last to an Anchor, without the Sentinels taking notice of it, on which they conjectur'd the Fortress was lost; *Antonio Moniz* call'd so loud to 'em, as being heard by those within, they went with the news to the Commander in Chief; here 'tis said, that the Sentinell asking who's there, a Souldier answered, *Garcia Rodriguez de Tavora*, which *Antonio Moniz* taking ill, reply'd, that he was the man came thither, and, if *Garcia Rodriguez* had not civilly and modestly tempered *Antonio Monits* just resentment, the Jealousie, (though time and reason were above so slight Quarrels) might have caus'd a greater Breach. *Dom John Mascarenhas* came to receive 'em, and with embraces told 'em, how much he valued their so seasonable Relief; he ask't *Antonio Moniz* where *Dom Alvaro de Castro* was, who in the Souldiers hearing answered him aloud, Sir you have him here with sixty Sail in *Madrefabat*, and with the first fair weather you'l see his Streamers; but between themselves he told him, that, after often putting to Sea, being forc't back again, he was yet at *Bacaim*,

The dangers of the Voyage.

They arrive at *Dio*.

The generous jealousie of two Gentlemen.

They tell news of *Dom Alvaro*.

caim, but so impatient of his stay there, that he would not wait for the time of year to come to his Relief; this news was so entertain'd, that the Souldiers with Dancing and Capering forgot their past Sufferings, in their hopes of the Recruit at hand; and those who had serv'd under *Dom Alvaro*, upon their experience of his Gallantry, warranted his coming, in spight of the Seas and VVinds.

125. *Dom John Mascarenhas* entertain'd his Guests on Saint *Johns* and Saint *Thomas's* works, where were the most ruins, Courting them, who had so well deserv'd from greater dangers, with those pastimes of VVarr. Our danger was not at that time less, though less apprehended. *Antonio Moniz* sent back the Vessel he came in to his Cousin-german *Luis de Mello de Mendoca*, who had begg'd it of him; there went on her some maim'd Souldiers, with Letters for *Dom Alvaro de Castro* from the Commander in chief, in which he gave him an account of all had past, telling him in short the straights we have before related. The Boat came back to *Bacaim* to the great joy of those who saw her, to hear the Fortress yet held out for the King, though that was allay'd with the dreggs of so many being Kill'd, of whom the most resented was *Dom Fernando de Castro*, who left behind him in so green Years so ripe a Memory. *Dom Alvaro* receiv'd it with the constancy of a Souldier, comforting himself with having his Sword in his hand to revenge him: and immediately that Evening commanded the Fleet to put to Sea, with orders to go away directly for *Dio*, and that no Ship should look after an other.

The Commander in chief adviseth *Dom Alvaro*,

who puts forth from *Dio*.

126. *Kumecaon* in the interim, seeing greater Execution done by Mines then Assaults, and having heard, by some Slaves who fled from the Fortress, of our Famine and Danger; of the grief ours were in for the miss of so many eminent Persons who were lost in the Mine, and of the scarcity of Ammunition and Provision, resolv'd to continue Mining, which was done with less

Rumecaon goes on with the Mines.

less Danger, and more Execution, and in pursuance of the design, commanded them to Sap at Saint *James's* work, and that part of the Wall which runs about it. All was done by crooked and cover'd Galleries, to hide the design from us, and secure the Work-men. *Dom John Mascarenhas*, cautious, and fore-warn'd, arguing from the short truce of the Enemy, that he was working in some other new Mine, affraid too of *Antonio Pecauha's* work, gave order for the Repairing it, and the opening some place to Listen at, by which he found they were working at that part of the Wall, which the Enemy found so strong, as to be proof against his Tools; an extremity he with Fire and Vinegar overcame. A proof the Enemies we had to do with in *Asia*, wanted neither Courage or Discipline, as some falsely write, who to lessen our Victories, take the Eastern *Moors* to be Raw and Barbarous; that day they begun to destroy the Wall, and presently *Rumecaon* commanded, that 'twixt Saint *Thomas's* Work and the round Tower the Mine should be made, which our men knowing, Counter-mind, and made up a strong Wall within; and wanting Materials, and VVork-men, those honourable Matrons help't in so difficult a Work, to favour the wounded and sick, who could neither endure nor excuse the Labour.

Our men labour to prevent 'em.

127. *Rumecaon* having perfected the Mine, resolv'd under protection of that, to make a general Assault, and calling to him the Officers of the Army, and those who were chose to Scale the VVall, 'tis reported he made 'em this Speech. "Those ruins you see, besmear'd "with the Blood of our Fellow-Souldiers, must this "day be our Grave, or our Quarters; they who keep "those shattered VValls are an hundred men, whose "strength is by hunger and wounds so abated, as we "only Fight with the shadows of those who have been "men, who miserably Sacrifice to our Semitars Lives "without Blood. All that honour, they with unhappy "Courage have won in this Siege, is to be Ours; for, "from

Rumecaon encourageth his men for an other assault.

" from the end of a Warr are the Atchievements nam'd, " and the World gives always the Courage to the last " success; Let's make an end of winning the Fortress, " Let's climb that mount of Triumphs, we shall with " only one Victory revenge infinite Affronts; Let's " deliver this Slave *Asia* from Prisons, and Taxes, Let's " free our Seas, which groan under the weight of their " Fleets; we shall by this Assault make an end of so " glorious a design, and the *East* will for whole Ages " joyfully remember so glorious a Day.

They fall upon Saint *James's* work.

128. Having ended his Speech, he spoke to, and animated particular Persons, with motives seasonable to the Time, and Persons, designing rewards to those who should first Scale the Walls, as would have done the most prudent and experienc't Commander of *Europe*. On the same day, the sixteenth of *August*, the Enemy with all their strength march't out of their Quarters, and dividing themselves orderly about the Works, left the main Body of the Army to fall upon Saint *James's*, where they hop't to open the Gate for Victory. Here they gathered Tumultuously, with rude Crys in their mouths, and letting fly, in great abundance, Arrows, and Darts, to summon our greatest strength to the Defence; here the Fight was at the hottest, till in the height of it, the Enemy, seeming to yield to our resistance, as on a sign given, suddainly retir'd; Our men who had been fore-warn'd, knowing the cheat of their feign'd fear in which they went off, quitted too the Work, looking for the springing of the Mine, which the *Moors* made play, and being resisted by the Counter-forts and Scarp of the Wall, which met with it, it sprung Recoyling towards the outward face of the Wall, and the Curtain flying, carry'd it with so great violence upon the *Moors*, that above three hundred were Kill'd, and many more Maim'd.

History of *India*, Dec. 6. Lib. 3. Cap. 2.

129. The Fortress was for some time hid in the Clouds of Powder, and Smoak, so as neither side knew their loss; as soon as the Air grew thinner, the Enemy came

came on in Troops to get upon the ſpoils and ruins of the Fire, with ſo much confidence of Victory as they hindred one the other, droven on out of Covetouſneſs of reward, or Ambition of honour; yet did Ours receive them on their Lances, ſending 'em back VVounded to thoſe whom the Mine had deſtroy'd; after them came on others, alſo after a long diſpute repell'd by ours, who were Gall'd with the multitude of Arrows, Darts, and Balls of VVild-fire which came from the Camp, with which they ſpoilt ſome of our men, and hindred the Souldiers, attent on both dangers, from the Defence; yet ſo Burnt and VVounded, not one quitted the place he kept, where they ſo Heroically behav'd themſelves, as is witneſs'd by the ſucceſs and inequality of the Fight. The fire, the *Moors* caſt into the VVorks, was ſo great, as Ours fought in live Flames, which the Commander in Chief remedy'd, by bringing Barrels of water, which mitigated, or put out, the fir'd Cloaths, and Bodies. The Enemies greateſt force being drawn hither, here it was our men made the greateſt oppoſition, which made the Fight the more terrible, Recruited every moment by the *Moors* with freſh men, and Re-inforc't with the preſence and voice of the General.

130. *Antonio Monits Barretto*, and *Garcia Rodriguez de Tavora* gave here eminent proofs of their Courage, enduring, with more then ordinary conſtancy, the weight of the Enemies, ſhewing, in the extremities both by Land and Sea, the ſame Gallantry. A great ſhare of the honour of the day is due to thoſe, never enough prais'd Matrons, companions not only in their labour, but danger. The good Old woman *Iſabel Fernandez*, with a Bill in her hands, by her words, but more by her example animated the Souldiers; and the others, amongſt the Arrows, Lances, and Bullets, either ſhow'd their own Courage, or aſſiſted it in others.

Ib.

The women continue their Courage.

131. In the other works, they were not idle; for to facilitate, by the diverſion, the entrance at Saint *James's*,

 where

where the Mine sprung, there was Fighting in all. *Rumecaon* gave order to Batter the Church in the Fortress, which, by being high, might be thrown down, believing too the offence in that place would be more sensible; but ours had so receiv'd the Enemy, as they now coldly and remissly went to Seale the Wall, kept back by the horrour of our Execution amongst 'em.

The Enemy retires with loss.

132. *Rumecaon* out of impatience Commanded the sounding a Retreat, leaving above five hundred Dead, without number the VVounded. Any one of ours might content himself with the honour he that day gain'd. That stout Souldier *Miguel de Arnide* so signalis'd himself, as he prov'd even that Body too little for so great a Soul, and accompanying so vast a Growth with proportionable Srrength, who ere was reach't by his first blow, excus'd him from a second. *Mojateeaon*, vvho vvas come to the Army vvith a great Recruit, and spoke vvith scorn of the valour of the *Portuguese*, by the experience of that day forming an other judgment, said they vvere vvorthy to command Kingdoms, and that the VVorlds good fortune consisted in their being so small in number; for Nature had, like Lyons, made them few, Locking them up in the Denns of the *West*.

Mojateeaon praiseth our mens Valour.

133. VVe lost that day seven Souldiers, those vvho vvere Scorch't vvere twenty two; and now the vvell vvere so few, as not to be enough to help the Wounded, less able to repair the ruins of the Fortress, for vvhich, time, Materials and Men vvere vvanting; but *Rumecaon* finding so tough resistance in the Assaults, had an other opinion of our strength. At this time three of our Slaves ran to the Enemy, vvho brought before *Rumecaon*, told him, there vvere not threescore Souldiers in the Fortress, vvho could bear Arms, and those very much vvore out vvith Hunger, and continual duty of Labour, and Centries; in vvhom nothing vvas to be found but obstinacy vvithout force. *Rumecaon*, on the certainty of this news, resolv'd the next day vvith all his

Rumecaon hath intelligence from three of our Slaves who ran away.

his strength to storm us, acquainted his men with the condition we were in, and gave order they should all hear it from the Slaves mouths, who running up and down the Army merrily spread the relation of our necessities. Ib.

134. As soon as the Day broke, the Army had orders to give the Assault; at which, as at the last of the Warr, every one would be present, some put on their Bravery, believing they went rather to Triumph then to Fight. They came out of their Tents with their Colours flying, playing on diverse Instruments, which seconded by the noise of the Camp, form'd Barbarous, and hideous Ecchoes, and having, by the intelligence we have spoke of, o'recome their fear, as soon as they came in sight they advanc't to Saint *Thomas*'s work, which being almost all thrown down help't them up by its ruins. The first company who fell on, with confidence of Victory, were *Turks*, who, by our mens casting amongst them some Pots of Powder, were forc't being all on Fire to retreat. Others came on with the same fury, and after a long dispute, as the first, gave back, of whom our Swords had drawn Blood; but *Rumecaon* not doubting but so continual resistance would spend us, as Iron which is blunted by cutting, by the slaughter of his own men guessing at our weakness, Commanded his Souldiers to go take possession of the Fortress, which had now none left to oppose 'em. Here tumultuously fell on a great Body of the *Moors*, engag'd on by their own credulity or the words of the General. These at their first speed got upon the Wall, and began body to body to Fight with ours, many and fresh, against a few, already wearied and wounded; yet deriving Courage from their gallantry, and necessity, the last found them as Valiant as the first. Some of the Enemies falling down, others came in their places, which often lost the Fortress. Here fell in *Don John Mascarenhas*, animating, as a great Commander, his Men, and Fighting, as the stoutest Souldier, himself; and provided

He gives another assault.

Our mens stout resistance.

ded for all the chances of Warr, had ready all sorts of Arms; which our men made use of, being by those stout Women, put into their hands. *Luis de Sousa* Commander of that Work, shew'd that day great Gallantry. *Antonio Moniz Barretto*, *Garcia Rodriguez de Tavora*, *Dom Pedro*, and *Dom Francisco de Almeyda*, did things worthy a larger History, and all the Cavalliers, and Souldiers, who were in the Action, purchast a most deserv'd Name.

Ib.

Rumecaon falls upon Saint *Johns* work and retires.

135. *Rumecaon* by the Slaves information, believing he should find free entrance, Commanded his men to fall upon Saint *Johns* work; but those few Defendants there were, so behav'd themselves, as the Enemy was forc't vvith loss and shame to retire. *Rumecaon*, amaz'd at vvhat he saw, said, vve vvere the Instruments of Heavens anger against *Cambaya*, and the second time, with certain Barbarous and Ridiculous expiations, vvent about the appeasing *Mahomet*; and because in storming, he lost a great many men vvithout success, and the Souldiers now grown Cowardly, did on the apprehension of their being so daily Butcher'd, slight their obedience, he set upon Mining again, as a vvay more effectual or more secure; and first he commanded the opening some Loop-holes in the VVall, which divided the Army, and our Fortress, by vvhich our men receiv'd no little harm, Fighting as in a plain Field, vvithout the protection of the VVall, vvhich vvas thrown down; and the showring of Musquets vvithout any intermission annoy'd us.

He endeavours to break down the Cistern.

136. He commanded his Souldiers to Batter the Cistern vvith a great Gun, because that being broke, as in a necessity past Cure, thirst vvould destroy us; this Cistern is at the entry of a Street, vvhich vve call the *Cova*, and vvas the *Moors* old Ditch, vvhere those vvho vvere not fit for Service retir'd; here fell store of Bullets, not vvithout doing mischief to the poor people vvho fled thither for Protection, and endangering the Roof vvhich cover'd the Cistern. The Commander in Chief prevented this fear by ordering an high defence of

VVood

Wood lin'd with Earth, which secur'd the apprehensions of either inconvenience, making holes too in the common joyning of the Houses, next the Fortress, by which they supply'd one the other securely.

137. The *Moors* in the interim work't in the Mine, vvhich vvas carried to Saint *James*'s vvork, and being by Ours found out, they on the inside put strong Abutements, and opened some Vents, that the Fire might spend it self, at the time of springing the Mine, it met vvith such resistance in the Scarp, that carrying vvith it part of the Work, it plaid vvithout the Fortress, Killing great numbers of those Souldiers and Miners, vvho were employ'd in it, not one of Ours miscarrying, by the Courtain of the Wall holding firm; it might be by chance, but that so extraordinary, as it appear'd a miracle. The *Moors*, vvhen the Mine plaid, did by vvhole Companies get up on the ruins of the Work, vvhere they vvere Resisted by our men, vvorn out by Watching, vveakned by their Fasting and Wounds, and more in Heart by the greatness of their Courage, then the force of Nature, yet so animated by honour and danger, as they seem'd to Fight with fresh, and entire strength, keeping off the wild Current of the Enemy with his own loss; The place was of reception for more to Fight upon, and the danger encreast by the inequality of the numbers. The noise of Arms, and confusion of Crys, interrupted all Commanding, and Obeying; of the *Moors* many fell, but by the diligence of the Commanders, others came in their place, by which they gave Ours no respite, who from a farr were thrown at by Darts and Arrows, and Fought clos'd hand to hand. Thus did they for many hours hold out the Fight. The Enemy gain'd so much as to plant three Colours on the VVorks, which their great numbers of Musquetteers defended; thence they descended by the VVall to the Apostle Saint *James*'s Church, which joyns to the same VVork, and placed themselves on the Top of it, so that one half of the

An other Mine plays with loss to the Enemy.

The great danger ours were in.

The Enemy plants three Colours on St. *James*'s work.

VVork and Church was kept by the *Moors*, and by us the other.

138. The night came on, and not Peace but Nature put an end to the dispute; yet did they with wandering and uncertain blows blindly continue the Battail. The Commander in chief gave presently order for the casting up a weak Work (which more divided then protected us from the Enemy) which was made by stealth, and with Swords in their hands; the Souldiers had no other Lodging then the place they fought on, where, not on their Arms, could they securely take a little repose, neither had they conveniency of time or place to dress their VVounds. The Commander indulg'd himself no rest from his Arms, less from his Thoughts; He that night Commanded the Levelling a Canon at the Door of the Church, which commanded the VVork, and with that gall'd the *Moors*, who while they kept possession of what they had got, receiv'd no little loss, till by a high Rampier they cover'd and secur'd themselves.

Luis de Mello departs from *Bacaim*.

139. The danger by Sea, was not less then that by Land; for immediately, upon the arrival of *Antonio Moniz's* Carvel to *Bacaim*, the next day (the fourteenth of *August*) *Luis de Mello* with fifteen Companions embark'd on her, and after him *Dom Iorge*, and *Dom Duarte de Menezes* with seventeen Souldiers in a Fly-boat. *Dom Antonio de Attayde*, and *Francisco Guilherme*, each in a Ship of his own, with fifteen Souldiers. *Luis de Mello* presently put to Sea, but for the contrary VVinds made but little way, the further he got off from the shore, he found the Seas higher, and the Carvel being but little, and loose, and the VVaves so great, as by the force of the Storm to break over and flowre her, she ship't the water on both sides, which the Mariners, every moment over-whelm'd, freed with Bucquets, upon which both *Grumets*, and Souldiers, grown fearfull, and out of heart, desir'd *Luis de Mello* to stand for his Port again, saying, that with men they could Fight, but

History of *India*, Dec. 6. Lib. 3. Cap. 3.

The dangers of his Voyage.

but not with the Elements; that 'twas now not Courage, but Obstinacy, to lose themselves for nothing; that against the wrath of God no Bravery could carry it out. *Luis de Mello* went to quiet 'em, alledging, that *Antonio Moniz* past in the same Vessel and same Storm; that he had not with him better men then he, nor did the Seas shew him more favour; that none without danger atchiev'd great things; that when their Friends, and Camrades were Fighting with the *Turks*, they were not to wait for calm Seas, and fair Winds to go and relieve 'em; that though the Waves swallow'd the Ship, he would, on his Sword swim to *Dio*; that they should go man the Sails, for God would help.

140. The terrour, and shame of these words, did for the present quiet 'em, so as that Evening and Night, they were striving with the Storm, expecting every Wave should overset 'em, and now wanting strength to furnish their Duty, seeing the Tempests likely every minute to grow bigger, Mariners and Souldiers agreed, by force to compell *Luis de Mello* to Tack about, which being told him by one *Gomez de Quadras*, a Souldier under his command, he took all the Arms, and laying 'em up in the Gun-room, with his Sword in his hand said, who ere spoke of going back, should be answer'd by Stabbs; that none of their Lives was more Valuable then his, that they should be afraid where he was lost, to lose 'em; that they should look forward, towards *Dio*, for that now, neither their honour, nor safety had any other Port. The Souldiers seeing this resolution, and the Mariners more afraid of the Commander, then the Storm, pursu'd their Voyage, with water always on Board, and drinking in Death, as if every puff of Wind had been to Bury 'em; thus were they Sailing in continual Shipwrack, till in the Evening they came in sight of the Fortress, whence they were perceiv'd with Joy and Amasement. The *Moors* at their coming over the Barr ply'd 'em with Shot, but they came without any hurt under the Fause-bray, where

He resists those who would return.

He arrives at *Dio* and tells news of *Dom Alvaro*.

where the Commander came with an Over-joy to receive 'em; who, was by *Luis Mello* assur'd, that *Dom Alvaro de Castro* could not be two days behind, news by every one entertain'd with such Rejoycing as reach't the *Moors*, on which they concluded the Relief was now at Sea, and *Rumecaon* resolv'd to streighten the Siege. *Luis de Mello* with his men were quartered on Saint *James*'s work, the most part of which was held by the Enemy, and which he had Garrison'd with the best men of his Army, put there to Dye in defence of what they had got. The next day arriv'd *Dom Iorge*, and *Dom Duarte de Menezes*, having scap't with the same resolution, as *Luis de Mello*, the same dangers; with this Recruit, more considerable in quality then number, the Warr seem'd to put on an other face.

The other Gentlemen arrive.

141. The new Guests importun'd *Dom John Mascarenhas* to let 'em see the Enemy, by setting on the driving him out of Saint *James*'s work, which he easily granted, and resolv'd to bear them Company. All provided against the next day, and when it broke, got upon those Walls the Enemy had made for his Defence; charging the *Moors* so Vigorously, as they forc't them from that place, maugre the Courage and Opposition they maintain'd themselves with; The noise before the news reach't *Rumecaon*'s Ears, who coming with all his Force to that place, again engag'd with Ours, on equality in the ground, but advantage in the number; Here both sides fought it out, Hand to Hand, and Body to Body, wounding one the other with short Weapons, every one with his Blood and Life maintaining the ground he stood upon. Ours with so inferiour a party shew'd so much Gallanty, as the *Moors* without the Works stood looking on with fear and wonder; yet, the Enemies force having so much the Odds, he regain'd that part of the Work he had won before, and re-inforcing it with a double Garrison, ordered the giving a general Assault to the Fortress. The Fight was every where at the same heat, many of the *Moors* drop't,

A fight in St. *James*'s work.

drop't, some ta'ne off by the Sword, others burnt with the Fire; but when the dispute was at the hottest, the day began to over-cast with a great storm of Wind, Rain, Thunder, and Lightning; as if in the Air was kindled an other new Battail.

142. The *Moors*, seeing our Match put out by the Rain, and that neither our Pots of Powder, nor any other Fire-works could do them any mischief, looking upon the course or variety of the Weather as Divine favour, came under covert in the midst of thick Rain, upon us without fear, and with Shouts, and Crys, as if they had Heaven on their side. This was the day, in which our men shew'd the greatest Courage, and the Fortress was in the greatest danger; because the *Moors* run upon our Lances and Swords; either Brutish, or Valiant. Six hours lasted this so resolute Assault, till the day turn'd clear again, and our men began to make use of their Pots of Powder, with which they Burnt not a few, whose sight cool'd the others Courage, making them Fight more Cautiously till the close of the Day, and *Rumecaons* sounding a Retreat; when he left, four hundred Dead, and above a thousand Wounded; of ours seven Dy'd, the Wounded were more. All the Gentlemen of the Recruit were in this Assault, giving the same proofs of their Courage and Birth; *Dom John Mascarenhas* play'd by turns the prudent Commander and stout Souldier, always present in danger, without prostituting his Command. Our men past that night with Watching, having for their so near Neighbours the Enemy, who had, for the straightness he held the Besieged in, receiv'd new Honours from the *Sultan*, and a Recruit of five thousand Foot was come to him, with many *Turk*-Officers, whom *Rumecaon* desir'd should be presently brought to face our men, that by shewing them with whom he had to do, he might justifie his Actions.

The danger the Fortress was in, and the Courage of our men.

Rumecaon retires with great loss.

The Enemy is recruited.

143. The day after the Assault, came over the Barr *Dom Antonio de Attayde*, and *Francisco Guilherme*, who found not the Seas less Boisterous then those we have

The other Gentlemen arrive at *Dio*.

spoke of; who reported *Dom Alvaro de Castro* could not be missing a day, having made the Fleet set out with this Order, that no Ship should stay for an other. The Souldiers, for this News and Recruit, kept Holyday with Musick, and continual Dancing, which made the dangers of the Siege go onely for a pass-time.

Rumecaon despairs of the design.

144. *Rumecaon*, having notice there were already arriv'd some Recruits at the Fortress, and thinking when the Weather opened, the *Portuguese* would not be backward to assist one the other in the greatest Dangers, began to despair of the design, seeing hardships shook not our mens Resolutions, and that his Souldiers in their Discourses did not allow the cause of the Warr, accusing the Breakers of that Peace we kept so inviolably; He was afraid of some dispositions he saw for a mutiny, which, by aggravating the miserable condition of Ours, and the infallibility of their Victory, he Labour'd to prevent. He paid the Souldiers, and commanded the **Cacizes* to Preach the certainty of Glory for all those who Dy'd in this Warr, and the Rewards, which for defending their Country, they were to receive from the *Sultan*, not forgetting to joyn the Temporal, with the Spiritual. And Mines not being so Dangerous as Storming, and of more Execution, he resolv'd to go on with them; on this design, he commanded the opening a great Mine, in that tract of the VVall which from Saint *Johns* work goes untill it end in *Antonio Pecanha's* Centry-house; but our men being caution'd (though subtil, and contriving *Rumecaon*, sap't under the other VVorks, commanding his men by night to make a noise there, by that diversion to keep from us his intention) *Dom John Mascarenhas* had notice of the Mine, against which, as at other times, he secur'd himself, the Gentlemen working to prevent it, whose example eas'd the Labour of the Souldiers.

History of *India*, Dec. 6. Lib. 3. Cap. 4.

* They are Judges, Preachers, and Governours of Colledges.

He opens an other Mine, which is prevented.

145. VVhen 'twas time to spring the Mine, the whole Army mov'd, and begun to surround the Fortress; there came before two *Sanjacks* commanding a Com-

It plays and our men defend the Breaches.

Company of *Turks*, who were to enter at the Breaches presum'd upon at the playing of the Mine, which with a hideous Noise carry'd into the Air the whole face of the Wall; The *Turks*, though blind with Smoak, and Dust, (the force of the Fire had rais'd) ran presently on, but found the opposition of an other VVall; the Fire either had not reach't, or had prov'd too strong; yet seeing *Antonio Pecanha*'s Watch-house open in three places, carrying thither their Arms, they endeavoured to gain it; but our men, as to the weakest place came its Relief, stopping the Current of the Enemy.

146. Here the dispute was for a while close and hot, the Besiegers and Besieg'd, as it were Fighting in a plain Campagnia, and *Rumecaon* believing, that there was all our force, Commanded 'em to fall on the other VVorks, where too the *Portuguese* entertain'd 'em with their Swords. The Enemy that day shot infinite Bullets into the Fortress, which, though That was almost raz'd, did no harm, an accident which for its rareness look't like a miracle. The Fight lasted some hours, the Enemy retiring with his usual loss, we with our ordinary good fortune. The Enemy retires.

147. *Rumecaon*, who now thought himself reproach'd by the length of the Siege, as one who to justifie himself, went in quest of dangers, and difficulties, the next day in Person fell upon Saint *Thomas*'s work, commanding several Officers to Scale the other VVorks, which made those days Storming go for a successive assault. The *Moors* fought here, more Desperately then Valiantly, making haste, though run through with Lances, and Swords at once, to Dye, and Kill; readier to offend, then save themselves, seeking Death as the gate to that imaginary Glory, promis'd 'em by the *Cacizes*, who in favour of the design, and to beget in the Souldiers a contempt of their Lives, continually prest that Diabolical incentive. In this heat, did they for some hours endure the Crisis of the Battail, with the loss of fourscore, upon whose Bodies they continued Fighting *Rumecaon* falls upon St. *Thomas*'s work.

Fighting, forc't on by the grief and loss of their slain Camrades. They in fine behav'd themselves with such resolution, as to keep that part of the VVork where the Fight was, planting on it their Colours, covering themselves with Trenches and Barricados.

How it went in St. *James's* work.

148. The dispute in Saint *James's* work was not cooler, the Enemies had twice got it, but met with so gallant a resistance, as at no little expence of Blood they again lost it; The fire the Enemy cast amongst us here was so much, that our men fought in Flames, having no other remedy for their Relief, then to cool themselves in Barrils of water. *Antonio Moniz Barretto*, was, with but two other Souldiers on the VVork, repelling the fury of the Enemy, and *Moniz* stepping off to allay the heat of the Fire in the Barril, was seis'd on by one of 'em, saying, Ah Signior *Moniz*, will you let the King's work be lost? I'me all on Fire (answered he) and go to bathe in the Tubbs, if your Arms (reply'd the Souldier) are well enough to Fight, all the rest is nothing; whose hints *Moniz* accepted, so pleas'd with the Souldiers courage as he got him his discharge, and brought him with him for *Portugall*, generously confessing his own backwardness, to the others advantage, and always calling him by an honourable Title, The Souldier of the Fire; neither do the relations of this Action, make him known to us by any other name.

The Enemy retires again.

149. In this, and the other VVorks they this day fought, with equal courage and danger, which we will not particularly relate, because the Circumstances do so agree, as looking like the same thing repeated, the Writing, and Reading would be tedious; yet, though the relation of this Siege doth not by its variety delight, who will deny this Action to be one of the most famous in human Story, which as so was valued by the most Warlick nations of *Asia*, and *Europe*? Upon the Enemies retiring, we fortify'd our selves in the ruins of the Fortress, where we were continually on our Guards.

150. *Dom John Mascarenhas* the next day, sent out *Antonio Correa* with twenty Companions in a Carak, a Souldier of great Courage, whose Birth (but by his Actions, which deserve, or suppose it Eminent) we know not. He got over the Barr, and Coasting the Island as was commanded him, without any Prize return'd; but as stout Souldiers satisfie not themselves with brave unless successfull Actions, *Correa* (more desperate then obedient) return'd to tempt Fortune five times on the same Errand; but that which seem'd chance, was Mystery, and Heaven decreed or permitted the stout Souldier should be obstinate in the design, who is to blame himself if his own fault procur'd his misfortune. He in fine, with too importune Curiosity, return'd, to provoke or know his Fortune, and standing up with the Island, perceiv'd a Fire at a distance, which made it seem less, but Rowing towards that place, leaving his Companions in the Boat, went on Shore, and walk't a while alone; till the light of the Fire discovered twelve *Moors*, who were warming themselves about it; immediately he return'd pleas'd to his Companions, bidding 'em leave their Boat, for now they had in their power the Prize they sought for, yet the Souldiers, either forgetting themselves, or Ministers of an higher providence, went not with him, making way for their Commanders fortune, who seeing the Souldiers base resolution, went alone to the *Moors*, having heart enough to go attempt that danger, he could not master; on a suddain he set upon the *Moors*, who surpris'd with so unlook't for an Assault, some fled, the rest, but Faintly and Timerously stood to their Defence, but coming to themselves, and seeing themselves Hack't but by one man, began with more resolution to resist him, those also who were fled came back to joyn in the Defence, and while *Antonio Correa* was at blows with some of 'em, others behind mastered him, and after taking him, like a Beast kept him Ty'd, and so carry'd him to *Rumecaon*, in credit of

Antonio Correa goes out to look for some Prize.

Sets upon twelve *Moors*, who take him.

of their Prize, shewing the Wounds they had receiv'd.

He is carry'd before *Rumecaon*,

151. *Rumecaon* commanded he should be loos'd, asking him how many men were in the Fortress? if the Governour intended to come to *Dio*? with what force, and in what time his Son was expected? he with great assurance answered him, that there were in the Fortress six hundred men, who were every day earnest with the Commander to lead 'em forth to the Camp; that they very shortly look't for *Dom Alvaro* to come with fourscore Vessels, who upon his arrival would Sally forth into the Campagnia, because some Galleys he brought with him wanted *Turkish* Slaves; that the Governour was preparing greater Forces, because at once he would determine the business of *Cambaya*. *Rumecaon* who knew the truth of our strength, envy'd so brave a Soul in so low Fortune, and esteeming him as a Souldier, who in Chains despis'd him, ask't him to turn *Moor*, that he might in a better Religion have better Fortune, and know the difference there was 'twixt serving a rich Monarck, and poor Pyrats. The stout Cavallier scandalis'd at the Affront of so base Civilities, told him, The *Portuguese* were always ready to shed their Blood for their Religion, and King; that *Mahamed* was an Impostor, infamous for his Actions and Doctrine; that if there were in *Cambaya* any Renegados, they were of other Nations, as was his Father *Coge-Sofar*, whom, as a Monster of the place he was Born in, his Parents and Country own'd not as their Son.

Who perswades him to change his Religion.

How he useth him.

152. *Rumecaon* not able to endure from a Slave the affronts of his Religion and Person, kindled with Zeal and Contempt, commanded, that before taking away his Life, he should in his presence be beaten and spit upon, believing the Punishment not so much to him as the scorn, then ordered, he should in disgrace and derision go naked through the Streets, a Barbarous inventor of so new a Punishment, first against Man,

then

then againſt Humanity; yet did this Souldier of Chriſt (like one, now a Souldier of an other Militia) with a ſofter Courage overcome by ſuffering. *Rumecaon*, after theſe affronts, ſaying, his Prophets honour demanded ſatisfaction in Blood, commanded he ſhould be Beheaded, and the Palm, he deſerv'd as a Souldier, he obtain'd as a Martyr; his Head was put upon a Pike, and ſet, where from the Fortreſs our men might ſee it, who as Souldiers, out of a natural but unjuſt Compunction vow'd to revenge his Blood, as Catholicks, envy'd his Death. The next day, thoſe who were in his Company return'd, whom the Commander, reſpecting the time, would neither ſee or puniſh; yet did they expiate their fault, by venturing on all occaſions, like men who loath'd Life without honour. Many of 'em accus'd by their Conſcience, deſign'd their own Death. The *Moors* at a diſtance mock't and geer'd at us, pointing at *Antonio Correa*'s Head, recompenſing ſo many loſſes with that ſatisfaction, and grown by it more daring, did in contempt of us ſome extraordinary Actions.

He commands he ſhould be Beheaded.

153. Between Saint *Thomas*'s and Saint *James*'s work was our Colours planted; which one of the *Moors* (believing he could without danger effect it, the Wall being Low, and not Guarded) had a mind to take away; coming by ſtealth and unſeen of our men, getting up by the Ruins, he got hold of the Staff, and though he by forcing mov'd it, yet could he not carry it away, and quitting out of fear his hold left it Leaning; ſeeing how little his firſt attempt coſt him, return'd with the ſame Caution in queſt of the Colours, and as he was reaching out his Arm to take hold of it, one of our Souldiers with a Muſquet-ſhot Kill'd him. This hapned in face of the Camp, who for his firſt exploit entertain'd him with Shouts and Praiſes, now look't upon him falling with a profound ſilence. Ours ran in great haſte to cut off his Head, which they ſo planted, as with it to confront *Antonio Correa*'s.

Hiſtory of *India*, Dec. 6. Lib. 3. Cap. 5.

154. The *Moors* who were fortify'd in Saint *Thomas*'s work,

work, went on at the purchase of their Blood, getting ground inch by inch, carrying always before 'em Mountains of Earth, and Boughs, with which they covered and fortify'd themselves. *Dom John Mascarenhas* commanded the bringing a great Canon to the Church door, which lying higher then the *Moors*, had 'em for a mark, from whence he so furiously Gall'd 'em, as to break their Defences, and with the loss of a great many, make 'em Dislodge.

The extremities of the Fortress.

155. The Fortress vvas now raz'd, and the *Portuguese* instead of Walls defended their own Ruins, the Enemy vvithin the VVorks at the gates of Victory; of the Provisions, some the time had Corrupted, the rest for their quality vvere Unwholsome, from vvhence proceeded so malign Diseases, as the vvell receiv'd more hurt by the Infection, then from the Enemy.

Dom Alvaro is forc't back.

156. *Dom Alvaro de Castro* vvas departed *Bacaim* vvith fifty Ships, (so they call any Boats in *India* be they *European* Carvels, or Vessels vvith Oars) and being Over-laded vvith Ammunition and Provision, not able to Live in so great Seas, they vvere, shattered and loose, forc't to alter their course, and recover diverse Bays and Creeks, as the vveather drove 'em. Amongst those Ships vvhich vvere scattered by the Storm, was that commanded by *Athanasio Freire*, vvho standing in for the Land, vvas cast into the Bay of *Cambaya*, almost quite sunk, and in such a condition, as by common consent they agreed to run on Shore at the first Land they made, counting Life more prisable then Liberty; accordingly they run a-ground near *Surat*, vvhere they vvere taken Slaves, and carry'd to *Sultan Mahumed*, vvho sent 'em away Prisoners, and commanded 'em to be put in the same Dungeon vvhere he kept *Simaon Feo* vvith other *Portuguese*.

Ruy Freire arrives at *Dio*.

157. *Ruy Freire* vvho came in Conserve vvith *Dom Alvaro*, in a Ship of his own, and Souldiers paid at his own Charge, did better keep the Seas, and Sailing that day and the next in the Storm, came in sight of the Coast

of

of *Dio*, whence he lay in for the Fortress, and coming over the Barr got to an Anchor under the Fausse-bray, where he was by every one welcomed, and told the Commander in chief the news of *Dom Alvaro*'s coming, as much expected as necessary, not then knowing any thing of his going back, of which we shall give an account.

158. *Dom Alvaro de Castro*, and *Dom Francisco de Menezes*, were with the general Storm forc't back to *Agacaim*, all shattered; where they quickly fitted themselves, and with most part of their Fleet ventured to Sea again, and over-coming the fury of the weather got sight of the other Coast near *Madrefaual*, whence they made at a distance a great Ship which came stealing by our Fleet. *Dom Alvaro* commanded the Captain to make up with her, as did two Ships more of the Company. The Ship presently stroke Sail, being the King of *Cambaya*'s, and coming from *Ormus*, she sent off two Merchants who came and presented *Dom Alvaro* their pass, sign'd before the Warr; who seis'd on the Ship, and sent her to *Goa*, that the Governour might determine if she was to be made Prize; The Commodities in her were Coral, Chamlots, Pintados, and Carpets, all which were judg'd to be lost. *Dom Alvaro de Castro* holding on his course arriv'd at the Barr of *Dio* with forty Ships, with their Wast-cloths, Streamers, and Pendents, making a show both warlick and pleasant. He saluted the Fortress with all his Guns, which, with the sounding of Drums and Trumpets return'd him the like answer. The Commander in chief made the Gates of the Fortress be opened to receive *Dom Alvaro*, all the Gentlemen, and Souldiers too, came to receive and welcome the Fleet, on which besides *Dom Alvaro* in Person, came Gentlemen and Cavalliers of eminent condition; they brought Ammunition and Provision for some time, the Governour not willing to have it at the Courtesie of the Seas, to deny or give passage to a second Relief. *Dom Alvaro*

Dom Alvaro keeps on his Voyage.

He takes a Ship of Cambaya.

He arrives at the Fortress with forty Ships.

His reception by the Commander in chief.

took up his quarters in the Work vvhere his Brother *Dom Fernando* fell, those who formerly had been under his Command came to serve under *Dom Alvaro*, and most of the Gentlemen, some as having bore a part in the sorrow for his Brother, others in his Victories; all too vvould take the word from him, as Admiral at Sea, not one being vvilling to be exempted from his Command, a thing contrary to the Time, and more to Discipline; yet *Dom Alvaro* told the Commander, he came to receive orders from him, which *Dom John Mascarenhas* taking for a Civility, answered vvith the same Courtship; but *Dom Alvaro* shew'd him his instructions, which vvere not the least part of the other excellencies of the Governour, to say, that, though by the Jurisdiction of his Place, and the King's Commission, he himself vvas exempt from any subjection vvhich belong'd not to the Governour of *India*, he sent his Son *Dom Alvaro* to receive orders from *Dom John Mascarenhas*, the great Honour he had gain'd in that Siege so requiring it; a temper in a man truly great, vvhere he had already lost one Son and ventur'd an other, to covet none of that Fame, he vvith his Blood help't to purchase, greater doubtless in this Neglect, then afterwards in his Victory.

159. *Rumecaon* knowing of *Dom Alvaro*'s arrival, said, there vvere now Prisoners in the Fortress to honour his Triumph, and commmanded his men to work more eagerly in the Mines. *Dom Alvaro* immediately dispatch't his Ship to the Governour with Letters, intimating in vvhat condition he found the Fortress; and *Dom John Mascarenhas* advis'd him of all had past. There vvere now six hundred men in the Fortress, all Souldiers of repute, whom, *Dom John Mascarenhas* thought capable of greater things, then only a Defence; he commanded the planting three great Guns against the Enemies Posts, vvith vvhich he so furiously Batter'd 'em, that *Rumecaon*, as Intent to defend himself as spoil us, re-inforc't his Fortification.

Both advise the Governour of the condition of the Fortress.

160. There

160. There was in the former assaults, Buried in the ruins of Saint *Thomas*'s works, a great Gun of an extravagant bigness, which the Commander was earnest to get up into the Fortress, and imploying Ropes and Machines, found it impossible, desiring so at least to secure it, as the Enemies might make no use of it, he ordered it to be ty'd there with great Cords. The *Moors* continued digging under the Walls of the Work, and striking on the bottom Stones, by the failing of the Foundation the VValls fell down, the great Gun remaining ty'd and suspended in the Air. The *Moors* came presently on to enter the Work, but found in their way *Dom Francisco de Menezes*, with others about him, who engag'd the *Moors* in a very hot dispute, and that being the first day of their seeing the Enemy, they charg'd him with such Vigour, as he was forc't to retire, leaving many of his men on the place. In the height of the Fight, some of 'em fasting a great Cabell to the Gun dragg'd it off, unseen of Ours, who engag'd in the Fight, did not take notice what the *Moors* were doing. The Enemy falls on again and retires.

161. *Dom John Mascarenhas* did vigilantly attend the designs of the Enemy, more afraid of their Mines, then being Assaulted openly; which coming to the knowledge of *Dom Alvaro*'s Souldiers, warn'd by the late example of *Dom Fernando de Castro*, and other Gentlemen, and Souldiers, who were Burnt to Death, they all agreed to Sally out and Fight the Enemy, fearfull where the danger was doubtfull, resolute where 'twas certain. Our men resolve to go out and seek him.

162. They said they would not by their useless obedience be Burnt to Death, when they might Dye in the Field, with Victory or Revenge; that knowing how to Fight like men, they would not perish like Beasts, fastned to their danger; that of two, they rather chose that they might overcome, then that they could not avoid. *Dom John Mascarenhas*, first by Reason, then by the Authority of his Place, and Person, did what he could to disswade 'em, but in vain, because (as their crime The Commander goes about to disswade 'em,

crime had some semblance of Virtue) they were proud of it, and expected rewards and praises for their Disobedience. *Dom Alvaro de Castro* help't to keep 'em back, much disgusted by so foul an obstinacy, saying, the King would be more sensible of the disobedience of one Souldier, then the loss of a Fortress; that it belong'd only to the Commander to Govern, to them to Obey and Fight. *Dom Francisco de Menezes* told 'em they were the first who would Defame the name of *Portuguese*; that they would go with their Honour lost, their Lives in no little danger, and though they scap't the arms of their Enemy, they could not free themselves from the just anger of their King, whom, by so base a Mutiny, they in the Person of his Commander, despis'd. For all this, with a fatal resoluteness did they provide to give Battel, saying, no fault could be such, as Victory would not excuse, and if they were lost, they were exempt from reward or punishment; that they stood up for the honour of the State, whose Custom, was rather to take places on the *Moors*, then lose its own.

as do *Dom Alvaro* and *Dom Francisco.*

163. All the mutinous Souldiers could be brought to, was to put off their Sallying forth till the next day, having left 'em for their Counsellour that so short time to consider, what was best for their safety, and honour; They, by a fatal unanimity, all rose resolute and ready for the Fight, telling the Commander if he would not command 'em, they would amongst themselves chuse a Head. *Dom John Mascarenhas*, seeing himself now forc't to go along with the unruly; and that standers by would judge more advantagiously of the daring, then prudent; resolv'd in Person, with *Dom Alvaro*, and most of the Gentlemen, to follow 'em; the Commanders by a new Discipline obeying, and the Souldiers commanding.

The Souldiers hold their resolution.

The Commander in chief and Gentlemen to prevent greater mischief resolve to go with 'em.

164. There were in the Fortress (as we have said) six hundred men, of whom one hundred staid to maintain the Posts, of the rest, *Dom John Mascarenhas* made

three

three Battallions, two he gave two *Dom Alvaro de Castro*, and *Dom Francisco de Menezes*, the other he took for himself. They immediately Sally'd out of the Fortress, and at the first charge got the Posts the *Moors* had made in the Ditch, who on easie terms quitted 'em. By this shaddow of Victory began our ruine; for our men ambitious, and out of order, assaulted the Wall. The first who got up was *Dom Alvaro*, seconded by two Brothers, *Luis de Mello*, and *Iorge de Mendoca*, who came up after him; *Dom Francisco de Menezes* entred at an other place; and amongst the first were *Antonio Moniz Barretto*, *Garcia Rodriguez de Tavora*, *Dom Iorge*, and *Dom Duarte de Menezes*, *Dom Francisco*, and *Dom Pedro de Almeyda*.

Our men Sally out, and in what order.

History of *India*, Dec. 6. Lib. 3. Cap. 6.

165. *Rumecaon*, *Juzarcaon*, and *Mojatecaon*, came with numerous Companies to receive ours, 'twixt whom the Fight began, maintain'd on our side with more Courage then Discipline; *Dom Francisco de Menezes* was forcing back the *Moors*, who not able to endure the weight of the charge lost ground apace, till reliev'd by a great many others, they stop't the Current of our men. *Dom John Mascarenhas* climbing up the Wall, at the same time with the other Officers, seeing diverse of the mutinous Souldiers, standing at the foot of it, without the hearts to get up, with sharp words, did aloud upbraid, first their Disobedience, then their Cowardliness, who without a word follow'd him, striving to answer by their Actions, and presently charging the Enemies who were engag'd with *Dom Alvaro*, made 'em quit part of their ground; but the party being so inequal, the *Moors* began to recover, so charging Ours, as to put 'em to disorder.

The Enemies resistance.

The Captain chides the Mutineers.

166. *Dom Alvaro* behav'd himself, as his Birth, Repute, and Courage promis'd, not being at a loss in Discipline, hard to be kept up when the day is lost; He was, as much as possible, Ordering and Leading off his men, Retreating honourably with his face always towards the Enemy, who had cut off some of his men, and

The Courage and Discipline of *Dom Alvaro*.

and the rest, not able to endure the force of the *Moors*, were leaving him; which *Iorge de Mendoca* perceiving, though Wounded, took *Dom Alvaro* in his hands to help him up the Wall, and not able by the bleeding of his Wounds to perform it, was help't by his Brother *Luis de Mello*; *Dom Alvaro* being upon the Wall, receiv'd a blow with a stone, which made him without any sign of Life fall down on the other side.

He gets upon the Wall, and with a blow of a Stone falls down.

167. After *Luis de Mello* had help't *Dom Alvaro*, he likewise sav'd his Brother, who was with *Garcia Rodriguez de Tavora*, *Antonio Moniz*, and other Gentlemen, repelling the fury of the *Moors*, till shot through with a Bullet he fell down for Dead; his Companions carry'd him off, and laid him on the VVall, thence was he brought to the Fortress, afterwards conveigh'd to *Chaul*, where he Dy'd of his Wound, deserving, by his singular Courage, if not a more glorious Death, a longer Life.

Luis de Mello is shot through with a Bullet.

168. *Dom Francisco de Menezes*, as he was Fighting stoutly, was tane off with a Bullet, at whose loss his men began disorderly to retire; here was the Execution greatest, for the *Moors* knowing our mens confusion charg'd 'em more Vigorously.

Dom Francisco de Menezes's Death.

169. *Dom John Mascarenhas* in this misfortune behav'd himself with Courage, and Prudence, some times Leading off his men, other times facing the Enemy, (whilst the Mutinous were retiring) by this course avoiding no little mischief; and having now secur'd the Walls, there went a report the Fortress was lost, on which the Souldiers like Routed men, began every one to disperse; in this so dangerous Conflict, *Dom John Mascarenhas* cry'd to his men, shaming them with their going off, and Fighting so couragiously that only with a few who stood to him he kept off the Enemy. The Gentlemen who were in the Fight, got a loud name in so unhappy a Day. *Lopo de Sousa* at the foot of the Wall defended himself against a whole Company of *Moors*, making them often retire, with such Bravery, that

The prudence of the Commander in chief.

that they charg'd him at a distance, till by a Dart which past his Breast he fell down Dead, leaving his Blood sufficiently reveng'd. *Antonio Moniz Barretto*, *Garcia Rodriguez de Tavora*, *Dom Duarte*, and *Dom Iorge de Menezes*, who had seventeen Wounds, made the Victory dear to the Enemy.

The Gentlemen who were that day taken notice of.

170. *Rumecaon* endeavouring to make the best of our Rashness, commanded *Mojatecaon* with five thousand men to march to the Fortress, to intercept those who were flying in the Rout, and falling upon Saint *Thomas*'s work, he found *Luis de Sousa* there, who with Canon and Musquet-shot, Kill'd great numbers of his men, yet the *Moors* emboldned with the heat of Victory, continued Scaling, but were so stoutly resisted, as with notorious loss to retire. *Dom John Mascarenhas* took such pains, as he Rally'd those men who were scatteringly going off, and making of them a close Battallion, led'em on to the Fortress, meeting by the way many of the *Moors*, who being careless in the security of Victory, he so Couragiously charged'em, as many left their Lives, more the Place. There were lost in this miscarriage five and thirty men, of whose number were the Gentlemen we have spoke of; the Wounded were above an hundred, but in so unbridled a design, the loss was not so much as the disobedience. The Commander in chief went presently to look out *Dom Alvaro*, whom he found yet Speechless, and by the judgment of Chirurgions in danger of Life, which lasted those days Philosophy calls Decretory or Critical; yet his pain abated, and *Dom Alvaro* recovered his health, to the satisfaction of those, who lov'd him for the quality of his Birth, and Person. *Nuno Pereira* was in the Fight, who behaving himself with known Courage, came off with fourteen Wounds; he desired leave for his Cure to go to *Goa*, having there a Family, and being lately Married to a great Fortune, most of which he spent in the King's service, till (as we shall tell hereafter) he lost his Life.

Mojatecaon falls upon the Fortress and retires.

The Commander in chief Rallies the Souldiers.

Our loss by this miscarriage.

History of *India*, Dec. 6. Lib. 3. Cap. 7.

171. *Rume-*

Rumecaon is encouraged by the success;

171. *Rumecaon* reflecting on this so unexpected Victory, got by our mens unruly Courage, had more hopes of success, and a stronger resolution to see the end of the design; for which he begun to find his mens obedience more pliable, having by this days experience lost a great deal of that fear they had of our Arms; he presently sent the *Sultan* news of the Victory, which was at Court solemnis'd with publick Rejoycings; and *Rumecaon* receiv'd from the King the honours of a Conquerour, being for the future better supply'd with Men, Ammunition, and Money, on the coming in of a great part of the Nobility, in hopes to go share in his Fortune: He presently commanded his men to go on with the design against our Work, stealing the Earth from underneath, that being unfurnish't the weight might sink it, by the failing of the Foundation on which it rested. *Dom John Mascarenhas* deluded this Plot, by ordering an other Fort to be made within, which took a less compass, and by containing less Earth was fitter for defence. This could not be hid from *Rumecaon*, who brought thither a great party of *Moors*, these with Stones, Darts, and Balls of Wild-fire, did without intermission charge our Work-men, some sure of their aim in those places the Wall discovered, others by casting over it, by which they Wounded our men, more intent on their Work then Defence, to avoid which, the Commander gave order they should by hidden Lights work by Night, laying the Stones by the marks and observation they had taken by Day.

goes on with his Mines and we with our Reparations.

172. *Rumecaon* high, and confident, on the countenance the Warr shew'd him in the last Fight, in contempt of the Governours coming, every day expected, began (as one who would in his imaginary Victory already enjoy the ease of Triumph) to Build a new City; whether 'twere to put his men in heart, or as a Credulous man, he grounded upon the prosperity of his imagin'd successes. He made Palaces for himself, with that Order and Grandeur, the wantonness of Peace would

Builds a new City.

would have allow'd off; He set out quarters for the Officers, by that, obliging 'em to defend their own Dwellings, shewing in the Fabrick, no less Skil, then Pride: He ordered the laying Boats across in that place of the River which goes from the Custom-house to the Town of *Rumes*, which being made fast with great Cabels, he fill'd equally with Earth, o're which; (as on a Bridge not steady, but secure) the Carts which provided the City had an easie passage. Upon *Rumecaon's* confident setting upon so costly a Fabrick, 'twas Voic't in many of the adjacent and remote Kingdoms from *Cambaya*, that we had lost our Fortress, which report pleasing the ears of the *Moors*, and *Pagans*, spread all over the *East*, till the *Sultan* receiv'd the Complements of many Princes who gave him the joy of the Victory. The sound of this News was with fear and silence listned to in *Goa*, and though at large, and without an Author, came to the Governours ears, who by the privacy and caution with which it went from one an other, did argue its probability.

173. This misfortune so much fear'd, seem'd confirm'd by the slowness of advice from *Dio*, neither was there any certainty what was become of *Dom Alvaro's* Fleet; those who would put by such thoughts in the Governour, seem'd rather to slight, then deny the news, and he as most concern'd, seeing the necessity of encouraging the people, seem'd not to lay it to heart, contradicting the News he fear'd, by the Face he put upon't.

The sollicitousness of the Governour.

174. This sollicitousness took up the Governour, (only diverted by the business and preparations of the Navy, which, omitting no diligence, he intended) when News was brought him, there was come to the Barr a Ship from the Kingdome, Captain *Dom Manoel de Lima*, who was parted from five more of the same Conserve, all under the Command of *Lourenco Pirez de Tavora*; the others were Commanded by *Dom John Lobo*, *John Rodriguez Pecanha*, *Fernand Alvarez da Cunha*,

Dom Manoel de Lima arrives from the Kingdome, at Goa.

Cunha, and *Alvaro Barradas*. The Governour thought *Dom Manoel de Lima*'s arrival very considerable, for the Person, and the necessity; he came Commander of the Fortress of *Ormus*, which the King had given him to put by some animosities which were 'twixt him and the Governour *Martin Affonso de Sousa*, whose return from *India* he expected, to demand satisfaction of him for some injuries. These disgusts the King took up, concern'd as a Father in the peace of both his Subjects. *Dom Manoel* would presently have been gon for *Dio*, with three hundred Souldiers at his own Charge; but the Governour disswaded him, desiring his Company in his Fleet, and his Courage and Experience in the management of the present Design.

The Governour receives news from *Dio*.

175. The Governour being more then ordinarily perplex't about the business of *Dio*, thinking no good of the want of advice, the Admiral, which carry'd *Dom Alvaro*, arriv'd at the Barr of *Goa*; She came in with her Wast-cloaths and Streamers, and by her joyfull Salutes, endeavour'd a farr off to tell the news she was fraught with. The greatest part of the people ran to the Sea-side, to enquire after their Children, Friends and Kindred, and those least concern'd, after the common interest of the State. The Captain was carried to the Governours Palace, satisfying by the way many repeated and troublesome questions; He found the Governour with the Bishop *Dom John de Albuquerque*, and Friar *Antonio do Casal* Guardian of the *Fanciscans*. The Governours first question was, if the Fortress yet held out for the King his Master? to which the Captain answered, it did and would do; At vvhich news the Governour falling on his Knees, vvith his Eyes to Heaven gave God thanks, not vvithout shedding some tears, vvitnesses, of his piety towards God, and his zeal for his Prince, and receiving presently his Letters, he heard the Death of his Son *Dom Fernando*, vvhich he receiv'd vvith so great constancy, as those about him perceiv'd no alteration in his Words or Countenance; as if to appear a Father, had

His piety and joy at the receipt of 'em.

His stout behaviour at the news of his Son *Dom Fernando*'s Death.

had been weakneſs, and to have the common affections of a man, diſhonour. He thank't the Captain, and ſent him to chear the City with the news; then retir'd, and in private wept for his Son, expecting time to grieve in, without leſſ'ning his place or courage. The ſame day came into Port the Ship which brought *Nuno Pereira*, who Dy'd at Sea of his Wounds. The body was Buried, with the Funeral ſolemnity due to the Perſon, accompany'd by the Governour, Nobility and People; the Gentleman leaving behind him a moſt endear'd Memory.

176. The next day there was made a ſolemn Proceſſion to thank God, at which the Governour aſſiſted, Cloath'd in Scarlet, comforting (a thing unheard of) the people for the Death of his own Son; He knew by this Ship, of our mens diſorderly and obſtinate Sally, which occaſion'd ſo many Deaths, and of the danger *Dom Alvaro* was in, moderating, or ſmothering his grief for't, as one who leſs valued his Sons Lives, then their Reputation. A proceſſion for Thankſgiving.

177. On the ſame day he diſpatch't *Vaſco de Cunha*, that Sailing along the Creeks and Bays of the Coaſt, he might bring together *Dom Alvaro*'s Fleet, and carry it into *Dio*; by him in his Letters, he Congratulated with *Dom John Maſcarenhas* for the honour he had gain'd, not leſs for himſelf then the State; aſſuring him, that in few days he would come and ſee him at *Dio*, with all the ſtrength the State could furniſh, for which he ſpar'd no coſt or diligence; and that while the Fleet was ſetting out, he would ſend him a Recruit, ſufficient to ſecure the Fortreſs, and bridle the Enemy, which he ſpeedily effected; for preſently after *Vaſco de Cunha*, he ſent away *Luis de Almeyda* with ſix Carvels, and four hundred Souldiers, with Ammunition and Proviſion, and plenty of other things which the neceſſity of the Siege requir'd; and ſo indefatigable was his diligence in providing himſelf, that in a very ſhort time all his Fleet was ready to Sail, only wanting the relief of He ſends relief to *Dio*.

Cananor

Cananor and *Cochim* to put to Sea; for with such affection and obedience, was he forwarded by every one, as the Ladies and Gentlemen of *Goa*, came and presented him with their Children and Estates; that Fleet carrying with it as many blessings from the people, as others use to carry tears and complaints.

Vasco de Cunha comes to Bacaim.

178. *Vasco da Cunha* following his Orders, was bringing together the Ships, which he found in the Creeks shattered by the Storm, and with them recovered *Bacaim*, where he found the Commander *Dom Jeronymo de Menezes* ready with fifteen Ships to go and relieve *Dio*; engag'd anew by his resentments of his Brother *Dom Francisco*'s Death, of which we have given an account, yet had he some days deferr'd his going, upon certain advice, that the *Bramaluco* would in his absence come and Besiege that Fortress, a diversion procur'd by the *Sultan*, in favour of the Besiegers. *Dom Jeronymo* looking upon himself more oblig'd to defend *Bacaim*, then relieve *Dio*, delivered his Ships to *Vasco da Cunha*, who setting Sail with 'em, met at Sea *Luis de Almeyda* with six Carvels, all of them in Conserve went into *Dio*, making shew by the number of the Vessels of a more considerable Recruit, yet was the Fortress secur'd from Famine and Danger, and the Souldiers being paid and furnish't, the Warr was less fear'd then desir'd.

History of *India*, Dec. 6. Cap. 8. Lib. 3.

He, with *Luis de Almeyda* goes into *Dio*.

Luis de Almeyda goes to look for the Mecca Fleet.

179. Now was the VVeather fair for us, and the States Ships began to Command at Sea; *Dom Alvaro*, as Admiral, ordered *Luis de Almeyda* with three Carvels (all of 'em under his Command, in two of 'em went Captains *Payo Rodriguez de Aravjo*, and *Pedro Affonso*) to stand for the Barr of *Surat*, and expect the *Mecca* Fleet, which would strive to recover that Port; who pursuing his Voyage, within few days saw two Ships crossing the Gulf, one great one, the other of a less Burden; as soon as *Luis de Almeyda* spy'd 'em, with all the Sail he could make, he stood up with 'em; the Ships came before the Wind, and seeing our Carvels tack't about,

about, but our Ships being light, and better Sailers, with all their Canvas abroad, were up with 'em present-ly. *Luis de Almeyda* Boarded the great Ship, which had for Captain a *Janizary*, a Kinsman of *Coge-Sofars*, who relying on the bigness of his Ship, his Guns and Men aboard, provided for his defence, provoking on all parts a very hot dispute, the Blood run down on both sides, the *Moors* fought out of necessity, Ours out of duty, and having the advantage of Courage and Discipline entred the Vessel, where the *Moors*, inspirited with despair fought to Dye reveng'd, till with the Death of the most considerable, the rest yielded. They found the *Janizary* full of Wounds, whom *Luis de Almeyda* made be carry'd aboard his Carvel, and his Cure attended. The other Ship on a slight resistance was made yield by *Payo Rodriguez de Aravjo*. After this action, *Luis de Almeyda*, while his Commission lasted, ply'd too and again in that Station, in which time he took some Boats of Provision going to furnish the Army, making others run on Shore, by which the Camp begun to feel some scarcity. With the Ships he had tane he presently came into *Dio*, with the *Moors* hang'd at the Yard-arms, torturing infinitely the Camp by so sad a spectacle. *Rumecaon* offered two and thirty thousand *Pardaos* for the *Janizary* Captain, who (as we have said) was of Kin to him; but *Dom Alvaro* commanded he should be hang'd, saying, he came not thither to Sell, but spill Blood, and that by the *Moors* he would get nothing but their Heads. *Rumecaon* was scar'd with his anger, the *Turks* with his contempt. *Dom Alvaro*, not to let his Souldiers Swords rust in the Scabbard, till there was a time of Action, sent forth some Ships of *Bacaim* and *Chaul*, to take the little Vessels which furnish't the Enemy, which succeeded so happily as they took fourteen, bringing them in with the *Moors* hung at the Yards, which was now less resented then trembled at, seeing our anger and vengeance had neither Limits or Compassion.

he takes two Ships,

he goes with 'em to *Dio*.

Dom Alvaro refuseth to release a *Janizary*, and commands to hang him up.

Our men take fourteen Barks from the Enemy.

180. *Dom John de Castro*, in the mean time, resolving with himself to Chastise the King of *Cambaya*, by whose example the Princes of *Asia* would Live in peace and reverence of the State, desir'd first to sound and try others mens judgments, that by their approving the design, he might find 'em more forward in the Execution of their own Councels; for this he call'd before him the Ecclesiastical and Civil Government of the City, with the Gentlemen and Souldiers of Eminency, to whom he declar'd his Resolution to go in Person to raise the Siege of *Dio*, and to Fight *Rumecaon* in his own Quarters; that though all knew it, in their particulars, he had a mind to tell it 'em in common, that in the approbation of the Common-wealth, he might carry with him the Justice of the cause as part of the Victory. Upon hearing the Governour, every one was affected, in the first place with his Modesty, that subjected an Independent Minister; then his great Zeal, that upon the yet reaking Blood of his Children, sacrifis'd his own Life for the Service of his Country. Upon giving their Votes in the business, their discourse was various; *Dom Diogo de Almeyda Freire*, Commander in Chief in *Goa*, whose experience was, by his Years and the chances of Warr, enlarg'd, did thus deliver his Opinion.

The Governour in Councel declares his resolution of going to *Dio*.

181. "The small force we now have, is by their ignorance of it formidable to our Enemies, all *Asia* reputing our strength, more by our Victories, then our Souldiers, so that the Fame only of what is past, keeps us up at present. Your Excellency hath in this Fleet brought together all the Power of *India*, in which we can hardly reckon two thousand *Portuguese*, and with so little Noise we design to fright the whole World. This Tree of the State (on whose Branches hang so many Trophies gain'd in the *East*) hath its Roots by infinite Leagues sever'd from its Body; its best way of preserving 'em, is by being underprop't, with Peace with some, and Awe from others. We

Dom Diogo de Almeyda's opinion to the contrary.

"can

"can never perform what is expected from our joyn'd "Forces, for one Victory will add but little to our "Reputation, and only one loss Destroys us. We have "already Reliev'd our Fortress, and to what end on a "Wound already Cur'd, to spend the Medicine which "is to serve for others? what new Prudence teaches "us in one only Fight to venture what hath been got "by so many Victories? we have an Army sufficient "as we are to maintain us so, not strength when we are "lost to repair us. No great Souldier without ne- "cessity ever gave a Field-battail, for where on both "sides the loss useth to be equal, the Conquerour "only keeps the Field and a useless Glory. At *Dio* we "neither covet, or can possess any thing but the For- "tress; with what blind Madness go we then to pur- "chase that with our Blood which is our own already? "what new Colonies have we to Plant the Island? from "what part of the World can we bring others who "are not *Moors* or *Pagans*, as fickle in their Loyalty to "the State, as those who now oppose us? We go to "Fight *Turks* and *Moors*, exceeding us in Numbers, "equal in Arms, and Discipline; if we have the worst "of it, we have no place to save our selves in, for the "Country is theirs; if we have the better on't, no ad- "vantage will come of the Victory. We have with our "Fleets Conquer'd *India*, with them must we keep it, "having the advantage of Vessels and Mariners. If we "look for Victory only in Fights, lets slight our Garri- "sons, and dismantle our Cities; if 'tis told me, 'tis for "the States honour, to destroy a Kingdome for an "affront, if all who have ta'ne Arms against us, had "receiv'd strict Punishment, the *East* had been already "unpeopled. Shall we blame *Affonso de Albuquerque* for "not Burning *Ormus*, after so many Hostilities and "Treacheries of its Kings and Governours? shall he "forfeit the great Name he atchiev'd there, because for "the Affronts and Quarrels of the *Samorim*, he de- "stroy'd not *Malabar*? shall *Nuno de Cunha* stain that

"Renown'd

"Renown'd fame for not making Warr upon *Cambaya*, "after the Treason of *Badur*? shall we set upon De-"stroying the *Turk* for his *Basbaw*'s daring to Besiege "our Fortress? shall we set out our Fleets against "*Achem*, because he hath so often invaded us in *Ma-*"*laca?* shall we put to Fire and Sword *Hidalcaon*, for "his taking every day our Provisions, and infesting our "Lands of *Bardes* and *Salsete?* what despair drives us "to offer the innocent States throat to the Enemies "knife. This Fleet, so terrible in appearance, so weak "in effect, is a Bridle to *Rumecaon*, to Ours a Defence; "but upon Landing so few Souldiers, the *East* will see "into the secret of our Forces, and all the Princes "endeavour to break down those weak Prisons in which "we keep 'em Fettered. *Quintus Fabius Maximus*'s "winning many Battails was the glory of the *Roman* "Empire, his avoiding one was its preservation. The "first Conquerours built us a House, we have nothing "to do but to keep it. If by storming *Dio* the Enemy "have lost an Army, what wants that action of Vi-"ctory? what of Punishment? Offence is undertaken "with equal strength, Vengeance with farr greater; "for to get satisfaction for one Affront, we are not to "venture a fresh injury, the rather, because Fortune "is in nothing so absolute as in the chances of Warr. "Victories are many times gotten by light accidents, "and lost by others. Will it be then just to put to the "Contingency of Success the Scepter of the *East*, "founded, with the dread and envy of Nations, upon "so many Victories? If we lose this Fleet in which is "amass'd together the whole strength of *India*, what "Treasures hath his Majesty laid up to set forth an-"other? we shall begin again, to Petition, or Conquer "the Princes of *India*; we shall bring back to its In-"fancy this Empire now grown Old; we shall Live on "the Courtesie of those Crowns we have provok't, "remaining their miserable Vassals, of whom we were "once Masters.

182. *Dom Diogo de Almeyda*'s Reasons satisfied those of his own Opinion, mov'd those of the contrary; yet *Dom John de Castro*, secure in the Resolution he had taken, thus Discourst against 'em. "That no ruling "Nation was content with a defensive Warr amongst "her Inferiours; that the State had made her self in "the *East* Arbiter of Peace and Warr, most of the "Princes of *Asia* coveting under our shelter to Live "secure; that all the Forts we had in *India* were to "be maintain'd by the same Arms which wonn 'em; "that the respect, the *Moors* and *Pagans* had for us, "would last no longer then they knew we could put "up an Injury; that all those Princes stood looking on "our Punishing *Cambaya*, and durst not yet with their "Auxiliaries come in to its Relief out of fear to be "crush t in its Ruins; yet if they saw us contented to "make up the ruins of our Fortress, and bind up the "Wounds they have opened, they would come again "to uncover 'em, and aim the second blow at the heart "of the State; that Reputation was the Soul of Em- "pires; Patience in particulars a Virtue, in Crowns a "Ruine; that we had in this Siege lost so many gallant "Gentlemen, so many Cavalliers and Souldiers of Ho- "nour, as the Wounds they receiv'd would cover with "Infamy the Surviving, if they saw 'em not Reveng'd; "what account could we give the World of this Siege, "but of our patience in enduring it; that the State "by Fame more preserv'd her self, then with all the "Spices of the *East*; which were only a valuable Com- "modity when we got 'em, not by Commerce, but by "Tribute. That, to conclude, he would not suffer "the first weakness of our Arms to happen in *Dom* "*John de Castro*'s time; that he was resolv'd to Fight, "the Blame should be solely his, every one should "have a share in the Victory. The Governour out of hopes of Success, or heighth of Courage, spoke these words with a Spirit presaging his fore-seen Triumph.

The Governours answer.

183. The Arms in *Dio* vvere not idle, for neither did the losses receiv'd, or our hopes of relief, fright stout and resolute *Rumecaon*; He knew the strength the Governour would bring in Person, (greater in report then appearance 'twould be) yet did not for that unbend his resolution of carrying on the Siege, and expecting the worst of Fortune. He commanded his men to under-mine the Watch-tower over the gate, where *Antonio Freire* had his Post; and though they work't with most profound silence, by diverse Stratagems diverting our attention, the Commander in chief (whom no Casualty, or Accident took unprovided) found out their work, which as at other times he prevented. The *Moors* on the 10th. of *October* play'd the Mine, which sprung without any hurt on the outward face of the Wall; the Fire giving back by the resistance of our Counter-forts, and the *Moors* saw within a new Wall rais'd, wondering at our fore-sight of all their designs, and that neither strength, or industry profitted 'em against so stout and cautious Enemies. Though *Rumecaon* found by Experience there was less Fruit then Labour in the Mines, yet to weary out our men, or keep his own in good Discipline, he began to open others, which too being known, were prevented, of which we speak nothing, because they had no memorable effect, and to avoid the tediousness things so alike have in their Relation.

Rumecaon begins another Mine,

which he plays without any loss to us.

THE

THE LIFE OF

DOM JOHN DE CASTRO.

The Third Book.

1. DOM *John de Castro*, (on the seventeenth of *October* of the Year one thousand five hundred forty and six) delivering up the Government of the City to the Bishop, *Dom John de Albuquerque*, and *Dom Diogo de Almeyda Freire*, set Sail directly for *Bacaim*, where he design'd to expect other Recruits and Provisions, which were not yet arriv'd, making it a point of honour that the Governour of *India* should not be one day Besieg'd in *Dio*, but with *Cæsar*'s Fortune, Come, See, and Overcome.

The Governour parts for *Dio*.

71.
Eys vem despois o pay, que as ondas corta
Co restante da gente Lusitana
E con forca e saber, que mais importa
Batalha da felice & soberana
Huns paredes subirodo escusaon portas
Outros a abrem, na fera esquadra insana,
Feytos faraon tan dignos de memoria
Que naon caibaon em verso, ou larga Historia.

72.
Este depois en Campo se apresenta
Vencedor forte e intrepido ao possante
Rey da Cambaya *e a vista che amedrente*
Da fera multidaon quadrupedante.

Cam. St. 71, 72. Can. 10.

71.
Lo, now the Father follows with full Sail,
And the remainder of the *Lusian* force,
He with strong hand, and head of more avail
Gives a brave lucky Battail to the *Moors*,
Where no way is he makes one with his Flail,
And where there is the Rampiers are his doors;
Such that days feats, so terrible the blows,
They will not stand in Verse, nor lye in Prose.

72.
Then lo, he to the great *Cambayan* King
Presents himself a Victor in the Field,
Pale fear into the face of him doth fling,
And of his furious Horse, which ground shall yield.

Sir *Richard Fan.* Translation.

The Fleet and Commanders.

John *de Barro's* Hist. of *India*, Dec. *6.* Lib. 3. Cap. *9.*

2. The Fleet consisted of twelve Gallions, of which the Admiral was the Saint *Denis*, on which went the Governour, the rest were Commanded by *Garcia de Sa*, *Iorge Cabral*, *Dom Manoel de Silveyra*, *Manoel de Sousa de Sepùlveda*, *Iorge de Sousa*, *John Falcaon*, *Dom John Manoel Alabastro*, *Lewis Alvarez de Sousa*. The Vessels with Oars were sixty, of which the chief Commanders were *Dom Manoel de Lima*, *Dom Antonio de Noronha*, *Miguel da Cunha*, *Dom Diogo de Sottomajor*, the Secretary *Antonio Corneiro*, *Alvaro Perez de Andrade*, *Dom Manoel Dèca*, *Iorge da Sylva*, *Luis Figuera*, *Jeronymo de Sousa*, *Nuno*, *Fernandez Pegado Ramatho*, *Lourenco Riberio*, *Antonio Leme*, *Alvaro Serraon*, *Cosme Fernandez*, *Manoel Lobo*, *Francisco de Azevedo*; *Pero de Attayde Inferno*, *Francisco da Cunha*, *Antonio de Sa* Native of *Romania*, *Vasco Fernandez* Captain of *Goa*, and Commander of fifteen Fly-boats, Barks, and other Vessels, on which went the *Canarins* brought up in *Goa*, and in company other Ships of *Cananor* and *Cochim*.

Arrives at *Bacaim*.

3. The Governour in six days came to an Anchor at *Bacaim*, where *Dom Jeronymo de Menezes*, his Brother-in-law, and Commander of that Fortress, came to him on Board, comforting one the other, in the loss of a Brother and a Son. The Governour unwilling his Arms should want employment, sent forth with six light Ships *Dom Manoel de Lima*, to take, in the Bay of *Cambaya*, some of those Vessels which Recruit, and Victual the

the Enemies Camp. He there ply'd for some days to and again, in which he took sixty Vessels of Provision from the *Moors*, whose Bodies he ordered to be mangled, and towing em, put 'em to Float in the mouth of the Rivers, for the Current to carry 'em to the Island, where they might be seen with horrour and amasement of the incenst *Portugue'e*, inventing every day new Cruelties. *Dom Manoel*, when his Commission was expir'd, came in, with threescore *Moors* hanging at the Yards-arms, a sight which sacrifis'd more to Vengeance then Humanity. The Governour, rejoycing at those Preludiums of the Warr he had undertaken, sent *Dom Manoel de Lima* out again with thirty Ships, and Orders to put to Fire and Sword all the Coast of *Cambaya*, that the memory of their Punishment might be Recorded in their Ruins.

4. *Lourenco Pirez de Tavora* Commander of the Ships which came from the Kingdome (as hath been said before) put in, with most of the Ships of his Squadron, at *Cochim*, there hearing the news of the Siege, he immediately parted for *Goa*, believing he should find the Governour on Shore; and upon knowledge of his being parted with the whole Fleet, set Sail directly for *Dio*, preferring the King's Service to the advantages of his Voyage. His example was follow'd by most of the Gentlemen who came that year from the Kingdome, the ruins of our Fortress being the first place they Landed at in *India*; Amongst whom was *Dom Antonio de Noronha*, (Son of the Vice-King *Dom Garcia*) with threescore Souldiers at his own charges: these were the Riches the Gentlemen of those times came for, to the *East*; wounds being then more prisable Commodities then now Diamonds. The Governour by those Ships receiv'd Letters from the *Infante Dom Lewis*, whose Copies we will put down, to shew the King's and Infant's attention to the least actions of Ministers, (forming a true judgment of 'em, by Rewards, or Punishments, to be even with 'em) and the simplicity

Lourenco Pirez goes after him,

and other Gentlemen,

simplicity of the stile, so free from the humour and height of other times; whose Memory to the Lovers of that Age will not be tedious.

The Infante Dom Lewis's *Letter.*

5. "HOnourable Governour. By your Letters to "my Lord the King, and my self, I have seen "an account of your Voyage from your parting from "*Mocambique* till your arrival in *India*, and what you did "there till the departure of the Ships; the condition "you found the Country in, the quality of the Persons, "the Licentiousness of Trade, the weakness of the "Fleet; how you behav'd your self to *Hidalcaon* in the "business of *Meale*; how in the affairs at *Ormus*; and "how to those Gentlemen, who were permitted by "*Martin Affonso* to carry thither Commodities; and "what more you said in those Letters; and because my "Lord the King answers all those things particularly, "I will not do the same but in short. Yet cannot I "forbear telling you, how I was here on Shore frighted "at the danger you scap't about the Island *Comaro*; "'twas seriously a great and wonderfull fortune, and "which I take as a good Omen, it seeming to me, God "in that would shew you he was to preserve you in the "difficulties of *India*, for which no less a miracle is "necessary, then that shew'd you in your scaping so "eminent a danger, for which I have given hearty "thanks and am glad to hear *Dom Jeronimo de Noronha* "bore you Company in it, since God hath likewise pre-"serv'd him, and 'tis for a man of his honour to share "in the extremities and troubles of his General. As "to the other things you write me, My Lord the King's "answer being particular, and I present at the dispat-"ches, 'twere I think too precise to write 'em to you "over again; for by his Letters you'l see his satis-

"faction,

"faction, in the way you design in those parts for his "Service, and in the good opinion the Country hath of "you, which he particularly commends to your care "in all businesses; what in that I have more to tell "you, is, that I'me very much satisfy'd with your ma- "nagement of affairs in that place, and with your "words as well as actions, for by those 'tis seen the "crossing so many Climates hath not altered you from "your self, or my constant opinion, which, you are not "content in shewing, by your actions, but your words "are a pledge you will continue doing the same, of "which I'me very well assur'd, that what by humane "power can be compast you will truly perform. His "Majesty is not less satisfy'd with your manner of wri- "ting, for your Letters came well digested, they con- "tain'd nothing superfluous, and by 'em is sufficiently "seen what I said before, that you both know what "you are to do, and have a desire and earnestness to do "it, without any temporary respect of interest or "affection, which I not a little rejoyce at to hear from "you; for though I am sure of your actions, 'tis yet a "sign of the great abundance of your heart and "virtue, your coveting to say so, which makes me con- "fident God will perfect all your good desires, and "bring you out of that Country, to your great satis- "faction and honour, for he cannot be unsuccessfull "who designs nothing but the service of God and his "King; and though that is to be purchas'd with no "ordinary difficulty, let me mind you, that 'tis there "resides merit, and that Our Saviour Christ was by "that to enter into his Glory; and if things appear "to you above your Mastery, remember, 'tis there God "puts in his helping hand, and seconds those who serve "him with your attention; and that men of them- "selves can furnish nothing but will and diligence, "which made Saint *Paul* attribute to himself nothing "but the planting, because God is to give the increase, "as he will give it to all those undertakings you plant "with

"with that zeal, I'me secure you have in all your "actions; therefore be not frighted at great things, or "slight little, poise equally, and remit the end to God "Almighty; and though some things succeed not as "you desire, be not transported by despair, while you "act with a just zeal, and clear intention, because God "often permits his servants to commit errors, thereby "to merit by their patience and trust in him, and for "the increase of their experience and perfection; do "justice according to your Conviction, always taking, "as you use, counsel and advice in business; preserve "your self in that clearness you practice in the temporal "injoyments, and advantages of that Country, then "happen what will, all will tend to a good end. Be "very exact in what relates to Divine worship for the "Conversion of the Infidels, for that's the Armory "must chiefly defend *India*. Endeavour to Banish "thence men's extravagant expences, the Effeminate-"ness and Luxury they Live in, and the excess of "Cloaths and Furniture, disposing them to't mildly, "and winningly, by your own and your Sons example; "and by Countenancing and Favouring those whose "practice is contrary; and if those things be above "your reforming let it not trouble you, because the "corruptions of time, must by time have their amend-"ment, and cannot be remedy'd on a suddain; con-"tinue therefore your good intention, managing things "according to the disposition of the time and persons "you have to do with, so, I hope in God, he will (as "you desire) direct all things, to his, and my Lord the "King's service and your honour. For your request, "of my solliciting your stay there may be short, I per-"ceive you have no little reason for your desire, but "my opinion is, it cannot be set upon till seeing your "Letters, which God willing we shall receive this year, "I therefore deferr answering that point till the next "year. I have spoke to the King in the business you "writ about your Son *Dom Alvaro*, his Majesty knows "him well, and is well inform'd of the qualities of his "Person, and desires to honour and favour him, yet "for some reasons his Majesty hath commanded to be "writ you, and as himself writes, that this year he signs "no Grants, he hath thought fit not to answer that "till the next; in the mean time, he hath sent "Commands for conferring on him that honour, you'l "find in his Letters Patent. I'me very carefull of put-"ting him in mind of all that concerns your Sons, and "hope in God 'twill be so ordered, that you shall re-"ceive from his Majesty honour and reward, as also "your Sons, whom he desires to use according to your "Deservings; and you may be confident his Majesty "very well knows your will to serve him, and is very "much satisfy'd with your way of doing it hitherto. I "spoke to his Majesty about *Affonso de Rojas*, and on "your consideration he immediately granted, what I "ask't him, but (as I said) because he tells those "who go to the *Indies* that this year he signs no Grants, "he hath diferr'd *Affonso de Rojas* business till the next, "and saith, he will then reward him: I'le take care, by "the grace of God, to send you the Letters Patent, and "am very glad of the good News you tell me of *Affonso* "*de Rojas*, and am apt to believe, that being Mr. *Ol-*"*medo's* Brother, and in your Company, he must prove "an honest man. What you sent me on the Ships "which came, was delivered me, I was very glad of it, "and value it as coming from your hands. *Almeirim* the "twenty sixth of *March* 1547.

The Infante Dom Lewis.

6. *Dom Manoel de Lima* setting Sail from *Bacaim* went by Night into the River of *Surat*, and getting up with the Tide came in sight of a great Village, which, though not Inhabited by the *Abissines*, had its name from 'em; the Village was on the *East* side of the River, spread on a great Plain; and, though in an open place, had

The hurt *Dom Manoel* doth about *Surat*.

History of *India*, Dec. 6. Lib. 3. Cap. 9.

two thousand Families, defended (without any other Fortification) only by some Trenches; on confidence perhaps of their first beginning the VVarr, and the strength of that Army they had in the Field. *Dom Manoel* went on shore; and our men, in the same order they Landed, fell upon the Enemy with more Courage then Discipline. The *Moors* were stout enough to expect, not to resist; less scar'd by their apprehension of our men, then the horrour of their own who first fell; whose Blood so frighted 'em, as they turn'd their backs. Many were cut off in the Flight, few in Resistance; the Slaughter was great, the Souldiers Sword sparing neither Sex or Age. *Dom Manoel* commanded his men to Fire the Houses, burning together Town and Estates; Covetousness was below their fury; only one *Moor* had his Hands ordered to be cut off, who was left Alive not to carry the News without signs of Victory.

He destroys the City of *Antote*,

7. The Fleet went out of the River, and Coasting along two days came in sight of the City of *Antote*, famous for its proud Buildings, and rich Inhabitants, whom their commerce by Sea had well enrich't; these, warn'd by others sufferings, resolv'd to Defend their Houses, or Dye in 'em, valuing so equally their Lives and Fortunes. *Dom Manoel* got on Shore, though not without loss; for the *Moors* waited for us, showing themselves Souldiers in their Resolution, not in their Conduct, who charg'd us divided into Companies, with wandring and uncertain Shot; betraying the same fear in their Resistance, they did afterwards in their Flight. *Dom Manoel* got ground of 'em, till he forc't 'em into the City, where, at the sight of Women and Children, they were made stand by their Compassion; here our men thought they had to do with Enemies, for they fought, with the Bowels of Fathers, Cowards in defending their own, stout in protecting the Lives of others; but their Courage not being natural, and proceeding from tender or timerous affections, their compassion yielded to their fear, which gave us possession of the

City,

City, Children, and Victory; and *Dom Manoel*, more designing Ruine then Conquest, gave up the City to the Flames. The cruelty out-went the destruction, for many *Bramenish* young Ladies, exempted from crime by their Sex, from the Sword by their faces, in Colour and Beauty not inferiour to those of our *Europe*, were not spar'd in the Victory.

8. *Dom Manoel de Lima* went Coasting all the Bay of *Cambaya*, destroying the Towns, so depopulating every place, as to seem not to be glutted, with Blood or Victory; at last retires with more Glory then Booty, and found the Governour with all the Fleet together at the Island *Dos Mortos*, the next day (the sixth of *November*) they set Sail for *Dio*, the Ships went light, and with the multitude of Pendants and Streamers, made a pleasant and beautifull sight. And other places, and retires.

9. At the Fortresses making the Fleet, such was the general satisfaction, as of men who after such a deluge of Blood, saw those who brought 'em Peace in Victory; the Fortress was round about full of Colours, the raz'd Ruins putting on contentment. The Commander in chief gave order for Shooting off all the Guns, answer'd by the Governour from Sea with an amazing Vollee, seconded by Instruments of Warr and Musick, solemnizing so frightfull a day with chearfull Vespers, the *Moors* too discharg'd a great many Pieces, shewing their joy or contempt for the Governours arrival. The Governour arrives at *Dio*.

10. *Dom John de Castro* kept that Night at Sea, and sent for on Board, the Commander in chief, *Garcia de Sa*, *Manoel de Sousa de Sepulveda*, *Iorge Cabral*, and other Gentlemen of the Counceel, whom he acquainted with the resolution he came with, to Fight the Enemy, upon which he ask't no mans Opinion, because the Governour of *India* drew not his Sword to Defend but Chastise, but in what manner he should fall upon the Enemy, he desir'd all their Counsels; *Garcia de Sa*, with such reasons, approv'd, and prais'd his fix't Resolution, as for his Person, and their weight were very taking with He holds a Council at Sea.

with the Governour. They discourst about the way of Fighting, and concluded of it, which was a secret till the Execution. 'Twas ordered the men should in the silence of the Night, be put into the Fortress; and on their Landing, Musick, Trumpets, and Shooting from the Ships should keep the design from *Rumecaon*. The men in three Nights by Ladders of Cords got into the Fortress; which was done with so much Caution, as not to be discovered by the Enemy.

Rumecaon's discourse.

11. *Rumecaon*, on the approaching danger shewing himself most Resolute, told his Souldiers, if the Governour resolv'd to come out and Fight in the Field, the *Moors* would march into the Fortress through the Gates, not over the Walls; that he hop't with the *Portuguese* Colours to sweep the House of their Prophet; that they fought for the Liberty of so many Princes, who sigh't under the heavy Oppression of Tribute, and Servitude; that they should reserve their Courage, in one day to revenge the Injuries of so many Years; that the State was crush't under the weight of so many Victories; that Fortune had so ordered it, to bring 'em together, at one Blow to cut 'em off. The *Turk* heightned this insolence, by Commanding all the Souldiers should have double Pay; his Army was of above forty thousand men, most of the Officers, *Turks*, old Souldiers, famous by the report of their Courage, brought thither by extraordinary Pay. There were come lately to the Camp seven hundred *Janizaries*, who proudly desir'd to Fight by themselves, that the *Moors* might see who gave 'em the Victory. *Rumecaon* supply'd the Posts, and plac't the main Body of his Army, so as to attend that place where he thought our Fleet would Anchor; neither did his Confidence disturb his Discipline. Thus expected he to be falln upon by us, ready for Defence, doubtfull of Success.

The number of his Army.

His ordering 'em.

12. The Governour having now got all the Souldiers into the Fortress, found diverse Opinions about falling on the Enemy, and all the Arguments striking on the

the Contingency of Success, they could not be approv'd or rejected, without the knowledge of what's to come, known to no body. *Garcia de Sa*, by the Authority of his Years Courage and Birth, discourst again about the conveniency of Fighting; but *Dom John de Castro* commanding silence said, that the Lot was already cast, that by the Valiant he should be well thought of, and from Cowards he car'd not for approbation; that those without should expect the success to give their judgments. He spent that Evening in disposing the Souldiers for the next day, not to alter by delay their Courage or Resolution; He gave order the Fleets Boats should for a sign expect three Roquets to be fir'd from the Fortress, and, at the same time our men resolv'd to Sally forth, Row toward that place of the Enemy which was most Obnoxious, with Drums and Trumpets sounding, crediting what they could their intentions of Landing, covering the entrance of the Boats with Lances, which would make the Stratagem probable, and that the Governours Boat should, by its place, Flagg Royal, and Adornments, be known at a distance; a Stratagem, which either gave, or furthered our Victory.

The Governour resolves to Fight.

His orders to the Fleet.

History of *India*, Dec. 6. Lib. 3. Cap. 10.

13. The day broke, which began the eleventh of *November*, Dedicated to the memory of the glorious Saint *Martin*, Bishop of *Tours*, who might, as a Saint favour, as a Souldier fight for us. The Governour, with the first Light, came with his Generals staff on the platform of the Fortress, his white Armour added so much to his Majesty, as his Charge was respected in his Person; Mass was said at an open Altar, that they might begg Victory of the God of Hoasts; the Governour and Major part of the Souldiers receiv'd the Sacrament, and the Guardian of the *Franciscans* proclam'd a Plenary indulgence to all those who Dy'd in the Battail; when this was done, he commanded the pulling down the gates of the Fortress, and the Dressing breakfast for the Souldiers with 'em, that the Generals confi-

dence and the despair of any shelter, might equally assist the Victory, making them stand to't out of glory, or necessity; He thus spake to the Souldiers. "We "are going now to a Battail, in which, if Conquer'd, "we shall honour our God with our Lives, if Con-"querours, our King with our Victory; The strength "of the Enemies Army, is *Turks* and *Janizaries*, who "like Souldiers of fortune desire Warr, hate Fighting; "the other part consists of diverse Nations, brought "into one Body by their Pay, but not to be forc't by "it, to be all unanimous. These are not stouter then "their Fathers, and Ancestors, there's no reason they "should be more Fortunate, all of 'em have by our "Arms been Mastered. This Empire of *Asia* is the "Child of our Victories, we have Nurst it in its first "Cradle, let's, now 'tis grown up, maintain it, that "after long succession of time it may point to the "World the glory of this Action; for me to encourage "you to Fight, were to forget my self we were *Portu-*"*guese*.

His Speech to the Souldiers.

14. The order he put his men in, was this; he gave the Van-guard to *Dom John Mascarenhas*, he claiming the greatest danger in recompence of his former; He had five hundred *Portuguese*, six hundred *Canarins*, and five hundred * *Naires*. *Dom Alvaro de Castro* commanded five hundred *Portuguese* more, part of whom were the Gentlemen, and Offiers of his Fleet. *Dom Manoel de Lima* had five hundred more; the Governour had the greatest Body, which was of about eight hundred *Portuguese*, with some *Canarins*, and *Malabareses*.

The order he put 'em in.

* The people of *Malabar* is divided into Nobility call'd *Naires*, and into Commonalty, call'd *Poleas*, 'twixt whom the difference and distinction is so great, as if a *Naire* be but by chance touch't by a *Polea*, he is bound by certain ceremonies to cleanse himself from that Contagion; The *Naires* have their Women in common, being bound from Marriage to be always ready to follow the *Samorim*, (i. e.) Emperour to the Warrs, without the partial concernment of Wives and Children; their Heirs are their Brothers or Sisters children; they must be of descent, the Emperour not having the power to make one; their Temperance is admirable, as is their Courage in incountring dangers or difficulties.

The *Poleas* are Tradesmen, and so bound to one Trade, as it is of necessity entail'd on the Family; a Carpenters Son cannot be a Taylor, nor a Taylor a Carpenter; They are too Slaves and Labourers to the *Naires*; if any women *Naire* mingles with a *Polea* she is counted Damn'd, and immediately put to Death. See *Barro*'s History of *India*, Dec. 1. Lib. 9. Cap. 3.

37.

Dous modos ha de gente, porque a nobre
Naires chamados saon, et a menos digna
Poleas tem por nome, aquem obriga
A ley naon mesturar a casta antiga.

38.

Porque os que usaraon sempre hum mesmo officio
De outro naon podem receber consorte
Nem os filhos teraon outro exercicio
Se naon o de seus passados ate morte
Para os Naires *he certo grande vicio*
D' estes serem tocados, de tal sorte
Que quando algum se toca per ventura
Com ceremonias mil, se alimpa et apura.

39.

Desta arte o Judaico povo antigo
Naon tocava na gente de Samaria
Mais estranhezas inda do que digo
N'esta terra vereys de usancavaria
Os Naires *sôs saon dados ao perigo*
D'as armas sôs defemdem da contraria
Banda o seu Rey, trazendo sempre usada
Na esquerda adarga, et na dereita espada.

40.

Bramenes *saon os seus' Religiosos*
Nome antiguo, et de grande preminencia
Observaon os preceitos taon famosas
De hum que premeyro pos nome a sciencia
Naon mataon cousa viva, et temerosas
Das carnes tem grandissima abstinencia
Somente no Venereo ajuntamento
Tem mas licenca et menos regimento.

41.

Geraes saon as molheres, mas somente
Para os da geracaon de seus maridos
Ditosa condicaon ditosa gente
Que naon saon de ciumes offendidos.
Estes, et outros costumes variamente
Saon pelos Malavares *admittidos*
A terra he grossa em tratta et tudo aquillo
Que as ondas podem dar da China *ao* Nilo.

Camo. Can. 7. St. 37, 38, 39, 40, 41.

37. Two

37.
Two Ranks they have of people, Nobles which
Are *Natres* stil'd, and those of base degree
Call'd *Poleas*. To both the Law prescribes
They shall not marry out of their own Tribes.

38.
And those who have been bred up to one Trade,
Ont of another may not take a Wife;
Nor may their Children any thing be made
But what their Parents have been all their Life.
To touch a *Naire* with their Bodies shade,
A scandal is to his Prerogative;
If themselves chance to touch them as they meet,
With thousand Rites himself he washes sweet.

39.
Just so the Jewish people did of Yore,
The touch of a *Samaritan* eschew:
But, when ye come into the Country, more
And things of greater strangeness shall ye view.
The *Naires* only go to Warr, before
Their King, they only stand a Rampier true
Against his foes. A Sword they always wield
With their right hand, and with the left a Shield.

40.
Their Prelates are call'd *Bramens* (an Old name
And (amongst them) of great Preheminence)
Of his fam'd Sect, who Wisdome did disdain,
And took a Stile of a more modest fence.
They kill no Living thing, and highly blame
All flesh to eat, with wondrous abstinence;
But other flesh their Law doth not forbid,
Yet they as prone thereto as if it did.

41.
Their Wives are common, but are so to none
Save those, who of their Husbands kindred are;
(O blessed Lot, blest Generation,
On whom fierce Jealousie doth wage no Warr.)
These are the Customs, but not these alone
Which are receiv'd by those of *Malabar*;
The Land abounds in Trade of all things, Isle
Or firm-land yields from *China* unto *Nile*.

Sir *Ric. Fanshaw*'s Translation.

15. The *Moors* daily encreased the Camp, and very lately were arriv'd *Alucaon* and *Mojatecaon* with five thousand Souldiers. The Governour commanded the Signal agreed on, of Firing the Roquets, should be given the Fleet, which, upon understanding it, betook themselves Lustily to their Oars, and being close to Shore discharg'd all their Guns in the *Moors* quarters. The smoak for some time hid the Ships, which made the Enemy fall on, not where the fear was, but where he apprehended; sollicitous in the imaginary, careless in the real danger. *Rumecaon* with the main Body of his Army, charg'd there to hinder our men from Landing. The Governour at that time, with Scaling Ladders in readiness to clap to the Wall, sally'd out of the Fortress. *Dom John Mascarenhas* with his men encompast the Ditch, to get up at that place where *Diogo Lopez de Sequeira's* work was. *Antonio Moniz Barretto*, who was of this Body, trusted with his Scaling Ladder three Valiant Souldiers, whose Blood was the first was spilt in that Victory they Liv'd not to enjoy. They were come but that year from the Kingdom, in *Lourenco Pirez de Tavora's* Fleet, Natives of the Town of *Torraon*; and brought recommendatory Letters to *Antonio Moniz* from his Mother, which they deliver'd as they were going to engage; He joyfully receiv'd 'em, telling the Souldiers, if they came off Alive, he would do 'em good Offices with the Governour; to which they unanimously reply'd, that, only for that day they needed his favour; that their Carriage should cut out their passage for the future; that they begg'd him to trust 'em with the Scaling Ladder, and be confident, they would Plant, and Defend it, with their Lives. *Antonio Moniz* seeing in such ordinary Souldiers such extraordinary Gallantry, confidently delivered it 'em, saying, he trusted 'em with the Ladder, and his Honour; and as soon as with unfortunate Courage they had planted it, a shot at randome took off their Heads.

16. Ile here give the Story of a strange Challenge, which

The Fleet Rows to shore.

Rumecaon came there to resist 'em.

The Governour Sallies out of the Fortress.

The unfortunate Gallantry of three Souldiers.

History of *India*, Dec. 6. Lib. 4. Cap. 1.

A strange Challenge.

which I should pass over were it not as Famous, as Compassionate. *Dom John Manoel*, and *John Falcaon*, Gentlemen of a great expectance, were for some sleight Jealousies (which in the Worlds opinion are heavy, as they are taken) fall'n out, and resolv'd to justifie their Pique in the Field, making Valour or Chance judge of their quarrel; The seconds, who engag'd with less pre-occupy'd judgments, endeavour'd to decide the quarrel by a more honourable Duel, alledging, the Governour was ready to engage; that a Challenge always a Crime, would be now a Scandal; that by the Edict they would forfeit their Lives; that *Dom John de Castro*, was not, though thought so, so indulgent a Father, he bore with faults, but not with insolences; that they might salve their Honours, where they ventured their Lives, by agreeing, that he who first, and with most Courage scal'd the Enemies Wall, should have in the particular and common Fight, the clearest Reputation; so by their Witty courage, inventing how to Dye with Rewards, and how to Fight Duels without a Crime, both the Enemies accepted the proposal, desiring their Kindred, and Friends, to hold their Ladders as to men who were to Fight for the States and their own honour; at the same time both began to climbe. *Dom John Manoel* laying one hand on the Wall had it cut off, relieving himself with the other, that too by a stroak was ta'ne away, and putting his Elbows to't to secure his hold, his Head was cut off by a Semitar. *John Falcaon* at the same instant seis'd on the Wall; and having mastered it, while he stoutly defended himself was cut in pieces. The Braves in the Army were of different opinions, who of these gave greatest marks of their Courage; in favour of both, wee'l say; he who gives all for it, owes no more to honour.

How *Dom John Mascarenhas* behaves himself.

17. *Dom John Mascarenhas* began with his men to plant Ladders, many getting up with as much Resolution, as Fortune, for though receiv'd with Lances, they o'recome the resistance; these had the honour to

to be the first in the Danger of being alone in the Camp, sustaining the weight of the *Moors* till their Companions came to 'em; how those who first scal'd the Walls behav'd themselves, may be guest by their posture of Fighting, the *Moors* fought on firm ground, Ours suspended in the Air. *Dom Alvaro de Castro*, and *Dom Manoel de Lima*, got over the Wall in several places, receiving most hurt in the stoutest Resistance; while they fought scattered, they lost some men, closing they made more room for the getting up of their Souldiers.

18. The Governour in the plain Field, met with greater Danger, then there was in Scaling; for he march't toward the Bridge, defended by a great Body of men, and great Pieces planted on it, the importance of gaining it equal'd the danger. The Governour eminently hazarded himself in falling on, his Courage was singular, his Fortune miraculous; for the *Moors* often put their match to the prim'd Guns, and not one took Fire, a successe, by the Miracle opportune, by the Accident unusual, yet would not Heaven have the whole Victory, for the coming of the *Turks* in greater numbers to the defence of the Bridge, with Musquets, Granados, and Pikes, stop't the fury of our Souldiers, some turn'd their backs to the Bullets; God perhaps, by that, shewing us, what we are when left to our selves; the Cowards fled, the Valiant stood to't; *Dom John de Castro*, below none in Courage, above all in Prudence, with some who follow'd him clos'd with the Enemy, crying aloud, Victory, the *Turks* run away: This noise was spread with so happy Ecchos, as our men once more Rally'd, and came to their Colours; the *Turks* fearfull, or Credulous, left the Field, this shout of the Generals being the gate of Victory. Our men did here the Execution of Conquerours, and now that past for truth, what was before stratagem. The Governour pursuing his Fortune, went up and down the Field, and, as Victory is exempt from Rashnesse, and Fear without Counsel,

The danger the Governour was in on the Bridge.

His miraculous deliverance.

He crys out Victory.

cel, *Dom John* surrounded almost with the Enemies whole Army, cry'd out Victory, and the *Moors* run away, without loss, but out of order: In fine, we had by him before the Battail the Victory; Those who engag'd with the Governour unanimously affirm, that he was the first got upon the Wall, and none but himself contradicted this testimony, who freely said, *Lourenco Pirez de Tavora* clim'd first; slighting repute so weakly proud; and desiring to be excus'd from stealing honour, he knew so well how to purchase.

and pursues it.

What he saith of *Lourenco Pirez.*

19. *Rumecaon*, upon advice of his mens disorderly Flight, came in with a Body of *Turks*, to stop, or interrupt the Victory; and retarding the fury of our Souldiers by the advantage of his Numbers, pois'd the Battail. The obstinacy of the dispute lasted some time; The Standard Royal was twice shot down, at which sight the Governour impatiently cry'd out, what means this *Portuguese*? shall they take out of your hands the Victory? shall they carry off the Standard? and charging the Enemy under cover of a Buckler which had sticking in it two Arrows, with words and actions so encourag'd the Souldiers, as with their fury, to make the *Moors* give ground, and the last fly, by the fright of the first.

The Governour fights in Person.

20. *Dom Alvaro de Castro*, and *Dom Manoel de Lima* being joyn'd, rais'd the envy of their Souldiers and Enemies; they charg'd *Alucaon*, and *Mojatecaon*, Valiant *Turks*, and the Chief Commanders of the Army, who, for no little time, made the Victory doubtfull; The blood Dy'd the Arms, Dy'd the ground, the rude noise of the *Moors*, did like a fresh danger fright the Camp, the horrour and confusion so mastered the Senses, as many before feeling their Wounds, felt themselves Dying. Number at last yielded to Courage, and the *Turks* with infinite loss quitted their ground. *Dom John Mascarenhas* charg'd *Juzarcaon*, whose Post he gain'd, not with less Valour, or worse Fortune. *Rumecaon*, without losing his Courage or Judgment by the first loss, expected

Rumecaon Rallies in the plain Field.

pected the second, forming his Squadrons in the open Field, out of necessity, or confidence, for in so numerous an Army the fright was more predominant then the loss; and as in extremities 'tis usual to accuse Fortune, *Rumecaon* in the hearing of our men, with superstitious Crys and Noises made his Atonements, as if so to appease the indignation of the Heavens.

The Governour and his Son falls on him.

21. *Dom John de Castro*, unwilling to lose one moment of so glorious a Day, joyn'd his small Army, and, giving the Van-guard to his Son *Dom Alvaro*, fac't the Enemy; who resolutely expected him, and putting out the Horns of the Half-moon in which he was form'd, came begirting our Infantry; yet *Dom Alvaro*, as if he would have to himself the glory of that Day, fell upon the Enemy with so much Gallantry, as he was the first of his men who Wounded the *Moors*, charging or opening with his Sword and Buckler a close Squadron. The Enemy in the first charge maintain'd the Field, afterwards unable to endure the weight of the Battail, retir'd in Disorder; our men Routing the disordered Ranks, rather chas'd, then Destroy'd the flying Enemy. Here the Victory began to be notorious; but *Rumecaon* with a great Batallion of *Moors*, and *Janizaries*, made Head against our men, who spread upon the pursute, neglected or not minded Discipline.

Dom Alvaro breaks him.

The danger and resolutenes of *Dom Alvaro*.

22. Here was *Dom Alvaro* given for lost, for his scattered Souldiers, unable to make any Resistance, march't off, leaving the Enemy the Camp, and Victory; nor were his Perswasions, or resolute Fighting, of force enough to Retain some, or Rally others, on so sleight accidents depends the fortune of Warr. *Antonio Casal* a Friar, (whose Religious courage is by Authors recorded) with a Crucifix lifted up, by pious, and moving Arguments, began to rebuke and animate our men, shewing 'em the Image of Christ expos'd again on the Cross to second injuries, it hapned that a Stone cast at randome, so unnail'd an arm of the Crucifix as to leave it hanging, the holy Figure shewing it self in the same

Fr. Antonio Casal plants a Crucifix.

 prospective,

History of India, Dec. 6. Lib. 3. Cap. 2.

prospective, inclin'd to the Believers, falln to the Infidels; Our men more animated by Heavens then the States injuries, shew'd in a different cause, different Courage, more engag'd by the Outrages offer'd their Creator, then by the severe Commands of their Monarck. On a suddain they all Rally'd, and recovering strength, were rather Instruments then Authors of the Victory. *Rumecaon* upon the Routing of his men retir'd, and *Dom Alvaro* engag'd with him at the same time entred the City, more hindered by those who fell, then by the resistance of the Living, who did not now defend themselves.

Our men are encouraged.

Rumecaon retires, and *Dom Alvaro* enters the City.

23. At that time came up *Dom Manoel de Lima*, as Couragious by Land, as Sea, who, where he was plac't broke the Enemy, till joyning with *Dom Alvaro*, and both entring the City, did bloody Execution on the *Moors*, who Routed, and Scattered, strove to save themselves more by Flight then Resistance, and the face of Warr look't more like Plunder then Fight, our men found *Moors*, not Enemies; many of 'em creeping into their Houses hid their own Estates, as stoll'n from the Victory; others cast away their Arms to fly nimbler. *Dom John Mascarenhas*, at an other place entred the City, ending that day so glorious a Siege.

Manoel de Lima joyns him,

and *Dom John Mascarenhas*.

24. The Governour fought still in the Camp, sollicitous for his mens Victory, secure in his own, when News came to him, that the Town was delivered, but *Rumecaon* (like a Mine) plaid again, retarding the Victory, with eight thousand Souldiers, so disposing himself, as to give or expect Battail, so great were their Numbers as with the leavings of the Field to manage a new Warr. About that time Sally'd out of the City, *Dom Alvaro de Castro, Dom John Mascarenhas*, and *Dom Manoel de Lima*, to joy with the Governour for the Victory; when they saw *Rumecaon* in the Field with an other Army. The Governour, that his suspence might not be mistook for fear, with the same Courage of the first, ingag'd in the second Battail, putting his men into three

Rumecaon offers Battail again.

three Squadrons, two fell upon the Enemy in the Flank, he himself in the Front; this was the order of his charging the Enemy, who more Desperate then Resolute receiv'd our first shock, afterwards fought without Courage or Confidence, and being seconded by his men with a faint and forc't Obedience, left us on sleight resistance the Field; though in all the Actions of Siege and Fight, *Rumecaon* shew'd himself no less Souldier then Valiant; but in adversity, Fame is sooner deserv'd then purchast.

The Governour defeats him.

25. The *Moors* opened their Front, the Governour (like an impetuous River carrying all before it) fell upon them undefended; now was the Execution without Fighting, the *Moors* look't like Enemies by their Flying, not by their Defence; and our men falling upon some Companies not yet broken, they, as for their advantage Disordered themselves, flying from one another with as much, rather more apparent Danger then from us; others not to pass for Enemies threw away their Arms, as Instruments which might mind us of their Offence and our Vengeance; there were in fine, in that Tragedy acted all those affections fear puts on. *Rumecaon* seeing all lost, put himself in a poor Garment amongst the Dead, exempting himself from Rage and Victory; but a Stone from an unknown hand, by his Death sav'd his waiting on the Triumph. Many stood to be the Authors of his Death, as formerly of *Galba's*, who had more Murderers then Wounds; and in our own Age and Kingdome have we seen the like accident.

The Victory gotten.

Rumecaon's Death.

26. I purposely omit the particular accidents of this Battail, because none can be prais'd without injury to others, wee'l only give a short relation of the Officers, and most eminent Personages, out of reverence to their Place, and Quality; besides in the confusion of a Battail 'tis difficult with the exact Rigour of truth to particularize accidents; and 'tis certain, those whose Pen finds out the Atoms of the most occult Carriages, endeavour to help out the History, or are very sharp sighted

sighted in finding out Events. 'Tis enough for knowledge, that so famous an Action credited then our Arms, now our Memory, and I believe that of all the designs in *Asia* no Siege out-went, or Battail equal'd this.

Diverse opinions of the Enemies numbers.

27. The numbers of the Enemies Army cannot with certainty be affirm'd, because with different Calculation, some raise 'em above sixty thousand, others say less, neither could the *Moors* who were ta'ne Prisoners, make any exact judgment of those they lost; but by all accounts, the disproportion of the Armies was so notorious, as was sufficient to amase the World with the report; and in forein Histories we find the Victory writ with more applause then in our own Memorials; and if our Country imitated the *Roman* Empires gratitude towards her Sons of desert, she would in proud Statues let the World read *Dom John de Castro*'s actions, which like Annals of Brass should be publick Volumes to all Ages; we find not that his Reward was suitable to his Merit, perhaps to raise it, he here met with the usual misfortune of *Heroes*; yet enjoy'd he as a more durable recompence, the glory of his Name.

Congratulating for his Victory.

The Princes of *Asia*, by ambitious Embassies gave him the joy of the Victory. The Chamber of *Goa* call'd him Duke, either to mind him of it, or to seem to desire it. The King *Dom John* honour'd him with the Title of Vice-King of *India*, the Fourth the State had there. The same Earth which covers his Ashes, Buries his other Rewards, his Posterity only Inheriting the glory of so great an Ascendent.

28. The Governour laid aside the King's share of the Booty, many Colours, and forty Pieces of great Canon, amongst which was that, we now have in Saint *Gillians* Fort; which keeps the name of the place whence 'twas taken. He delivered up the City to Plunder, not reserving for himself the point of a Lance, a constant despiser of the Riches of the *East*; 'twas for this and other Virtues, the Governour (as the *Moors* affirm) was always assisted by some Divine power, for on the top

The plunder of the City.

Our assistance from Heaven.

of

of the Church they saw a Virgin, whose brightness they were not able to behold, at whose sight their hearts fail'd, on which they quitted their Arms, some out of fear, others out of reverence. This favour from Heaven is not above belief, if we consider the justice of the Cause, and piety of the General. There Dy'd of the *Moors* five thousand, amongst them were *Rumecaon*, *Alucaon*, *Accedecaon*, and other *Turks* of Name; the Prisoners were six hundred, who afterwards honour'd the Triumph; we lost of Ours thirty, the Wounded were neer three hundred.

History of *India*, Dec. 6. Lib. 4. Cap. 1.

How many the *Moors* lost.

Our dead and wounded.

29. The Governour had but few days rest in the repose of Victory, being immediately seis'd on by the Anxious care of Re-building, rather founding the Fortress from the first Foundation; a Work, for the Necessity of it indispensable, for our Straights impossible; for the expences of so long a Warr had drain'd the States Revenues, so pawn'd besides, as only to be redeem'd by a Peace of long continuance; yet the Governour, not Disheartned by these difficulties, went about beginning the new Fabrick, with a new design; for in the judgment of the Skilfull, 'twas requisite to enlarge the Situation, to make the Walls thicker, the Bastions nearer, to Build *Magazins* in a dry place for the keeping Ammunition, and Provision, that it might be preserv'd well conditioned, which it had not been formerly, but by the moistness of the Soil corrupted. Materials could not be bought, or brought, without pay, or wages; Stone-cutters, Pioneers and Work-men ask't satisfaction for their Labour.

The Governour Builds up the Fortress.

The Governour had neither Plate, or Jewels to serve his occasions, so as to be forc't to try other Pawns, Valuable by his honour, not their own nature. He commanded the Bones of his Son *Dom Fernando* to be ta'ne up, to send 'em in an unheard of Pawn to the City of *Goa*, but the Earth having not quite corrupted the Body, he cut off some hairs of his own Beard, on which he ask't twenty thousand *Pardaos* of the Chamber of

Pawns for it the hairs of his Beard.

Goa; his affection for his Country finding him out a strange way, never light upon by those Loyal *Decios*, *Curtios*, and *Fabios*, of whom *Rome* yet proud, preserves their Memory in the Ruins of her Empire. The pawn was accompany'd by this following Letter.

A Letter writ from *Dio* by the Governour *Dom John de Castro* to the City of *Goa*.

Gentlemen, Magistrates, Judges, and People, of the most Honourable and always Loyal City of Goa; *I writ to you some days since by* Simaon Alvarez *one of your Citizens the news of the Victory God gave me against the Commanders of the King of* Cambaya, *and that you might without any allay enjoy the pleasure and satisfaction of the Victory, I spoke not in my Letter, of the great streights and necessities I was in; but now I think fit, no longer to dissemble, and to give you an account of the urgencies which are upon me, and to desire your assistance to supply, and remedy things of so great moment as are now in my hands; for the Fortress of* Dio *is so beaten down to the ground, as not one foot of the Wall can serve again, so as 'tis not only necessary this Summer to Build it up again, but with such Skil, and in such a form as the King of* Cambaya *may lose his hopes, of being at any time able to take it. To this trouble is added an other as great, or greater, to me incomparably above all others, which is the trouble and perplexity the* Lasquerins *put me to for their Pay, which I have secur'd to 'em, else would they be all gone, and I should be left alone in the Fortress; which would put me into no little danger, and consequently all* India; *for the Commanders of the King of* Cambaya, *with those men who are left of the Defeat, quarter at* Suna, *two Leagues from this Fortress, and the King every day sends 'em Horse and Foot to increase their Camp, as if they would return and*

try

try their fortune by giving an other Battail, wherefore I am in great want of a considerable sum of Money, and, because it concerns the service of our Lord the King, and complies with your Honour, and Loyalty, I earnestly begg of you to remember your old Custom, and great Generosity, which oblig'd you (as good and Loyal Subjects) always to relieve the urgent necessities of his Majesty, and for the great and intimate affection I have for you all, you would lend me twenty thousand Pardaos, *which as a Gentleman I promise, and on the Holy Gospel swear, before a years end to see you Repaid, though I should be set upon, by greater necessities, and extremities, then those by which I am at present environ'd. I commanded the taking up my Son* Dom Fernando, *whom the* Moors *kill'd in this Fortress (fighting for God, and our Lord the King) to pawn to you his Bones, but they were found so, as 'twas not fit to take 'em out of the ground, by which I am without any other Pawn, but part of my Beard, which I hear send you by* Diogo Rodriguez de Azevedo, *for as you know, I have neither Gold, Plate, Houshold-stuff, or any thing of Value to secure your Estate, only a plain and naked truth given me by God Almighty. But that you may more certainly rely on your Payment, and it may not be thought by some, that (what hath at other times fallen out) some intervening accident may keep you from it; I here send you an order for the Treasurer of* Goa *to be paying you out of the Tax for the Horse, engaging all can be made of it, till you are re-imburst; for the manner of the paying it you are to fix it with him; Excuse me for not affecting words to heighten to you my extremities, being, from what I have said before firmly perswaded, that you will in this Conjuncture, do what you can, and above your abilities, without any other mediation, then your accustomed Nobleness, and our reciprocal Affection. I recommend my self, Gentlemen, to your Goodness.* Dated at *Dio* the twenty third of *November*, Year 1546.

30. Upon the Messengers arrival at *Goa*, the people furnish't him with more then he demanded, seeing they had

The Citizens of *Goa* return 'em.

They are yet preserved.

had a Governour, so little proud as to ask, so great as to defend 'em; they return'd him those honourable Pawns, which are at present preserv'd in the hands of the Bishop, Inquisitor General, his most deserving Grand-child, who put 'em in an Urn or Pyramid of Crystal, set in a Basis of Silver, on which are Engraven several Disticks, which make an ingenious Memory of so famous an Action; this honourable Relique remaining with his Posterity, to make Hereditary the virtues of *Dom John de Castro.* With the Money was carry'd the following Letter.

The Chamber of *Goa*'s Letter in answer to the Governours.

History of *India*, Dec. 6. Lib. 4. Cap. 4.

Most Illustrious, and Excellent Captain General, and Governour of India, *for the High and Mighty, and most Excellent Prince our Lord the King.* Diogo Rodriguez de Azevedo, *arriv'd at this City on Monday the sixth of* December, *and the next day delivered a Letter to the Chamber from your Illustrious Lordship, which was read with no little pleasure, and satisfaction, because, by it we were assur'd of your Health; which good news we always covet to know, and desire encrease of, and for it, this City, and People, in general, and by themselves, give God many thanks, and are confident in our Lady, the Virgin* Mary, *the Mother of God and our Advocate, that as long as the people of* India *hath your Illustrious Lordship: for their Captain, and Governour, we shall never want the Divine assistance in our affronts and troubles, in recompence of your most Catholick and modest Life, your Carriage, and Actions of most commendable Virtue, on which hope we now enjoy our present quiet; for, the late and glorious Victory atchiev'd by your prudent Conduct, great Courage and Magnanimity, the raising the Siege of* Dio, *the routing and defeating the King of* Cambaya*'s whole Army, besides above twenty thousand others,*

others, Moors, Turks, Rumes, Coracos, *and Renegade* Christians, Germans, Venetians, Genuese, *and* French, *and diverse other Nations*, (*considerable numbers of whom were Kill'd by our Lances and Swords, as this City is assur'd by honest men and eye-witnesses*) *these good Services are certain signs, that for the future, by God's grace and protection, we need not fear any other troubles which shall appear from a fresh Army of the King of* Cambaya, *or other Neighbouring Kings and Potentates, or whole* India, *who are certainly our implacable Enemies, besides being Infidels, and haters of our holy Catholick Faith, from neither of whom can we have any secure or firm Peace, though some shew of a double and cousening Friendship. As for the Loan, which in the name of our Lord the King you ask of us, the Cities answer is, That we the Inhabitants will now and always do our duty in serving his Majesty with our Estates, Lives and Souls; and because the Cities, and every particular man's design is to serve your Illustrious Lordship with an Eye that such a Loan is very much for the service of our Lord the King, whose the City is, and we are all, with a great deal of diligence and care, from the day that* Diogo Rodriguez de Azevedo *delivered his message, to the present* (*which is the seven and twentieth of* December) *have we rais'd twenty thousand, one hundred and forty six* Pardaos, *and one* Tanga, *at five* Tangas *the* Pardao, *which the City lends, that is Citizens, and People, as also the* Bramens, *Merchants, Traders, and Goldsmiths; and by our Letters we assure your Lordship, that this City, and its honourable Inhabitants, are bound for your service to lay down our Lives more chearfully then for our own honour and interest. As for the Pawns your Lordship sent us, the City and Inhabitants think our selves injur'd by your Lordship to rely so little on us, and our Loyalties; for in a business that so concern'd the service of our Lord the King, and his Royal State, such honourable and glorious Pawns were not necessary, our Loyalty obliging us to serve the King, and present necessity, after that your Obligations on us, and your Lordship great affection and love to this City and Inhabitants,*

 for

for which, and what besides we confess owing to you, we kiss your hands, and begg of God Almighty your enjoying perfect health, and prosperity, in much honour, and great Victories over the Enemies of our most holy Faith. My Lord, Diogo Rodriguez de Azevedo *returns to carry you back your Pawns, and he, and* Bertholamew Bispo *Procurator of this City bring you the Money, which the City, and People lend you, of their good and free will; they carry too, the order you sent hither to the Treasurer for the payment of the Money; and our desires, you would accept all, as from Loyal Subjects, we profess to be to our Lord the King, and men oblig'd to your Lordship.* Dated at the Chamber the twenty seventh of *December*, 1547. and I *Lewis Tremessaon* Clerk of the Chamber gave order for the writing it, and sign'd it, by the authority I have so to do. *Pero Godinho, John Rodriguez Paez, Ruy Goncalvez, Ruy Dioz, Iorge Ribeiro, Bertholamew Bispo.*

The works ... on at the ...ortress.

31. The works at the Fortress went on with so great satisfaction to the Officers, and Labourers, as it advanc't without time, and the pay of Work-men and Souldiers was so punctual, as the State was only poor; for the Governour, besides what the City lent, the Ladies, and Gentlewomen, sent him in a Cabinet their Diamonds, and Jewels, by which Female impotency sacrifis'd both to Glory and Vanity; an offer which expected neither interest, or recompence, whence is seen, how much better the People supply the Virtues, then Tyrannies of Regents.

And the ...arr against ...mbaya.

32. He commanded *Dom Manoel de Lima* with thirty Ships to go along the Coast of *Cambaya*, and Burn all the Villages, to shew the *Sultan*, his Revenge was not satisfy'd by the Victory; but not to put in at the City of *Goga*, because the intelligence said, that there were imbody'd all those who scap't from the Battail. *Dom*

Dom ...anoel de ...ma Wageth

Manoel, (who again look't for good fortune in that Bay) went Sailing along the Coast, and in a few days of being out, was surpris'd by so violent a Tempest, as to to be forc't by the necessity of the Storm, to put into the Port forbidden by his instructions. The Citizens having their imaginations fill'd with the late dangers, at the sight of the same Arms which wounded 'em quitted the City; the Souldiers, as well as the unserviceable Rabble, in the same distemper flying to the Mountain. There was at Anchor in the Port a *Moorish* Vessel, belonging to the *Camalake*, (one who was in good correspondence with the State) which observing the flight of the *Moors* hal'd to our men to fall upon the City. *Dom Manoel* not understanding the sign, concluded that in defiance they bid him Battail, and 'twixt anger and impatience making ready, perceiv'd the City emptying, and the poor people running in confus'd multitudes towards a small Mountain, which was in sight, believing the distance, and cragginess of its situation would secure 'em from being fall'n upon by our Souldiers; *Dom Manoel* found out the design of the Ships hawling, and put to't, 'twixt the opportunity, and his obedience, brought the business to Council; and amongst Valiant Souldiers, Gallantry being the best interpreter of Orders, 'twas voted they should enter the City, because the Governours instructions could not take in all accidents, who, if there, would be the first should leap on shore; the Counsel was immediately follow'd by Execution, *Dom Manoel*, almost without any resistance entred the City, the pillage of the Souldiers was great; and what was below the covering, was committed to the Fire, which burnt Estates and Houses; the Dammage was greater then the Victory. *Dom Manoel* took three *Baneans* Prisoners, by whom he was told, that all the Inhabitants had sav'd themselves in a place of the Mountain not farr of; he resolv'd to invest it, that the fugitives and opposers might have the same Punishment; at break of Day he went to the place, taking with him for guides the *Baneans*, forc't by miserable necessity to deliver up their Children and Kindred, and those who thought themselves secure in the

Goes to the City of *Goga*.

History of *India*, Dec. 6. Lib. 4. Cap. 3.

Which he Sacks and Burns.

the ſhelter of the Mountain, ſaw over their Heads the Sword, before the Enemy. The ſlaughter differenc't not cauſe from cauſe, perſon from perſon, natives and ſtrangers, guilty and innocent with their Lives paid for their own or an others offence. From Perſons the affront paſt to Religion, he caus'd many to be Hang'd up in the Temples of their Idols, an outrage in the Superſtition of their Religion, inexpiable. He cut the Throats of all the Cattel, ſprinkling the Moſques with Cows blood, an Animal, which as the depoſitary of Souls, they adore with abominable worſhip.

He returns on Board, and is in danger.

33. *Dom Manoèl de Lima* return'd to his Ships, and venturd to croſs the Bay, where without a Storm he fear'd Shipwrack; for the Tide is there ſo unruly, and impetuous, as is ſufficient to looſen the Veſſels. In Sailing he came in ſight of the City *Gandar*, peopled by *Pagan* Merchants, rich by its Commerce, weak by its Inhabitants. This was in the firſt Onſet yielded, and burnt, the Natives diſcovered their Eſtates as a ranſome for their Lives, which neither by oppoſing nor yielding could they ſave, for the anger, rather inhumanity of the Souldiers more coveted blood then booty. He deſtroy'd many other places of the Bay, whoſe aſhes and ruins for many years kept up the memory of their Deſtruction. Thoſe Natives who ſurviv'd the miſeries of their fellows, retir'd to the Inland of the Kingdome, where in ſecure poverty they preſerv'd themſelves.

He deſtroys *Gandar*.

Returns for *Dio*.

34. *Dom Manoel* return'd for *Dio*, where he found the Governour employ'd about the new Fortifications, in whoſe ſight the Works advanc't; diverſe buſineſſes re-demanding him at *Goa*, he had a mind to leave the Fortreſs in a ſtate of defence. *Dom John Maſcarenhas*, either wore out, or ſatisfy'd with the difficulties of the Siege, before his time was out reſign'd, his Government, deſiring that year to return for the Kingdome, to enjoy that Fame of which he ſo well deſerv'd. The Governour endeavour'd to diſſwade him, fearing none would accept it after him; for by the late Victory and

alteration of the Trade, the Spurrs of honour, and profit, were Blunted, the greatest incentives men Bow under. But *Dom John Mascarenhas*'s resolution to go for the Kingdome, in *Lourenco Pirez de Tavora*'s Fleet, put the Governour upon finding out a Commander for the Garrison, which some Gentlemen had refus'd to be, out of Dislike to a place which had been the Seat of so many Victories, perhaps out of the hazard there is to succeed Persons of extraordinary Eminency; yet *Dom Manoel de Lima* offer'd to remain on the place, out of either complacency to the Governour, or confidence of himself.

Dom John Mascarenhas leaves his Command.

Dom Manoel de Lima offers to continue in it.

35. The Governour in the mean time provided for his passage to *Goa*, and ordered *Antonio Moniz Barretto* with some Ships to look out for the Fleet of *Cambaya*, which (by his private intelligence) he knew were to Visit the Coast of *Por*, and *Mangalor*, which *Moniz* meeting at Sea, Boarded, and carry'd into *Dio*, their Lading help't to bear the States charges. The King of *Cambaya* in his resentment of so many losses, burst forth into a most barbarous Revenge, commanding two of our innocent Prisoners, taken during the Warr, to be Kill'd, taking his satisfaction for so great Outrages on so little shadows.

Antonio Moniz takes some Ships.

The barbarous revenge of the King of *Cambaya*.

36. The affairs of *Dio* being concluded, fortune began to alarm the State with new accidents; The Governour had from *Ormus* repeated intelligence, that the *Turks* with a mighty Army had thrown out of *Balsora Mahomet As-Cnam*, a Loyal friend to the State, who summon'd our Arms, as Auxiliary forces, to resist the common Enemy. The dangers, and consequences of having so unruly a Neighbour, were of no difficult discovery, for whom and us the World, much less the State, would be too narrow; The importancy of *Balsora* was weig'd, as a Foundation laid for greater designs; whose situation we will briefly acquaint you with. *Balsora* is a Colony of four thousand Families, seated in *Arabia* the Happy, in twenty four degrees of

News from *Ormus*.

The description of *Balsora*.

Northern Latitude, not farr distant from the River *Euphrates*. 'Tis from the Fortress of *Ormus* two hundred Leagues, from *Babylon* a little above forty. Ships go from *Ormus* thither along the Coast of *Persia*, having on that side more convenient Ports and Watering. 'Tis inhabited by *Moors*, Schismaticks from the *Turks*, for though all Worshippers of *Mahomed*, yet differ in their Belief, these following the Rites and Ceremonies of the *Persian*, whom the Divel in different Cups makes to drink of the abominations of *Mahomed*; here the *Turks* fortify'd themselves, and began to gain upon the Neighbouring *Arabians*, on some by Arms, on others by Benefits, setting up a new Prince in *Balsora*, who being of the Race of their antient Kings was lik't of by the *Arabs*, and would be faithfull to the *Turks*, whose Liberality, under a shew of friendship, Veyl'd their ambition of ruling. This mans pretensions, whom the *Turks* saluted for King, others write at large, I omit the relation, as importune to the Reader, and from the design of the History.

The *Turks* fortifie themselves in it.

37. The Governour resolv'd to send *Dom Manoel de Lima* for the Fortress of *Ormus*, (which came to him by the Death of *Dom Manoel da Sylveira*) that as the Perquisits of the place he should take on him the obligation of managing the Warr against the *Turks*; the Fortress of *Dio*, being once more left as a Stone of offence, rejected by the Builders; for no Gentleman would remain there, with only the care of the Fortifications, *Dom John Mascarenhas* carrying away with him the glory of the danger. I know not if the affairs of *India* are now held in the same respect. The Governour was troubled the Theater of so many Victories should be laid aside, which *Dom John Mascarenhas* hearing, offer'd that Winter to continue in the place, a thing taken very well by the Governour, who told him, whilst the Fortress was finishing, 'twould be Wall'd by his reputation; and that it may be known how facil this so great Personage was in confirming other mens

Dom Manoel de Lima goes for *Ormus*,

And *Dom John Mascarenhas* returns to his Command in *Dio*.

mens deserts, I'le set down a Letter he writ to his Son *Dom Alvaro*, upon *Dom John Mascarenhas* going to *Goa* to take passage for the Kingdome. "There comes by "this occasion *Dom John Mascarenhas*, the same the "*Pagans*, and *Moors* take him for, I who am a good "Christian make the same confession of his Courage, "having, in all the Fights found him always at my side; "He goes to embark for the Kingdome, I ask it of you, "to entertain him, as you would my own Person, and "not to consent he should Lodge any where but with "you, which yet is below his merits; I hope in God "he will in a little time return to these Parts, to cor-"rect my Defects. He also writ largely to the King of every mans Desert, said nothing of himself, betraying his partiality for other mens services, his ingratitude for his own.

What the Governour writes of him to his Son *Dom Alvaro*,

and to the King of every one.

38. Order being taken about *Dio*, the Governour left *Dom Iorge de Menezes* with six Ships, to hover the rest of the Summer about the Bay of *Cambaya*, and gave him instructions to proclaim in all the adjacent places, That all the *Moors*, and *Pagans* might return to Inhabit the Island, for under shelter of his Justice, their Persons and Commerce should be secure, enjoying their Antient peace and freedome; and truth being credited by Courage, the *Pagans* as much sought for the protection of our Arms, as Laws, there coming in great numbers of Merchants and Inhabitants to improve the Trade, counting that Peace secure, which begun on the confines of Warr.

He leaves *Dom Iorge* on that Coast.

39. The Governour took Shipping for *Goa*, expected there by the general applause of all people, the articulate Ecchos of his Victory; in ten days he came into Port, where the Bishop, the Commander in chief, and Magistrates came to Visit him, desiring him to stay at *Pangim*, whilst the City prepar'd the Triumph they intended for his Reception, that the World might not think 'em uncivil, barbarous, or ungratefull; that so deserv'd a Triumph, was not the ambition of the Person, but

Embarks for *Goa*.

Arrives, and is visited at Sea.

but glory of the State; that Kings carry away the advantages of Victories, Subjects the honour; that he might scorn the Reward, without refusing the Memory.

A Triumph is decreed him.

40. The Governour suffer'd himself to be o'recome by the kindness of the People, as one who could not sleight the honours of a Triumph, without injuring those who bore him Company in the atchievement, nor limit the popular Rejoycing, without envying the common prosperity; their festival Solemnities having their excuse in our Fortune, their example in the *Cæsars*. The fifteenth of *April* of the Year 1547. was appointed for the day of the Triumph, the first, and last, our Arms ever saw, us'd to purchase Fame without glory. The City Built in Saint *Catherines Basar*, a great Arch, covering the Materials with diverse Carpets. The gate of the City was from the top of the Wall thrown down, the Stones appearing humble, or gratefull; the Hangings of the Walls were of Rich cloth of Gold, greatness could do no more, the general satisfaction was not content with less. In many places the Adornment was of diverse Colour'd Velvets, that the Gold might set off the Majesty, the diversity of Colours the pleasantness. On the Walls on each side the Gate were two gilded Lyons, upholding in their Paws the wheels of the *Castros*, always Famous, now Triumphant. There run along by the Arch a dilated Thicket of Trees, which with intermitting shades, qualify'd the heat, without hindring the light. The Sea appear'd all cover'd with Ships, Galleys, Boats, and Brigantines, which came from the Nighbouring Islands, all with their Streamers and Wast-cloaths. There was in the Court of the Palace a Fortress, design'd for the Model of *Dio*, within it some Guns charg'd without Bullets, and other Fire-arms, a pleasant Representation of former Horrours. In the same Fortress was hid exquisite Musick, which with Tunable voices kept time in singing the praises of the Governour, delighting by their sweetness, the

The Fabrick of it.

History of *India*, Dec. 6. Lib. 4. Cap. 6.

the Ear, by their words, the Judgment. The general correspondency in the adorning the Streets, was as if design'd to shew the Riches of the *East*; The Embroidery, as common, was look't upon with scorn. The Cloaths of the Citizens were in all kinds such, as if the People had Triumph'd; Neither, if their hearts could have been seen, would the applause of their souls have seem'd less, being the voluntary Demonstrations of inartificial affections.

41. The Governour came from *Pangim* in a little Gally, differenc't from the rest by its Adorning; he had with him the old Cavalliers, his Companions in the Expedition, who shar'd equally of the glory and danger. The Galleons of the Fleet went on Head, in their Stern follow'd the Vessels with Oars, with their Sails furl'd in the Brayles, and all shadow'd with the Verdure of several Boughs, appearing from the Land, a loose Wood, or moving City. When they came in sight of the Fortress, by the horrour of their Salute, the Warr seem'd rather real then apparent; the Guns also from the Shore, gave 'em so terrible an answer, as the senses could not distinguish whether it were a Fight or Triumph; all the Fleet opened to make way for the Governours Gally. He was richly Cloath'd, giving the Season its due, and became them as well, and sprightly as his Arms; He had on, a French suit of Crimson Satin, with Gold twist about the Slashes and Seams, and not to forget he was a Souldier, he put on a Coat of Mail wrought on Cloth of Gold with Buttons of Plate, Feathers in his Hat, and the Guarniture of his Sword Gold. Upon the Key, the Officers of the Militia, Nobility, and Magistracy of the City waited for him, with whom he entred the first Gate, where one of the Consuls made him a sober Speech in Latin, shewing, that by the advantage of his Valour we had humbled the proudest Scepter of the *East*, whose Ruins would be his Fames best Trumpets; that *Portugal* had now secur'd the State, born again in his Arms, who fought as

The Governours entry.

well for Religion, as Empire, so laying his designs, as the Voice of the Gospel reach't Parts so remote; that now the *Moors* and *Pagans* could not but believe that God to be Great, who was the God of so great Victories; that after long Revolutions of time in the *East*, men Sailing by would point at the place of the Battail, the Destruction of *Cambaya* going in Tradition from Nation to Nation, from Kingdome to Kingdome; that Parents would tell it their Children, to fright 'em with the memory of former Dangers; that now our Colours gloriously Roll'd up, might rest in the Temple of Peace, having opened that of Victory. He discours'd largely upon the passages of his Government, yet in the thoughts of the people, was rather sparing, then extravagant in his Virtues, greater in the Eyes of strangers, then in our praises. The end of the Speech had its Cadence in the Harmony of differing, and agreeing Instruments; immediately were Shot off some Guns, charg'd instead of Bullets with diverse Comfits, which falling at a little distance, made a pleasant, though running Banquet for the common people. The Magistrates of the City receiv'd the Governour under a Canopy, and presently a Citizen of quality, reverently bowing, took his Hat from his Head, putting him on a Crown of Triumph, and in his hand a Palm. The Guardian of the *Franciscan*'s Order walk't before, with the Crucifix he held up in the Battail, the Arm unnail'd, and hanging, (a Signal by which the Divine Majesty not only in that but this Age hath secur'd to us our Kingdoms and Victories *) there follow'd the Royal

They receive him under a Canopy.

The order of the Triumph.

* *Dom Antonio de Sousa de Macedo* (now Secretary of State in *Portugal*) in the third Chapter of the third Book of his *Lusitania Liberata* (Printed at *London* 1645.) saith, The design of shaking of the King of *Spain* being Compleated, by Killing the Secretary, and Proclaming *John* the Fourth Duke of *Braganza* (at that time at his House in the Country) the Nobility, in the King's absence desir'd the Arch-bishop of *Lisbone* to Govern the City; who going in solemn Procession to the Palace, as he past by Saint *Anthonies* Church, and was praying to the Saint to intercede for the good of the Kingdome, and his Native Country, the Arm of a rich Crucifix which was carry'd before him, Miraculously unnail'd and held it self forth to the people, who receiv'd the Miracle, with acclamations crying out, God stretcheth out the hand of his power to free the *Portuguese*, and decide their cause against the *Castillian*, who had said, he only desir'd God should be Judge. This is the Miracle hinted at by the Author, and compar'd to the Crucifixes having an Arm unnail'd in the Battail, as was related in the 22. Parag. of this Book.

Banner

Banner of our Cinks, beheld by the *Moors* and *Pagans* with fresh admiration; immediately came the Standarts of *Cambaya*, dragg'd on the ground in the sight of *Juzarcaon*, and other Commanders pinion'd, who represented the Tragedy of their Fortune, for them compassionate, to us pleasant; there were seen six hundred Prisoners, dragging their Chains after them, after them the Field-pieces, with different and numerous Arms. The Ladies from their Windows sprinkled the Triumpher with distill'd waters of diverse Spices. The Officers through whose hands past the Gold, and other rich Commodities, came and made him voluntary offerings, the equal disposition of their affections being more Valuable then the Triumph. The beautify'd, and open Churches shew'd their acceptance and thanks. In this order he went to Visit the Cathedral, the Mother-Church of the *East*, where the Bishop, and Clergy receiv'd him with the Hymn *Te Deum Laudamus*; being entred into the See, with Religious offerings he acknowledg'd the Author of Victories, and it being now late, with little Ceremony retir'd to the Palace, one days time being too narrow for the Majesty of the Triumph.

THE LIFE OF DOM JOHN DE CASTRO.

The Fourth Book.

THere were but few Kingdoms in the *East*, which in the Government of *Dom John de Castro* did not Alarme that State, by diverse Rumours of Warr, by either Arms against us, or against one the other; inviting our Forces to make Peace, or forward the Victory; the *East* also saw him often gird his Sword for the cause of Religion.

Franciscan Friars go for *Ceilan*.

1. King *John* had sent to the Island of *Zeilan* some *Franciscan* Friars, exemplary in their Lives and Doctrine, that by Martyrdome and Preaching, they might bear witness of the truth of the Gospel, that being our Prince's greatest concernment, whose Banners *Asia* saw oftner display'd in reverence to Religion, then ambition of Empire. These Friars on their Landing in the Island were by the King of *Cotta* civilly entertain'd, the Sun of Righteousness beginning once more to rise in the *East*. That *Paganism* began to Listen to the Voice of Heaven, and that Barren ground to answer the pains by its Improvement, by the coming in of infinite Sheep to the Sheep-fold of the Church.

History of *India*, Dec. 6. Lib. 4. Cap. 7.

They preach the Faith in *Candea*, and the King hearkens to it.

2. Those Embassadours of the Gospel went forward, to give News of the Light to the King of *Candea*, in the

the heart of the Island, whom they found Courteous in the entertainment of their Persons, flexible to the obedience of their Doctrine; He was instructed in the mysteries of our Belief, that with a stronger Faith he might wash in the waters of Baptism. He gave the Friars ground, Materials, and Money, for the Building a Church; that being the first Fortress the Conquest of the Gospel rais'd in the Island against the delusions of Idolatry; for of the Preaching of the Apostle, Saint *Thomas* (if it reach't so farr) neither had their Understandings any light, nor their Country memory.

3. That Prince shew'd himself obedient to the precepts of our Religion, but not constant, for the fear of his Subjects revolting on his change of Doctrine, made him, not to lose what he Esteem'd, forsake what he was Convicted of; for as a Plant not yet Rooted, the force of human perswasion enclin'd him either way. The Religious men endeavour'd to take those Rubbs out of the way of Life, by assuring him that under the protection of our Religion, and Arms, he might secure both Crowns, for the State was at that time Govern'd by *Dom John de Castro*, who for the propagation of the Faith us'd to venture his Blood, for his Friends, the State. He is inconstant. The Friars encourage him.

4. The King listned to the proposition, saying, if the Governour would send him Relief, he would not only himself profess the Faith, but preach it to his Subjects. One of the Friars carry'd this resolution to *Goa*; the Governour, certify'd of the cause of his coming, desir'd the Conversion of that Prince, as his greatest business in the *East*, not less zealous in giving Children to the Church, then Victories to the State. He immediately dispatch't *Antonio Moniz Barretto* with seven Fly-boats, and Orders, that if he found any of our Ships at Sea to carry 'em with him; writ honourable Letters to the Prince, which he accompany'd with several Presents: but leaving *Antonio Moniz* at Sea, we will (to observe the order of time in the His resolution. The Governour desires that Conversion, and sends to him *Antonio Moniz*.

 the

the Relation of ſucceſſes) ſpeak of the taking of *Barobe*.

5. The Governour had diſpatch't from *Dio*, *Dom Iorge de Menezes*, to commit all imaginable Hoſtilities in the Bay of *Cambaya*, to ſhow the *Sultan* the edge of our Arms was not Blunted, by their former Execution. *Dom Iorge* took ſome Veſſels of Proviſion going to furniſh the Enemies Ports, that thoſe the Sword had ſpar'd, might be made an end of by Famine. He came one Evening in ſight of the City *Baroche*, whoſe ſtately Buildings preſented him with the Politeneſs of *Europe*. 'Twas ſituated on an Eminency ſurrounded with Brick-walls., which were more for ſhew, then defence; yet were there diverſe Bull-works to be ſeen, made not without ſome in-ſight in Fortification, furniſh't with ſtore of Ordnance, which commanded the entrance into the Haven. The height of the ſituation diſcovered the Gates to be of ſquare Stone poliſh't, and the correſpondency of Turrets and Windows, argued the wealth and policy of the Inhabitants. The Trade of the place was in very fine Silks, a Commodity exported thence to many Ports of the *East*. *Madre Maluco* was Lord of the City, and had Tributary the Neighbouring Villages, which, by their fertility and bigneſs, made him up a moderate Seignory.

The Situation and Fortifying of *Baroche*.

Madre Maluco Lord of it.

6. Our men had by chance taken a little Boat of Fiſher-men, Natives of the place, who upon enquiry told what we have related of the City, and upon *Dom Iorge*'s deſire to know what Garriſon was in the place, had ſaid, that *Madre Maluco* had carry'd all the Souldiery to *Amadabat*, the *Sultan*'s Court, and at preſent were remaining only ſome Artiſans, and other Trades-men. *Dom Iorge* thinking the occaſion opportune for aſſaulting the City, though his ſtrength was not proportionable to ſuch a deſign, yet (events depending on accidents) reſolv'd to run his Fortune; and to amuſe the Inhabitants in ſecurity, ſteer'd an other courſe, Sailing by a different *Rumbe*, taking along with him the Fiſher-

men,

men, to be his Pilots in the entrance. At night the whole Fleet tacking about, stood up with the Port, and getting all on Shore, (the Enemies confidence, or negligence, being unprovided of any Defence, or Sentinel) fell upon the Unarm'd, and weak Multitude, when the Night, Confusion, and Sleep, run 'em upon the danger they avoided, miserably wandering; they shun'd their own as Enemies, flying from those who fled themselves. The skreeks of the Children stirr'd not up in their Parents any Compassion, less Vengeance, for the suddain fear gave 'em over to the basest affections of Nature; the Crys and Laments of the Women discovered them, their, Ah me, being their greatest danger; those who by flying into Houses scap't the Sword, were in them consum'd by the Fire, the poor people having no remedy against, but choice of their Death; the Invasion, and Sack was at the same time; the Slaughter, as in a Fight without resistance; the Plunder, as in a City forc't to deliver. *Dom Iorge* in fine purchas'd in this Action, Fame without Danger, Victory without an Enemy; yet doubt we not that had he found more Opposition, his Courage would have atchiev'd what his Fortune effected. He commanded the City to be Burnt, where, in a few hours, the Nobility and People, Gardens and Houses became compassionate Ashes, without any distinction of nature, or separation of place. He put on Board some of the smaller Guns, broke in pieces the great. This Action being so famous amongst our Souldiers, as to give him who was call'd *Menezes*, the Sirname of *Baroche*, as the Ruins of *Carthage* gave *Scipio* the name of *Africanus*.

Dom Iorge enters by Night.

7. *Maluco* came with five thousand Horse; soon enough to deplore, too late to help, and seeing the Fire and Sword had left nothing in its own shape, return'd inpatiently to the King of *Cambaya*, as one whose green Wound very sensibly smarted. He represented to him the Destruction of the City, as an Outrage aggravated by being the latest of so many; The

Maluco comes too late.

Sultan

Sultan seem'd touch't with this new accident, and Vow'd once more to set upon *Dio* the stone of offence, on which was broke the strength of so vast an Empire; but while the Heart-burnings of *Cambaya* vent themselves in an imaginary Revenge, we will speak of the Spirituals of *Candea*, which as Seed choak't up by Thorns came not to produce any Fruit.

The King of *Cotta* is against the King of *Candea's* Conversion.

History of *India*, Dec. 6. Lib. 4. Cap. 8.

8. *Madune* King of *Cotta* came to know that the King of *Candea* endeavour'd by the change of his Religion to get the protection of the State, (who as those *Pagans* are zealous observers of their errors) sought for arguments to perswade him, that Idolatry was necessary for his Crown, telling him, his new Belief would make his Subjects rebell, the Neighbouring Kings his Enemies, himself Ingratefull to his old Gods, who had for so long prospered the Scepter of *Candea* in his Royal Progenitors; that the Governour of *India* must of necessity be the most Insolent man upon Earth, who suffered not the World to have any other King, or God, but that, he Obey'd, and Ador'd; that he deny'd not the *Portuguese* Religion, to be either better, or more fortunate, since they serv'd the God of Victories; yet 'twas sufficient for him to serve the Gods of the Country he was Born in; without coveting a better Posterity, or greater Fortune then his Predecessors; besides, who knew that the Governour under pretence of Religion design'd not the usurpation of his Scepter; that he ought not to receive on the Island, men of such a temper as could not be satisfy'd, without being the Lords, to be any where; that if the *Franks* promis'd him, to furnish him with a better Creed, and inlarge his Territories, what sound judgment would credit so unusual goodness in men he never saw, especially when they were not so great despisers of Temporalities, but to come from the end of the World to Domineer in *Asia*? that if example had with him any Authority, he should find more Kingdomes destroy'd by 'em, then indoctrinated; that 'twas true, their *Ioques* (by them call'd

call'd Priests) did willingly Dye for their Religion, but did it, either out of an ambition of Name, or prodigality of Life; if there were not in the *West* more Fools, then in other Parts, who were all possest with that dangerous obstinacy of instructing the World; that in fine, he Counsel'd him as a King and Ally to cut off the Relief he expected from the *Franks*, in expiation to his old Gods, justly incenst to be thrown off for a forein Divinity; that were it their Pride in pretending to come and enlighten his Understanding, or ambition to usurp his Kingdome, the Circumstance of either fault deserv'd this Punishment; that in prosecution of it he would assist him with Arms, and Souldiers, making that a common Cause, which was the Outrage of all their Idols.

9 The unfortunate Prince not able at once to throw off the weight of his old Errors, suffered himself to be perswaded by the Arguments of his Barbarous, and Treacherous friend; his Eyes yet darkned with the Clouds of Idolatry, not being able to endure the Dawning of the Light of Truth, and immediately, wanting prudence or resolution, conspir'd in *Madune's* Treachery, like a Diseas'd Frantick, angry with the Physicians: In fine, they expected their Guests, resolv'd to put in Execution their plotted malice. The King of *Candea* consents.

10. *Antonio Moniz* being parted from *Goa*, found some of our Ships in several Ports, which, according to his Orders, he joyn'd to his Fleet; having doubled the Cape of *Camorim*, and past the Quick-sands of *Manar*, he steer'd for *Baticalou*, to go from thence by Land to *Candea*. He had with him twelve Fly-boats, out of which he took one hundred and twenty select Souldiers, and with them march't, in the security that he was going to a Prince, a Friend, and one obliged by the State, above all, if not yet a Convert, at least gratefull, and a well-willer to the truth of that Doctrine we profest; at his coming to *Candea*, by every ones being in Arms, the Treason could not be kept so close as that *Antonio* *Antonio Moniz* Voyage. He comes to *Candea*, and finds all things altered.

Moniz had not notice of it by diverse advices, and by their pretending to divide his Souldiers, so to Kill 'em more securely; besides, the King in Person would not see 'em, perhaps, not to discover by his Affections, his Timerous, and guilty Conscience. *Antonio Moniz* march't presently out of the City, Commanded all the Impediments and Baggage to be Burnt, to be thus more at liberty, to Defend and Retreat, and assembling his Souldiers spoke to 'em;

He endeavours to resist.

11. "Friends and Companions, you all know the "Treason plotted against us by this *Pagan* King, whom "we come to serve and assist; I have intelligence they "will set upon us by open Force, having now a reason, "or cause to hurt us, they had not before, that is, that "we have found out their Treachery. None of us hath "any more Life, then he can Defend; Courage, and "Discipline may save us; we expect no Relief, for it lies "in our selves; and the Infidels will not persist in their "Treason, if they find it Costly; and what is it? if in "this Conjuncture we do that for our selves, we came "to do for them, that is, lose our Lives. The passages "which go to *Baticalou*, where our Fleet is, must be "suppos'd Lin'd with the Enemy; wherefore I am of "opinion, for us to go to the King of *Ceitavaca*, a "faithfull Friend to the State, where we shall find en-"tertainment and secure protection to go from thence "in quest of our Fleet.

Is set upon by the Enemy.

12. As soon as *Antonio Moniz* began to march, the Enemy appear'd in Companies, charging us with Arrows, Darts, Stones, and other such Weapons, with which they Wounded some of our men, and made account by this importune way of Fighting to Destroy us without danger. The Enemy appear'd to have a Body of eight thousand men, Commanded by their Officers (by them call'd *Modeliares*) expert in that wild way of charging and retiring, out-going us in number and agility, and without doubt would one by one have Destroy'd us, had not our Musquets made 'em stand off, from

from which they receiv'd no little Dammage, and greater fear, for fear'd, by seeing some drop down Dead suddainly, the rest follow'd us with more fear and caution; they thus continued Gawling us all that day, one while Venturous, another Cowards: with this unequal and troublesome chase, they gave us a slow, but un-interrupted charge.

13. By the coming on of the Night our men had more security, then repose, for they were so disquieted with wandring and roving Shot, that the poor Souldiers could not take any little rest upon their Arms, eating their Biscuit with their Eyes toward the Enemy, and their Hands on their Weapons; so past they till the next day, when they discovered the *Pagans*, more Venturous and Daring, for that first horrour our Fire-arms bred in 'em, was either quite lost or moderated. They at last arriv'd to the confidence to charge us with short Arms, on which *Antonio Moniz* was forc't to stop his March, and sometimes front 'em, in this we cut off some of their men, and took Prisoner, amongst the rest one of their *Modeliars*, who by his Habit and Arms seem'd to Command the party, as also, by their venturing and daring to recover him, making several Charges, in which they were worsted, yet so constant in their resolute attaquing us, as our men quite worn out could no longer maintain it. The difficulty he was in.

14. Some were of opinion to face the Enemy, and either by Fighting free themselves, or Dye reveng'd; but *Antonio Moniz* told 'em, that the greatest proof of their Courage would be enduring, and the only way to save 'em; that they had already Conquer'd the greatest part of the way; that Marching with care and in a Body, they could not receive much Dammage; that the greater the danger was, more would the pleasure be, when they should tell it gloriously, and securely. Thus did the Commander encourage 'em, and Bridle the despair of so tedious a Resistance, till the coming of the Night made 'em some amends for the Days difficulty; for His prudence in moderating his men.

for the *Pagans* being also broken, gave our men some time to rest; yet at break of Day did they assault us more furiously, asham'd perhaps to find amongst so few so stout opposition. They now came on more boldly on our men, who defended themselves, though with less strength, with their usual Courage.

15. *Antonio Moniz* commanded one to break the *Modeliars* Leggs he had taken Prisoner, and cast him in the way, whom his own men, leaving off Fighting, immediately went to Relieve, mov'd by their affection or pity, to see their Leader or Companion, in so compassionate a condition; Our men, were for some time as if without an Enemy, yet suddainly Fir'd with Commiseration, or Revenge, did they violently fall upon us in a narrow passage, which ended in a Bridge made over a great River not to be Foarded; here *Antonio Moniz* shew'd extraordinary Courage, facing the Enemy with nine more, till his Souldiers got over, and when he had 'em on the other side, broke a part of the Bridge, a diligence, which stopp'd the *Pagans* passage, and pursute. *Antonio Moniz* by so Heroick a defence got not popular applause, yet the few who know how to Value extraordinary Actions, voted this Retreat worthy the Fame of a signal Victory; they got at last to the King of *Ceitavaca*, where they had kind, and hearty Reception, and recover'd their Hunger, Wounds, and hard March in a free and courteous Hospitality, who offered 'em his Forces to revenge so just a quarrel.

His courage in Fighting.

His retreat.

16. The poor King of *Candea* repenting of the Crime, the perswasion of a Neighbour Prince induc't him to commit, and abhorring the Treachery, as hatch't in an others Brest, sent a Messenger to *Antonio Moniz* with ten thousand *Pardaos* for the expence of his Fleet, and a Letter, that the sorrow was his, the mischief an other mans; that coming to him when an Infidel, he should not now forsake him when a Christian; that the God on whom he began to believe, was therefore so great, because he pardoned offences; that he ought not to

The King of *Candea* repents.

Sends a Messenger.

to suffer those tender Flowers which were Blossoming in the Garden of the Church, to be unshelrered, expos'd to the scorching of Idolatry; that his coming in Arms being to weed that Wood of *Pagan* superstitions, he should not wonder to get off hurt by the Briars, and Thistles of Infidelity; that, the God they Preach't to him, being so Gratious, did not in his Justice, without Mercy save the World; that Earth ought not to despise him, who was not cast off by Heaven; that he entreated him to come to his Succour, who was ready to Sacrifize all he had, for his Protection, and his Life for Religion.

17. *Antonio Moniz* on this Letter resolv'd to return to *Candea*, looking on the Interest of Religion to be more considerable then the hazard of his Life; but the Souldiers cleaving fast to the Plank they scap't on, would not quit the protection of a Prince their Friend, saying, The first cheat was a false Traitors, the second would be a Credulous, and Incantelous Commanders, that they would not return to trust that Viper which had once bit 'em; for if when oblig'd by a voluntary relief he would have Kill'd 'em, what would he now do when provok't by their affronting his bafled Army? that they would thank God for one Miracle without asking an other; that the Governour sent them not as Apostles, but Souldiers; that if they went to Dye for the Faith, they might go without Arms, but their Calling was not to Preach, but with their Sword defend Religion. *Antonio Moniz* seeing the Souldiers cool'd in their Zeal, and obstinate in their Obedience, considering, that if God would save that people, he would find out the means, resolv'd to recover his Fleet; and while he is at Sea, we will to the business of *Hidalcaon*, which we have Retarded.

Antonio Moniz desir'd to return,

His men are against it.

He goes to his Fleet.

18. *Hidalcaon* alarm'd by *Meale*'s being in *Goa*, endeavoured by the Cure of Arms to purge those Disquiets, and because the Warr of *Dio* had weakned the State, thinking to surprize the Governour in the confidence,

Hidalcaon sends Souldiers upon the Continent.

confidence, or careleſneſs of his Victories; knowing alſo his abſence from the City of *Goa*, he fell upon the Territories of *Bardez* and *Salſete*, in the ſecurity of Peace unguarded; He ſent four thouſand Souldiers, who without drawing their Swords took poſſeſſion, making the Peaſants bring in their Fruit, and the Annual Cuſtoms they paid the State. The news of their Incurſion reach't *Goa*, and caus'd no little trouble by taking them unprovided to reſiſt the Enemy. They reſolv'd to expect the Governours return, whoſe name was ſufficient to take down *Hidalcaon's* Pride, only in the Interim to Garriſon the Fortreſs of *Rachol*, with this ſmall Curb to Bridle the invaſion of the Enemy.

History of *India*, Dec. 6. Lib. 4. Cap. 9.

19. Upon the Governours arrival at *Goa*, he beſtow'd the firſt Days on the pleaſure of his Succeſs, but would not paſs any more in eaſe, as one who counted Peace a Vice, Warr his Profeſſion; He immediately went to *Agacaim*, thence diſpatch't *Dom Diogo de Almeyda Freire* with nine hundred men to Diſlodge the Enemy, who with four thouſand Souldiers quartered in the Neighbouring Villages; when the *Moors* heard our men were on their March, without ſtaying to hear our Drums, or ſee our Colours, they retir'd to the Mountain, out of reſpect (as was thought by all) to the Victories of *Dio*, whoſe Fame had ſeis'd the whole *East* with fear and reverence. The *Campagnia* was again brought under our Obedience, enjoying with the Jealouſies of Warr, an inſecure Peace, as was to be expected from a Male-content and Neighbour Prince. *Hidalcaon*, taking himſelf affronted by his mens Flight, made the reputation of his Arms an other cauſe to raiſe Warr, and ſent eight thouſand Souldiers to take in that ground which was in diſpute, whilſt he was making greater Levies, with an intention (as he gave out) where his Kingdome lay at ſtake, to venture his Perſon; but whilſt *Goa* is unalarm'd by the noiſe of his Forces, we will ſpeak of the affairs of *Malaca*, and *Maluco*, diſpos'd by the Governours prudence, and finiſh't by his Fortune.

They retire for fear of ours.

20. *Ber-*

20. *Bernadim de Sousa* was sent Governour to the *Maluco*-Islands, which by their distance from the heart of the State, were of a more fickle Obedience, both for the Subjection of the Natives, and Libertinism of the Governours, who behav'd themselves as Absolute and Independent. *Jordaon de Freitas* had sent the King *Aeyro* to *Goa*, in Chains unbecoming a Crown, and with a false Process drawn against him; which *Dom John de Castro* commanded should be prov'd according to Law, and absolving the poor King from the imputed Crimes, after a Royal entertainment, restor'd the injuries of the innocent Scepter with favour, and honour, Commanding *Bernadim de Sousa* to give him possession of the Kingdome, with more reverence then had been us'd to other Kings, by our Governours, that that Nation might take notice of the States clemency and justice, which held the Scales even betwixt Friends and Subjects.

John de Barro's History of India, Dec. 6 Lib. 1. Cap. 8.

The King Aeyro sent Prisoner to Goa.

Absolv'd by the Governour,

21. *Bernardim de Sousa* arriv'd at the Island of *Ternate*, and getting on Shore, went into the Fortress, without those Ceremonies, the ambition of that people Customarily us'd in the reception of their Governours. *Jordaou de Freitas* who read in the suddain coming of his Successour, and his own guilty Conscience, the Process of his extravagancies, was not a little disquieted, knowing *Dom John de Castro*'s impartiality, that permitted not the Governours, to do, or receive any injuries from the Confederate Kings, and that by *Aeyros* being Justify'd, he must necessarily be Condemn'd; yet gave *Bernardim de Sousa* possession of the Fortress, to whom immediately repair'd *Aeyro*'s Children, more to know their Fathers punishment, then expect his return, so Timerous are mens judgments in their desires; *Bernardim de Sousa* bid them go fetch him to Shore in such State, as it might appear, he rather went to plead Services, then answer Accusations. His Children, though not trusting to the pleasure of such unexpected News, went running to the Sea-side, follow'd by multitudes of

Is brought to Ternate.

of the people, who look't upon, as a thing unusual, Justice against one so Powerfull, admiring the equality of our Laws, so indifferent to Natives, and Strangers. *Aeyro* came on Shore, saying, we had against our selves, given him the Victory, and that he would with his * Finger in his mouth always speak of the Governours excellencies; He carry'd in his hands the Fetters he had on at his departure, making pass-time of the memory of his grievances; by this Justice things in the *Malucos* were for many years in a gratefull Obedience.

* A sign of Admiration amongst them.

Diverse Kings conspire against *Malaca*.

22. *Malaca* at that time enjoy'd a most profound Peace, setled by the friendship and commerce of the Neighbouring Princes; yet the King of *Viantata* finding he had Force enough to set upon any great design, was by strength, and ease put in mind of many forgotten grievances, which his Predecessors had receiv'd from the Kings of *Patana*, and having good correspondence with the Princes of *Queda*, *Pam*, and other Borderers, found a way to bring 'em into a League, making them take their parts in revenging an others Injuries; they put to Sea a great Fleet, and by Capitulations agreed, that the King of *Viantata* should be satisfy'd in being reveng'd on his Enemy, and they go away with the Booty of the Warr for Venturing their Lives in an others quarrel.

How the Commander behaves himself.

23. In this Conjuncture, *Simaon de Mello* was Commander of *Malaca*, and on knowledge of the Breach betwixt those Princes, writ to *Diogo Soarez de Mello*, who was in the Haven of *Patane*, to come to that Fortress, for all those Kings being Friends to the State, he had rather arbitrate then side in their differences; besides, it was in Policy, reason to let 'em be broke by a Warr, that being drain'd, they might Live with more Subjection under the peace and obedience of our Arms, considering time might furnish 'em with an opportunity, and their strength with Courage, our Dominion over them being a sufficient cause for them to hate us, and for a Warr, a strong Army look't for no other pretensions.

24. *Diogo*

24. *Diogo Soarez* not refusing the advice dispatch't some Ships Laden for *China*, and parted himself with two little Galleys for *Malaca*. The King of *Achem* was at this time with twenty great Vessels looking out for Prizes, with the force of a Prince playing the part of a Pirat; He took some Junks of Provisions, and at Sea behav'd himself insolently to some Ships of his Friends, his success heightned his confidence, Landing by Night in the Port of *Malaca*, only to say he had set footing on ground that Liv'd under our obedience, and with this glory wonn solely by stealth, He immediately return'd on Board.

The King of Achem Lands, and immediately retires.

25. The City was in an Uproar, and the fear and night encreas'd the danger, many flying from their own shadows; the Crys of the fearfull only reach't the Fortress, for they were surpris'd with fear without danger. The Commander in chief sent out *Dom Francisco d' Esa* with some Souldiers, who going into the Colony of the *Chelins*, saw in every ones fear and confusion the face of a Warr without an Enemy, who was by this time on Board, carrying with him only the imaginary vanity of having Landed; *Simaon de Mello* was as sensible of the King of *Achem*'s Cowardise, as if it had been an Outrage; so sacred were the Walls of that Fortress, as if to march towards 'em had been an Insolence, to look on them a Crime; He presently set forth a light Vessel, to find out the King of *Achem*'s course, whilst he put to Sea two great Carvels, and six Fly-boats to find out the Enemy. *Diogo Soarez de Mello* with the two Galleys we spake of came at this time into the Haven, as if steer'd by our Fortune to help the Victory. *Dom Francisco d' Esa* was nam'd Commander of this Squadron, who, though ill fitted out, like one who hastens to a suddain quarrel, put to Sea, with instructions, that if in ten days he saw not the Enemy, he should return to Port, not having Provisions for longer time.

The Fleet goes out to find him.

26. They Sail'd eight days without sight of the *Armada*; and arriving at an Island had news the Enemy

was come to an Anchor at *Queda*, a Voyage of two days. *Dom Francisco* resolv'd to proceed, but the Souldiers mutiny'd, alledging, 'twas like a raw Commander to chase a flying Enemy; that their Provisions were already spent; that they came not to Fight with Famine; that if by the Governours orders they were limited to ten days, their Obedience would be better then the Victory; yet *Diogo Soarez de Mello*, though Inferiour in Command, higher in Authority, said, what Captain soever tack't about, he would set upon him first, for he should do the King better service in sinking disobedient Souldiers then valiant Enemies. One fear thus laid with an other, they set Sail for *Queda*, where they heard the Enemy was in Port eight Leagues off, *Dom Francisco* resolv'd, having him so near, to persue; here was the Souldiers murmuring greater then before, though less insolent, seeing the hazard of their fear out-go that of the danger, so as they follow'd the Admiral with greater signs of satisfaction then ever, either to Gild over their former apprehensions, or their souls, presaging the Victory, created more honourable affections.

The Commander hears News of him, and resolves to follow him.

The Souldiers mutiny.

Diogo Soarez quels 'em.

They see, and set on the Enemy.

27. That evening they saw the City *Parlez*, where the Enemy was at an Anchor, in a Bay form'd by the River, at a little distance from the City. The Commander of the Squadron made some of his sound the River, and with Boughs laid out the Chanel, to avoid the Shelves, and knowing by the soundings there was water enough for the Carvels, lay in, as the Enemy with two Galleys, and other Ships, was coming to find out our Fleet; for he was told by his Spies; who from the Shore had only seen the great Carvels, (the Fly-boats, and Galleys being covered by the shelter of a crooked winding Point made there by the River) there were none but Merchant men. The Enemy had sent before two Galleys, which were Convoys to a Fleet of Fly-boats, and finding those Souldiers they imagin'd Merchants, strove to tack about, but the River being narrow,

row, and they coming before the Wind, could not do it, before we first came up with 'em; being in a little time come to Grapling, the Arms and River were Dy'd in Blood. *Diogo Soarez* with fifty Souldiers Boarded the Admiral Galley, and found in the *Moors* such resolute resistance, as all Dy'd, not one yielded, the rest fought with as brave resolution. The Victory was known by the Vessels, not by the Prisoners, it seem'd by so honourable obstinacy that none would out-live his freedome; the Enemies resistance was the proof of our mens Courage, who fought not only with men Valiant, but Desperate.

Diogo Soarez takes the Admiral.

28. The King of *Viantana*, and most of the Confederates had in the mean time receiv'd so good satisfaction from the King of *Patane*, as a Peace was ty'd with stronger Knots, and knowing our Fleet was gone to Sea, by that, concluding the Fortress was left without sufficient Garrison, they design'd to try if that occasion would make their way to free *Malaca* of so troublesome a Neighbour, and made Bold by their hating us, and Cowardly by their fear, they design'd in the semblance of Peace, to disguise a Warr; they sent an experienc't Commander to *Simaon de Mello*, to Condole with him for the King of *Achem*'s destroying our Fleet, and advise him, that on the joy of the Victory he was joyning more force to come upon the Fortress; that he having so few Defendants, Courage must necessarily yield to multitudes, since numbers and opportunities give Victories; that as Friends to the State, they desir'd leave to Land at that Port, and with their Lives redeem the Fortress from so inevitable Ruine, that the World might see they were better Friends in exigencies, then prosperity; besides so Cautelous a message, the Envoy had instructions to observe what Souldiers were in the Fortress, and find out by the Governours countenance what Courage or Fear he betray'd at the news of the loss of his Fleet; the Heart being a more faithfull interpreter of the affections, then the Tongue.

The Embassage of the Confederates.

29. *Simaon*

The Governour of *Malaca's* answer.

29. *Simaon de Mello* perceiving the offer Treachery, and the Messenger a Spy, resolv'd to beat 'em at their own Weapon, making use of Stratagem against Stratagem; He gave 'em thanks for their offer of so seasonable succours, and in return of so great friendship, Challeng'd from 'em the usual gifts for good news, for just then he had receiv'd fresh advice of the Victory his Fleet had obtain'd against the King of *Achem*; and that he had in the Fortress Men and Ammunition to spare, for their service against their Enemies; that the King of *Achem* went flying out of that Port; that in the persute the *Portuguese* had some difficulty, none in the Victory. These words were Credited by the security of the delivery, and the *Moor* being Dismist, Credulous and Discontented at the Governours resolution, and the Victory of the Fleet, reported to those who sent him, that the Governour either understood the design, or was above the apprehension.

News wants from the Fleet.

30. *Simaon de Mello* as things stood was not a little Disquieted, for the stay of the Fleet made the News possible, and accus'd himself for being rash and inconsiderate, to engage the strength of that place against an Enemy, whose Peace brought us no profit, or Ruine glory; for having overcome him, when we were Inferiour in force; 'twould be but a small proof of our Valour to worst him when equal; thus discourst the Governour, as if without a fault there could be no miscarriage; there were gone on the Fleet the Inhabitants of *Malaca*, whose Wives, and Children, with untimely tears bewail'd the Victory, they knew not of; complaining of the Governour, who with other mens Lives acquir'd glory; when an honourable Peace was more suitable to the States exigencies, then an unprofitable Victory; the popular Tumult had grown to Libertinism, if *Franciscus Xaverius* (whom *India* then honour'd as a Penitent, the World now reverenceth as a Saint) had not Bridled the people, by Preaching to them patience in adversity, not only as a Virtue, but Remedy, cautiously, but

The people complain.

Franciscus Xaverius quells 'em.

but compassionately encouraging 'em, with the hopes of better News, which then look't more like a Friends comforting, then a Prophets prognosticks; when, on the day of the Fight, as he was Preaching the ways of Life in the presence of a great Multitude, he was suddainly rap't into a profound Extasis, as taking in the Heavenly secrets in a soft silence, till waking from the Mysterious intermission of his senses, His pleasant Voice burst forth, in Commanding us prostrate before the Altars, to give thanks to the Author of Victories, for at that time had God with our Arms destroy'd the Enemies Fleet; the people out of reverence to the Divine interpreters fore-sight, with gratefull and pious tears prais'd God in his Saint, from the extreams of grief beginning a more secure content. That very Evening as he was in a Chappel instructing the people, he so particularly related the passages of the Battail, as if acquainted with the success from the Author of the Victory; we believe the glorious Saint was the Intercessour, and Oracle of this happiness, whose presaging Soul had by diverse other Divine revelations a fore-sight into hidden secrets. *Malaca* afterward, enjoy'd an hononrable Peace, secur'd by the Victory we have related; but the Governour in *Goa* with his Arms reaking in the Blood of one Battail, was summon'd to an other.

Fore-tells the Victory, and the manner of it.

31. *Martim Affonso de Sousa*, (as we have said before) left things, betwixt *Hidalcaon* and the State, dispos'd for an open Enmity, in which *Dom John de Castro* could not refuse satisfaction without a Warr, or give it, with his reputation. Upon the *Moors* retiring, the Territories of *Bardez* and *Salsete* were under our Obedience, and the fruits of Husbandry grew under the protection of our Arms. *Hidalcaon* seeing the Land before his face, and that likewise the Injury was continued in a Retention, by him counted unjust, did every day by Arms mind us of his Title; alarm'd also by *Meale's* being in *Goa*, (a Poyson which seis'd on the heart of the Kingdome) and considering his stoll'n, and sud-

Hidalcaon's perplexity.

dain Inroads, more provok't then weakned the State, and that by keeping from us Provisions, he impoverish't his Subjects, and inrich't his Neighbours, from whose Ports we were furnish't; He consulted how to set-upon us in open Warr, in which he would venture his Kingdome and Person, leaving the fortune of a Battail to decide the justice of his or our Arms; and being grown Rich by Peace and Tyranny, the expence of that Warr he was to make at his own Doors, was easie. He immediately sent eight thousand Souldiers to get possession of the Land in dispute, whilst more Forces were raising to maintain what they recovered.

He sent's Forces on the main Land.

32. The Governour on the first advice of the Inroad sent *Dom Diogo de Almeyda Freire* with nine hundred *Portuguese*, some paid *Canarins* and a Troop of Horse, to go meet the Enemy, staying himself in *Pangim*, to come with the rest of the Forces to his Relief, if *Hidalcaon* came in Person, a report cast out by the *Moors*, which they would have perswaded us, or were perswaded of themselves; *Dom Diogo de Almeyda* departed with those men, and made a Halt at the Fortress of *Rachol*, before which he had some light Scarmishes with the Enemy, who would not engage, or accept the Battail we offer'd, knowing perhaps we could not endure a long Warr for want of Provisions, and inconvenience of the ground, which was Marish and cut into Rivulets, where we could not Lodge dry, or make use of our Cavallry in all places of the *Campannia*, in some for the wet which hindered our passage, in others for the unevenness; which were disadvantages more easily Conquer'd by the *Moors*, who being Natives of the place better knew the passes, and from their Birth were us'd to the difficulty of treading the Boggs with nimbleness and agility, besides being of the Country were more plentifully provided. *Dom Diogo* seeing at last, 'twas at the Enemies choice to Fight or Retire, and that he wanted Provisions, advis'd the Governour, who sent him Orders to retire with his men into the Fortress

Dom Diogo de Almeyda goes out to him.

The Governour orders him to retire,

tress of *Rachol*, whilst what was to be done was resolv'd.

33. The Governour return'd from *Pangim* to *Goa*, where he put to Council the State of things, and his desires of quelling *Hidalcaon* with a sharper Warr to avoid the troublesomeness of so repeated Inroads, so to have his hands at Liberty to attend other business, which he could not do, leaving so importune a Neighbour arm'd, and unpunish't; yet all were of opinion to deferr the Warr till a fitter opportunity, which would be the next Summer, when our men might Encamp on dry ground, and with more force, Recruited with the Souldiers from the Kingdome, expected by the next Ships; the design of Action not being haste, but Victory.

and debaits the Warr in Council.

34. The Governour though warlick, and impatient, subjected his will to his understanding, expecting a time to call *Hidalcaon* to a more severe account for his insulting; which being agreed on, he ordered *Dom Diogo de Almeyda Freire* to retire with his men, leaving a sufficient Garrison in the Fortress of *Rachol*, so to bridle the courses of the Enemy. The Governour indefatigable in the exercise of Arms, being without a real Warr past his time with the Representation of one. He every day went in the Field, where he commanded the Souldiers to throw the Barr, fence, form Squadrons, encouraging some with Rewards, others with Praise, increasing those Virtues by emulation and exercise; making a quiet and politick Government; a School of Arms, these were the Dances and Comedies, where the people Recreated themselves with usefull and warlick passtime; the frequency of these preludes so well Disciplining the Souldiers, as no occasion of a real Warr, no Accident, or Alarm found 'em wanting. Passing once through the Street call'd our Lady of Light, he saw in a poor House quantity of Arms in a Press kept so clean and bright, that their Lustre and Order in which they were dispos'd so much pleas'd him, as stopping his Horse, he

'Tis deferr'd till an other time.

He exerciseth Warr in Peace.

He countenanceth the Souldiers.

he ask't who Liv'd there; the Master himself hapned to answer him, who was *Francisco Goncalvez*, a Souldier of Fortune. The Governour, after commending his curiosity, and well employing his time, commanded thirty *Pardaos* to be given him to cleanse his Arms, though in his Government there was but little time for Arms to gather Rust.

Receives advice from *Dio*.

35. 'Twas now *August*, and the Governour, as foreseeing future exigencies, lost no time in providing and fitting the Fleet, when *Francisco de Moraes* Commander of a Vessel arriv'd at the Barr of *Goa*, with Letters from *Dom John Mascarenhas*, advising him, that the *Sultan* of *Cambaya* had joyn'd all the forces of his Kingdomes, and gave it out he intended to lay a second Siege before the Fortress, that 'twas necessary this Summer to show him our Arms, that being employ'd to secure things at home, he might forbear his disturbance abroad, chiefly, if our Fleets took from him, the liberty of Sailing, and advantage of Commerce, he would be brought to see, that his Peace with the State, was that on which depended his prosperity.

He communicates it to the Senate, and desires their help.

36. The Governour assembled the Magistracy of the City, to whom he communicated *Dom John Mascarenhas*'s Letter, desiring their help to quell, or reduce this Enemy; though this contribution came immediately on the former Loan, yet was the Governours proposition so well taken by them all, as they offered him Lives and Estates, as if the States service had been the Breeding, and Inheritance of their Children, *India* had not so happy a time in the other Governments. *Dom John de Castro* desir'd of them ten thousand *Pardaos*, which the people readily furnish't; and some rich Citizens Wives, sent him a considerable quantity of Jewels, with a Letter full of honourable Complaints, for his not accepting and spending them, when first offer'd; the Ladies of *Chaul* also, though second in example, shew'd themselves more splendid in their Offer; yet the Governour, sparing in the use and expence of so Loyal presents,

They offer him their Estates,

and the Women their Jewels.

presents, return'd them, with a gratefull acceptance, paying them for so Liberal and Opportune a Service in the honours conferr'd on their Husbands and Children; He advis'd the Inhabitants of *Bacaim* and *Chaul* of the Commander of *Dio*'s intimation, of the charges of the Fleet, and his necessity of their Assistance, who so willingly comply'd with the King's occasions, as if they took new occasions of danger and expence, in payment of former Services.

He adviseth *Chaul* and *Bacaim*.

37. As the Governour was busie in fitting and providing the Fleet, he receiv'd News that two Ships from the Kingdome who had Out-sail'd their Conserve were come to an Anchor at the Barr of *Goa*. That year there came from the Kingdome six Ships, without any to command the Squadron; the Commanders of those which arriv'd were *Balthasar Lobo de Sousa*, and *Francisco de Gouvea*, of the four which were missing, *Dom Francisco de Lima* in the Saint *Philip*, who came with a Commission to be Admiral of *Goa*, *Francisco da Cunha* in the *Zambuco*, these two departed late in the Year, and arriv'd at the Barr the three and twentieth of *September*. The Commander of the other Ship call'd the *Burgalese* was *Bernando Nazer*, who Wintred in *Sacotora*, and came to *Goa* the latter end of *May*. The other was Commanded by *Dom Pedro da Sylva da Gama* Son to the Lord Admiral, design'd for *Malaca*, and by the unskilfulness of the Pilot lost amongst *Angoxa* Islands; yet the men scap't, who got to *Mocambique*, and thence Ship't on several Vessels came to *India*. These Ships brought the Governour orders to enlarge the Fortress at *Mocambique*, upon the News of the * *Rumes* coming thither, and 'twas necessary to secure the Inhabitants, and Port (which was the chief Scale of our Ships) taking from the Enemy the possibility of hindering our Trade with *Sofala*, and *Cuama*.

Ships arrive from the Kingdome.

The orders they brought.

* *Rumes*, are Natives of that part about *Constantinople* call'd *Romania*, (which the *Turks* now call *Rumeli*) from the priviledge granted by Pope *Sylvester* to *Constantine* the Great, upon his removing the seat of the Empire, to call *Constantinople*, *Rome*.

 38. The

Warr resolv'd against *Hidalcaon.*

38. The Governour had three thousand *Portuguese* Souldiers, and some Auxiliaries of *Naires* from *Cochim*, the greatest Army he ever had in *India*, and considering *Hidalcaon* (taking his opportunity when no Body was left in *Goa* able to resist him) might in his absence molest the State, He resolv'd to find him out in the Inland, and force him to Fight; having for so necessary a Warr, his time and strength Limited; He acquainted the Magistrates of the City, and Heads of the Militia, with this resolution, who all agreed in the seasonableness of the occasion. The Governour more then ordinarily quick in Execution, having his men ready, divided the Souldiers (as the manner of *India* is) into five Squadrons, commanded by his Son *Dom Alvaro*, *Dom Bernardo*, and *Dom Antonio de Noronha*, (Sons to the Vice-King *Dom Garcia de Noronha*) *Manoel de Sousa de Sepulveda*, and *Vasco da Cunha*. *Dom Diogo de Almeyda Freire* went also with two hundred Horse, and the Inhabitants of *Goa*, to whom joyn'd themselves the Bores of the Country, in all one thousand five hundred. *Francisco de Mello* with three hundred *Portuguese*, and some foot of the Natives, was Commander of the Fortress of *Rachol*, to whom the Governour sent word to come and joyn him at *Margaon*.

The order of his men.

Embassadours from *Canara* come to the Governour.

39. At this time came Embassadours to *Goa* from the King of *Canara*, desiring a League with the State, to assist him in disturbing his Borderer *Hidalcaon*. This Kingdome, is for the greatness of Empire, the most famous of the *East*; for the story of its beginning, the most fall'n, telling a thousand Apocryphal traditions, which flattery makes use of to adore the Prince. The Governour gave Audience to the Embassadours, with Ceremonies suitable to the King's ambition, and the States grandeur; and immediately concluded a Friendship on conditions honourable for both Crowns. *Hidalcaon* understanding the Governours resolution, retir'd his In-land Garrisons, as if avoiding the blow of the first invasion, endeavouring to weary out the State with

He hears, and dispatcheth the Embassadours.

Hidalcaon retires his men.

with a suddain and incursive Warr; to them easie, to us intolerable.

40. The Governour had intelligence the *Moors* were got together at *Ponda*, protected there by the Artillery of their Fortress; some of the Commanders were not for the Governours following the Enemy who fled, this opinion was Countenanc't by the most experienc't Souldiery; but *Dom John de Castro*, unwilling to put on his Arms in vain, Commanded the marching on, saying he would at his own Home chastise *Hidalcaon*; this resolution was agreeable to the Souldiers who believ'd, that in the Fortune of the General was much of the Victory. The Camp that day march't two Leagues, and was in the Evening in sight of the Enemy; who with a Body of two thousand men, had made an halt on the other side of a River to hinder their passage.

The Governour follows them.

41. *Dom Alvaro de Castro* who Commanded the Vanguard leap't into the River, at the same time Wading and Fighting; the Enemy charg'd them with their Musquets, and Kill'd some of his men, yet without hindering, or retarding the rest who went forward; most of the Commanders in diverse places past the River, and gotten over found *Dom Alvaro* engag'd with the *Moors*, who already were so prest as to give ground; for not intending to Fight in the open Field, we having Conquer'd the River, they gave over opposing us, retiring in good order to their Fortress of *Ponda*. The Governour commanded his men to follow 'em, which they did that day over Crows-feet, which Wounded many; when come to *Ponda*, they saw all *Hidalcaon*'s Officers drawn up in a posture, to give or accept Battail. The Governour keeping the same pace of his March, commanded his men to fall on; the *Moors* seem'd in their resolution to distinguish the person of *Dom John de Castro*, and as if yielding to the report of his Name quitted the Field, where only his respect got the Victory. The Enemy retir'd to the Mountain, where the difficulty of the way kept off the persute. *Dom Alvaro*

Dom Alvaro Fights in the Vanguard.

The *Moors* fly.

The Governour commands his men to follow.

They retire to the Mountain.

Alvaro went into the Fortress, which he found forsaken; many mov'd for the sleighting it, but the Governour voting more Haughtily, ordered that Refuge should be left for the poor Fugitives. 'Twas done in scorn, yet look't like compassion.

42. The Land was once more under our obedience, without a firm Peace, or continued Warr. *Hidalcaan* was strong enough to hinder us of the Crop, but not enjoy it; and now fought more for his Reputation then the advantage of the *Campagnia*. The Governour return'd to *Goa*, where the Fleet was ready to go Northward, having no other place to rest in but the Sea, or Field; and the season calling on Board, and success satisfying the Souldiery, neither proclamation or diligence was necessary for their Embarking.

He returns to *Goa*.

43. The Governour put to Sea with one hundred and threescore Vessels, Commanded by *Dom Alvaro de Castro*, *Dom Roque Tello*, *Dom Pedro da Sylva da Gama*, *Dom John de Abranchez*, *Dom Iorge* of '*Eca*, *Dom Bernardo da Sylva*, *Vasco da Cunha*, *Francisco de Lima*, *Francisco da Sylva de Menezes*, *Dom Iorge de Menezes Baroche*, *Manoel de Sousa de Sepulveda*, *Cide de Sousa*, *Duarte Pereira*, *Diogo de Sousa*, *Garcia Rodriguez de Tavora*, *Dom John de Attayde*, *Dom John Lobo*, *Gaspar de Miranda*, *Dom Bras de Almeyda*, *Iorge da Sylva*, *Dom Pedro de Almeyda*, *Pedro de Attayde Inferno*, *Antonio Moniz Barretto*, *Cosme Eanes* Secretary, *Melchior Correa*, *Sebastion Lopez Lobatto*, *Antonio de Sa*, *Alvaro Serraon*, *Dom Antonio de Noronha*, *Diogo Alvarez Tellez*, *Antonio Henriquez*, *Aleixo de Abreu*, *Antonio Diaz*, *Balthasar Diaz*, *Balthasar Lopez da Costa*, *Damiaon de Sousa*, *Manoel de Sa*, *Fernaon de Lima*, *Alonso de Bonifacio*, *Antonio Rebello*, *Antonio Rodriguez Pereira*, *Melchior Cardoso*, *Cosme Fernandez*, *Nuno Fernandez*, *Francisco Marquez*, *Duarte Diaz*, *Diogo Goncalvez*, *Francisco Alvarez*, *Francisco Varella*, *Luis de Almeyda*, *Francisco de Britto*, *Goncalo Gomez*, *Gregorio de Vasconcellos*, *Gomez Vidal* Captain of the Governours Life-guard, *Antonio Pessoa* Purveyor of

Goes again to *Dio*.

of the Navies Provision, *Goncalo Falcaon*, *Goncalo de Valladarez*, *Galaor de Barros*, *Gaspar Pirez*, *John Fernandez de Vasconcellos*, *Fernand' Alvarez*, *John Soarez*, *Ignacio Coutinho*, *Joaon Cardoso*, *Joaon Nunez Homem*, *Joaon Lopez*, *Lopo de Faria*, *Manoel Pinto*, *Lopo Soarez*, *Manoel Pinheiro*, *Lopo Fernandez*, *Manoel Affonso*, *Marcos Fernandez*, *Nuno Goncalvez de Leaon*, *Pero de Caceres*, *Pero de Moura*, *Ruy Pirez*, *Pero Affonso*, *Pero Preto*, *Luis Lobatto*, *Simaon de Areda*, *Francisco de Cunha*, *Simaon Bernardez*, *Thome Branco* chief Pilot of the Coast, *Coge Percoli* Interpreter; the Ships also which came from *Cochim*, were Commanded by our men; there were in this Conserve some Ships of particulars, who out of kindness to the Governour freely serv'd the State.

44. The Governour with all the Fleet came to an Anchor at *Bacaim*, whence he sent some Spies to *Cambaya*, to observe the Enemies force and design, whose strength was in all those Ports talk't of with fear and amasement, and the *Guzarats* out of pride, or credulity, gave it out, the *Sultan* might at that time bring the State under his Lash; here the Governour had intelligence, that *Caracem*, Son-in-law to *Coge-Sofar*, on presumption of the Neighbourhood of the Army, was with a small Garrison in the Fortress of *Surat*; *Dom John de Castro* desiring to set on some of those places which took shelter under the Enemy, sent his Son *Dom Alvaro* with sixty Sail, to go up the River of *Surat*, and to employ some Person of trust to observe the state of the Fortress, or get intelligence with what Provisions or Garrison *Caracem* was there, and if he thought he could by Scaling take the Fortress, immediately to give an assault, for by the print of his footsteps he would come to his Relief.

Arrives at *Bacaim*.

Sends *Dom Alvaro* to *Surat*.

45. *Dom Alvaro* arriv'd with his Fleet at the first Road lying in the mouth of the River, and presently sent off *Dom Iorge de Menezes Baroche* with six Fly-boats to survey the Fortress. *Dom Iorge* went up the River, Rowing softly, till coming in sight of the Fortress they

Dom Alvaro sends *Dom Iorge* before,

Shot at him; those in the Boats, either out of fear, or caution, immediately went about, though *Dom Iorge* hal'd 'em to stay. Here was the greatest danger where none was apprehended; for from a Colony of the *Abessines*, which lies upon the River, came repeated Shot, which *Dom Iorge* observing went on Shore, and entring the Village, gain'd the Guns of the Redouts with so great courage and presence of mind, as to carry 'em on Board, maugre the resistance of those who came to the rescue; this security heightned the opinion of our strength, the Enemy perhaps measuring our force by our daring.

and two other Captains.

46. *Dom Alvaro* having sent *Dom Iorge* before with the Fly-boats, sent after him two more, Commanded by *Francisco da Sylva de Menezes*, and *John Fernandez de Vasconcellos*, who desiring some intelligence from the Shore, came to Anchor at a Road a little short of the Colony of the *Abessines*; whence they sent off some Mariners to water, who getting on Shore walk't about a Canon-shot. *Caracem*, at the report of the Guns, (which as we now said were Shot from the *Abessines* Colony) sent five hundred *Turks* to their Relief, who found the Posts lost, and the Guns on Board, and Marching on were discovered by the Mariners who were getting water, and gave the Alarm to *Francisco da Sylva* that the Enemy appear'd, *Francisco da Sylva*, seconded by *John Fernandez de Vasconcellos*, went to their Relief, and forming a close Body, invested the *Turks*, and Routed 'em, some remaining Dead on the place by the Shot of our Musquetteers. *Dom Iorge* in his return, seeing the Boats at an Anchor, and our men Fighting on shore, turn'd his Ships head to the Land, and came seasonably to charge the Enemy, who retir'd flying; leaving some of their Companions dead on the place. This Victory cost us one Souldier.

Their success.

They return to *Dom Alvaro*.

47. Our men got on Board, and in Company of *Dom Iorge* went toward the Fleet, who reporting his success and observations to *Dom Alvaro*, 'twas thought by the Officers,

Officers, the atchievement was not seasonable, the Fleet being discovered, and the Coast alarm'd; only *Dom Jorge* obstinately insisted, that they ought to fall upon the Fortress, his height of mind being the best argument; but the contrary opinion was so strongly urg'd, that the most happy success could not have been faultless.

48. While *Dom Alvaro* was in the River of *Surat*, the Governour at *Bacaim* dispatch't diverse affairs; and being Facetious as well as Valiant, gave out He was going to surprise the *Sultan* in *Amadabat*, where in sight of the *Turks* who guarded him he would roast him Alive, and this report being, by so great Victories, credited, 'twas current amongst these timerous and credulous *Moors*. The Governour to advance their fear or his own gallantry, bespoke some great Spits, as one who in the interval of more weighty business delighted in Witty diversion. The Souldiers of those times us'd to wear at their Girdles little bright Axes, which serv'd to cut the Rigging and Tackling of their Prizes, as also to break open Chests and Bundels, this was the true use, the first a pretence. The Governour not liking Arms design'd for so mean service, and seeing by chance *Fausto Serraon de Calvos* a spruce Souldier, pass by with an Ax, told him, that only a Sword became men of honour; Sir, answer'd the Souldier, without this Ax your honours Spits will be of little use, because we shall not be able to Roast the King of *Cambaya* whole.

What the Governour did at *Bacaim*.

History of *India*, Dec. 6. Lib. 5. Cap. 7.

49. The Governour went to joyn his Son at the Barr of *Surat*, where he had intelligence the Fortress was Reliev'd; from thence with all his Fleet together he went to *Baroche*, from that Port dispatch't *Francisco de Sequeira* (Commander of the *Naires* of *Cochim*) to sound the River, and see what was to be done, informing himself by his sight of the conditions of the Fortress. This Captain went up the River till he came in sight of the *Sultan*'s Army; which o'erspread a very large Plain; the report was, he had brought into the

He goes to joyn his Son.

Field

Field two hundred thousand Souldiers; the truth is, the multitudes were so great as to cover that and the adjacent *Campagnia*. He reported what he had seen to the Governour, who heightned to see himself so fear'd, would for the credit of his own Fame face the Enemy; He gave orders for the weighing of the Fleet, and Sail'd up, till he cast Anchor in sight of an Army whose numbers drunk up Rivers; and going on Shore, laid out his ground and presented Battail to the *Sultan*. So stout an Action, as amongst the most memorable of the World ought not to be the second. The *Sultan*, neither accepted or deny'd Fighting, but expected to be fall'n on as well as found out; he saw the Governour, but would not see his Sword. *Dom John de Castro*, hunting after new glory in extraordinary Actions, assembled the Officers and Gentlemen of name, to whom he spoke to this purpose.

Makes a Speech to his men.

50. "We have before us the greatest King of *Asia*, "and greatest Army, Fortune is seeking out occasions "to make us glorious, that after this Victory, we may "lay up our Arms in the obedience of the *East*. I allow "the great inequality betwixt the Armies, but we "count not our Troops by number, but gallantry. "Those are the same we so lately beat at *Dio*; we need "not give 'em new Wounds; only make the Incision "greater of those which are yet open; their numbers "heighten their fear, seeing all ways of saving them-"selves Obstructed: if but yesterday when they held "us Besieg'd they left us the Field, how will they stand "in our way when Victorious? They who have lost "their own honour, are but ill maintainers of their "Kings; our strength is greater then the Enemies, on "our side fight Fame and Victory; I believe there's "none here; who would part with his share of this days "glory.

The Gentlemens and Officers answer.

51. The Gentlemen and Souldiers disswaded the Governour from so hazardous an attempt; for in so disproportionable Forces the very Victory was blameworthy;

worthy; that great men trusted more to Reason then Fortune; that he should look to his preservation having an over-plus of Fame; that 'twas enough to have Landed, and on his own ground bid the *Sultan* Battail. The Governour suffered himself to be overcome by those Reasons, more apprehending the fault, then danger. *Dom Iorge* desir'd five hundred Musquetteers with them to Skirmish with the Enemy; but as they had put by *Dom John de Castro's* full Blow for the Battail, he seem'd unwilling to give the *Sultan* so sleight a Wound; He staid three hours in the Field without the Enemies moving, then re-imbark't his Souldiers, so unscar'd and full of security as if in one of the States Ports; the most glorious Action we ever perform'd without Blood.

He stays three hours in the Field, and goes on Board.

52. The Governour from *Baroche* crost over to *Dio*, and sent some Ships into the Bay of *Cambayu* to destroy those places on the Coast our Sword had pardoned; these spoil'd the Gardens, and Groves of Plam-trees Planted for the Inhabitants maintenance and recreation; burnt store of Ships, pull'd down Stately buildings, whose destruction and memory is yet preserv'd in their waste Ruins.

The hurt he doth.

53. The Governour recovered *Dio*, where the Commander in chief came to receive him at the Sea-side, and the Natives of the Island made Holy-day, as proud to be under the subjection of so Valiant an Enemy. *Dom John Mascarenhas* put him in mind of the leave he had obtain'd to go for the Kingdome, which the Governour was unwilling to grant, nor could deny; some Gentlemen had refus'd the Government of the place, fearing, as appear'd, not to have the same opportunities as their Predecessours. *Lewis Falcaon*, who came from being Governour in *Ormus*, came then into Port, before him had come to the Governour some complaints of his Carriage, tolerable, because not discrediting the Courage and Justice of his Government. The Governour in private acquainted him with the accusations

Arrives at *Dio*.

Dom John Mascarenhas resigns the Government of the place.

laid to his charge by his Enemies, which as a Friend he was willing to forget, could not as a Magistrate; that he might by new Services silence all former miscarriages, remaining in that Fortress, which had so on it the Eyes of his Majesty and the whole World. *Lewis Falcaon* accepted it, thanking the Governour for so honourable Correction, offering besides to spend in the place what he had got in *Ormus*, or possest in the Kingdome. *Dom John de Castro*, with signal favours, commended, and provok't this Gallantry.

The Governour gives it to *Lewis Falcaon.*

54. Upon concluding the business of *Dio*, the Governour set Sail directly for *Bacaim*, going in sight of the Coast of *Por*, and *Mangalor*, where he Burnt the Cities of *Pate*, and *Patane*; the Inhabitants to avoid the Lash, sav'd their Lives and part of their Estates in the Mountain; wanting Courage or Conduct to defend themselves or Dye in their Houses; one hundred and fourscore Vessels which lay in several Ports were Burnt by his Order, the poor owners with unprofitable tears looking on. The crys and groans were heard at a distance, and despis'd by Anger, and Victory. The Governour gave order, to spare some Old men, and Children, who could not save themselves; Compassion, importune to the Souldiery; pleasing to Humanity; the Booty was given up to the Fire, the Prize not being so notable, as the desolation; many other places on that Coast, of no name, were Destroy'd; this Siege of *Dio* being more famous for Vengeance then Victory.

Sets Sail, the mischiei he doth.

His compassion.

55. The Governour went from hence to *Bacaim*, resolving to spend the rest of that Summer in the Warr of *Cambaya*; thence he sent some Spies to observe the March of the Enemy, who inform'd him, that in the Court at *Amadebat* there was not a Family without tears; and that the *Sultan* by a severe Decree had forbid the mentioning the Siege and Battail of *Dio*; as if Laws could command grief and memory. The Governour heard by the same Envoys, that the Fortresses of *Surat*, and *Baroche*, were quitted at the sight of *Dom*

He goes to *Bacaim*,

is sensible of the not taking *Surat*,

Alvaro's

Alvaro's Fleet, and that he might by Scale have taken them, had he not been hindered by the disswasions of his Officers; which *Dom John de Castro* took so to heart, as if 'twere necessary to divine opportunities, and his temper burst forth into words, which accus'd the Commanders of the Fleet of neglect and remisness.

56. The Governour employ'd the short Leisure he had at *Bacaim* in writing for the Kingdome, making so honourable mention to the King of those who had serv'd him, as amongst so many eminent Virtues, this zeal, or gratitude seem'd to be singular, and the Souldiers thereby improv'd in Courage, having security that their General would not be wanting in his Zeal or Rewards.

puts the King in mind of those who had serv'd him.

57. *Hidalcaon* considering that the States strength was, though Triumphant, broken with so many Victories, came in again to get possession of the In-land with an Army of twenty thousand Foot, under the Command of *Casa Batecaon*, a stout *Turk* born in *Dalmatia*, experienc't in the Languages, and Discipline of *Europe*; He without any opposition subjected the Country, forcing some few of our Souldiers to retreat to the Fortress of *Rachol*, who advis'd *Goa* of the strength of the Enemy.

Hidalcaon renews the Warr.

58. Upon this advice, *Dom Diogo de Almeyda*, by Counsel of the Bishop, (then Governour) and of some Gentlemen and Souldiers, resolv'd to dislodge the *Moors* with the standing Militia, before they Encamp't themselves, and increasing in strength and boldness fac't the Walls of *Goa*, the Metrapolitan City. The men who were to go with him being appointed and ready to March, the Magistracy and Government of this City came expostulating and protesting against their going; that the Head of the State was not to be ventured on so disproportionable Forces; that the Governour was at *Bacaim* with a Fleet full of Victorious Souldiers, able to chastise the Enemy, against whom he would bring, as a second Army, his Fame and Fortune.

The Commander at *Goa* desires to go against him.

The City hinders him.

59. The

Adviseth the Governour.

59. The dispute continued so hot betwixt the Souldiers and Citizens, as to come near Sedition, and Mutiny, these standing for the preservation of the City, the other on the reputation of our Armies; the difference was at last decided and compos'd, that the Governour being so near, should be acquainted with the business, who understanding the Civil Government intermedled in ordering the Warr, chid sharply their animosity, allow'd and confirm'd *Diogo de Almeyda's* resolution of finding out the Enemy, sending him orders to stay with his men at *Pangim*, where he would in few days joyn him.

He immediately goes on Board.

60. *Dom John de Castro* had scarce laid down his Pen, with which he writ for the Kingdome, when he again took in hand his Sword; the same day he receiv'd the advice, he commanded a great Gun to be Shot off to warn the Fleet to be in readiness to weigh, and the next, set Sail with the whole *Armado*, and Coasting went in sight of the City *Dabul*, famous for the marks our Arms had before left there, and now the chief Scale of *Hidalcaon's* Ports; at a distance were seen a great many Gardens, Orchards, and proud Buildings, which shew'd the Luxury and Grandeur of the Inhabitants; the City contains about four thousand Families, hath two Forts, and some Redouts which defend the entrance into the Harbour, and though the Action requir'd much Deliberation, the Governour resolv'd on the undertaking.

Goes in sight of *Dabul*.

61. The Fleet that Evening went Coasting in sight of the City, observing its Anchorage and Defence; the next Morning by break of day the Governour commanded his Son *Dom Alvaro* with two thousand men to go into Boats and get on Shore, he being one of the first, who amongst many repeated Shot got footing; here was the Enemies resistance in hindering, or retarding our passage; the Battail was for some time without inclining, the place and cause heightning their Bravery in Fighting; the Crys of Women and Children

Dom Alvaro gets on Shore.

in

in their Ears, made them receive Wounds without pain or fear; the Dead who fell were not an example for their Fear but Vengeance. The Blood ran down on both sides, and the resoluteness of both parties made the success Contingent, when the Governour with the rest of his men came in, and charg'd the Enemy so home, as he began to abate in his Defence; they were by degrees giving ground, till by a declar'd flying they left us the Victory. The Governour mingled with the *Moors* entred the City, where many Dy'd in sight of their Wives they could neither forsake nor defend. The slaughter was succeeded by Covetousness, the Booty was not inferiour to the Victory; the Vessels of the Fleet could scarce take in the pillage. The City in a few hours was Consum'd by a Lamentable fire, its deplorable Ruins once more preserving the memory of this and a former Destruction. We lost in this Action five Souldiers, the Enemy two hundred, the number of the Wounded was greater.

The Governour follows him, and takes the City.

62. The Governour leaving the City in Flames re-imbark'd, and steer'd for *Agacaim*, where he expected *Dom Diogo de Almeyda* with one hundred and fifty Horse, and the standing Militia, and with store of Barks to pass the men; the Governour staid here one day, to inform himself of the Enemies force, and design, and on the next (the Apostle Saint *Thomas*'s Eve) resolv'd to fall on the *Moors*, and in the Battail invoke the name of the Saint, not to deprive him of the honour of the Protection of *India*, purchas'd by his Preaching, and shedding his Blood on the Cross of his Martyrdome.

Arrives at *Agacaim*.

63. The Enemy was quartered at a Town call'd *Morgaon*, not farr from *Agacaim*; the Governour having notice of it, form'd his men into two Battallions, he gave the first to his Son *Dom Alvaro de Castro*, the Companion of his Victories, with him were the *Naires* of *Cochim*, and Citizens of *Goa*; the second (which he kept for himself) was made up of all the Gentlemen and Souldiers of the Fleet, who in their Wings had the

He falls on the Enemy.

City-horse, in this order did he March, sending some Horse before to discover the Camp.

64. The *Moors* were spread without Order or Discipline, as men who neither fear'd nor expected an Enemy; some of their Souldiers, who went up and down the Camp, spy'd our Colours, and by their sight, or intelligence, knowing the Governour look't out for 'em, went in a fright to advise *Cala Batecaon*, aggravating our strength, which their fear, and the distance made greater. The *Turk* alarm'd at the approach of so Victorious Arms, was not Master of more consideration, then by his Flight to be an example to his men; they left in their quarters, Tents, Provision, and Baggage, and what meat was for Supper, then almost ready; for the difficulty of our March a most necessary and pleasant Booty. The Governour by this Flight began to be in possession of the Land and Victory.

They fly.

65. The *Moors* went over a deep River, only to be past by some Loggs of Wood laid across instead of a Bridge, which the Enemy to hinder our persute cut in pieces, yet in so much haste, as the Earth which fell down, left open a passage, not without difficulty, though without danger. *Dom Alvaro* in this place set upon passing the River, beginning to wade by few at a time, as the straightness of the ground permitted.

Dom Alvaro follows 'em.

66. The Enemy was not so out of himself as to lose the occasion of Fighting on so eminent advantages; He turn'd with his men to the River, shewing us that so cautious fear was Stratagem. The *Moors* charg'd our men as they were passing, and so were timorous, few, and disordered; The Governour, with his Voice, command, and presence, encourag'd them to go over, but fear o'recame their Obedience; the first turn'd back, not without loss of Blood, and with worse marks then their Wounds. At this time the Governour's impatience attempted the River in different places. *Dom Diogo de Almeyda* waded it with a Troop of Horse, finding where he went better Foording, and Fortune, for he fell

They turn.

fell in with the *Moors* General who was on Horse-back, ordering and encouraging his men, whom he set upon with great Bravery; The *Turk* with the shock fell to the ground, but rising again without loss of his judgment laid hold on his Semitar, and went after *Dom Diogo*, who though he lost not his Saddle, was for a while with the force of the Blow dis-inabled, but coming again to himself the second time charg'd the *Turk*, and (though two Souldiers endeavoured to rescue him) left him with many Wounds measuring the ground. *Dom Diogo* kills the General.

67. The other Commanders, though with difficulty, crost the River, put upon't by the Governours example, whom they saw engag'd with the Enemy, and was more envy'd then obey'd by his own Souldiers, who scattered and disordered, some cautious, others heady cast themselves into the River; but when all his men were over, he so Vigorously charg'd the Enemy, as not able to endure the shock of the Battail he gave ground. The Governour, sparing no accident favourable to his Fortune, so prest the *Moors*, grown fearfull and out of order, as in a little time to Rivet the Victory. Few of ours Dy'd, the Wounded were more; the Slaughter was great amongst the *Moors*, and greater in the Chase then Fight, for our men making no Prisoners, did with the same stroke take off those who resisted or yielded. *Dom Alvaro de Castro* by Commanding, and Fighting, never more appear'd the Son of such a Father, then in this Action; The other Gentlemen and Cavalliers so equally behav'd themselves in their Courage, as not one deserv'd to be nam'd second. By the calling on Saint *Thomas*, and on his Day, was this Battail won, who gave the *Eastern* Catholicks an eminent proof of his Patronage. This so memorable Defeat is yet, so many years afterwards, sung by the young Ladies of *Goa*, who in the easiness of unforc't Verses, have invented Praise without artifice or flattery.

The Governour Fights, got the Victory.

On Saint *Thomas's* day, and by his mediation.

68. The Governour disbanded his men, and went to rest

rest himself at *Pangim*, excusing keeping *Christmas* at *Goa*, in a just contempt of Palmes, and martial Triumpes, since his Name was now in the Vogue of the World above all other applause; here he dispatch't the Ships of Burden which were to go for the Kingdome, on which went *Dom John Mascarenhas*, a Man more constant in the difficulties of *Asia*, then in the adversities of his Native Country; he was receiv'd by the King and Nobility, with extraordinary honours, yet were not his Rewards answerable to his Services; He was of the Council of State to the King *Dom Sebastion*, afterwards one of the Governours of the Kingdome. He Marry'd *Dona Elena* Daughter to *Dom John de Castellbranco*, by whom he left a most Renown'd and Loyal Posterity.

He dispatcheth Ships for the Kingdome.

Dom John Mascarenhas's praise.

69. *Dom John de Castro* thought not *Hidalcaon* yet sufficiently Curb'd by our Arms, and resolv'd with a sharper Warr to bring him under; He secur'd with a strong Garrison the Territories of *Salsete*, leaving there *Dom Diogo de Almeyda* with six score Horse, and one thousand Foot of the place, and ordered some Ships to lye in the Rivers of *Rachol*, to defend the Neighbouring Villages, the Labourers having quitted the grounds, seeing their Dominion, by the ficklenes of Warr, casual and uncertain. The Governour also understanding how easie it was to pull down a declining Kingdome, carry'd on the Warr against *Hidalcaon*, desiring the States Rivals might take warning by his Punishment; He embark't those Souldiers he had always in readiness, by being their Companion in dangers, and Father in difficulties, and setting Sail, went along all *Hidalcaon's* Coast, which he so impartially Destroy'd, as not to leave one place to comfort an others miseries, none was freed by their resistance, some by their distance.

The Governour carries on the Warr.

What hurt he doth.

70. There was another *Dabul* call'd the upper, two Leagues from the Shore, which by its strength and distance, was the Rich depository of a great many Estates; but the protection of the In-land was not sufficient to exempt

He destroys upper *Dabul*.

exempt it from the Fortune of the rest, for the Governour march't to it, giving the first danger of the Van-guard to his Son *Dom Alvaro*, (these were the favours of that Father, and those times) who coming to the place, found the *Moors* had secur'd their Persons and Estates in the Mountain, nothing being left to recommend the Victory; what was, serv'd only for Destruction, for the Buildings which could be no Boory pay'd for't by their Ruine. The Mosques and Temples were thrown to the ground, and the Idols broke and prostrate, our Anger not differencing stone from stone, and the *Moors* and *Pagans* bewail'd with the same tears their Gods and own miseries; The fury of our Arms went to the Desolating the *Campagnia*, destroying the Flocks, and Groves of Palmes, that the Warr might be attended by Famine, a Sword not to be scap't by Flight or Resistance. All was in fine so wasted, as the difference berween the Villages, and *Campagnia*, was not by the sight, but memory. and the *Campagnia*.

71. The Governour retreated to *Bacaim*, whence he design'd his Arms for the Warr of *Cambaya*, setting forth some Vessels to Endammage all that Coast, and make Prize of the *Meca* Fleet, which came to an Anchor in the Ports of that Bay; this was happily perform'd by *Dom Antonio de Noronha*, and *Dom Iorge Baroche*, who by their Prizes, and Victories, rais'd the States strength, and reputation; our Arms in *Dom John de Castro*'s time being so fear'd or respected, that most of the Princes of *Asia*, Borderers, and Remote, became (to defend, or secure their Kingdoms with the protection of our Forces) by voluntary Obedience the States Tributaries; of this truth the Kings of *Campar*, and *Caxem* were no sleight Arguments. Goes to *Bacaim*. Spoils *Cambaya*.

72. Our Chronicles (and Forein with greater amasement) relate that famous Seige of *Dio*, held out by *Antonio da Sylveira*, by whom the *Turks* Arms in *India* receiv'd the first, or greatest Baffle; Their General in this expedition was *Rax Solimon*, who, after the loss A Character of *Rax Solimon*.

See *John de Barro's* History of *India*, Dec. 5. Lib. 4.

loss of a great part of his *Armado* in the Siege, for fear of our Ships at Anchor in the Port, retir'd Flying, and left on Shore his Baggage and Wounded; and seeing he could not atchieve what he promis'd his Master, (whose Pride, and Imperiousness us'd not to receive satisfaction for miscarriages, or misfortunes) ventured, rather then his Head, his Loyalty; He went into the Port of *Adem* under Colour of Friendship, where the King sent to Visit him, with Regallios and Refreshments from Shore, but was cautious and vigilant to preserve the City, for the *Bashaw's* Force and Loyalty was suspitious. The *Turk*, who saw his Treason fear'd or discovered, design'd to surprise the City by Scaling, but was afraid of the Fortress of the place, and Courage of the *Arabians*, and on that, had Recourse to an other Stratagem, more base, and more secure, which was to excuse himself to the King for not coming into the City, in fear to lose the favourable Wind; that he desir'd to see him on Board, for he was to communicate to him some business from the Grand Signior to the great advantage of his Kingdome. The poor King, facil, or credulous in the good of his State, went immediately to meet the *Bashaw* at Sea, secure in an innocent Conscience; but the Tyrant forgetting Faith, and Humanity, made him with Scoffs and Derision, (a cruel delight in so foul a Treason) be Beheaded in the Galley. 'Twas easie for the *Bashaw* upon the Death of the King to seise on the City, frighted and confus'd at the violent Murder of their Prince; and because the *Turkish* Neighbourhood cost the State blood, and trouble, we will in brief give you this relation of the place.

His coming to *Adem*.

Beheads the King.

The situation of *Adem*.

73. It is situate on the Coast of *Arabia* the happy, in twelve degrees, and fifteen minutes of *Northern* Latitude, protected by a little Mountain, which with some Castles defends the entrance of the Harbour; it lies in the mouth of the Straight, the Port bold, capable to Anchor Ships of any burden, though expos'd to *Westerly* winds, which are the *Monsones* in Summer. Art and

Nature have made it Tenable by Land, securing it from the ambition of the Neighbour Princes and the incursions of the Mountainous *Arabs*, who molest the Country with troublesome Inroads; there is in the Port a little Island, tolerably Fortify'd, call'd by the Natives *Cira*, before it is an other safe Harbour, sheltered from many Winds, where the *Mecca* Fleet use to come to an Anchor. There are no Rivers or Fountains to water the ground, it doth not sometimes Rain for two or three years, whether it be the nature of the Clime, or some hidden Judgment, so as they fetch their water at a distance with *Caravans* of Camels. The chief Commodity of the place is Rubarb, but that which brings in most profit is the Anchorage of Ships which pass the Straight. The Nation is Warlick and Cruel, goes willingly to the Warr, though more for Plunder, then Victory.

74. The *Bashaw* having seis'd on the City, and seeing himself, though an Intruder, obey'd, began with diverse Oppressions to break the people, unarming 'em, that their fear, and subjection might make them more easily Govern'd; he Cut off, and Confiscated without any reason those who were Eminent, their Lives being a fault, their Estates a crime; the poor Peoples suffering was more their Virtue, then Cure, for the Tyrant was irritated at the so servile patience of the innocent. *Marzaon* succeeded him in the Government of the City, as also in his Tyranny, being so Cruel as quite to wear out the patience of the miserable Inhabitants, who resolv'd rather to endure him as an Enemy, then Governour; They found out ways to offer their City and Obedience to the King of *Campar*, saying, they would with any Relief fall upon the *Turks*, grown careless, in a peacefull and almost hereditary Dominion, much more in their Contempt of those men, who (as they thought) had lost all memory of their Liberty, and Injuries.

Soliman seiseth it.

The Inhabitants offer it to the King of *Campar*.

75. The Neighbouring King, with words full of Com-

The King accepts it, and what he doth.

Compassion and Gratitude accepted the offer, whether out of ambition, or humanity; He selected out of his Army, a thousand Souldiers well-deserving of so honourable an Action, and would himself be their Companion, and Commander; they began to March in the silence of the Night, and being come to the City, the Conspiritors possest 'em of a Gate, at which they entred, making themselves with a weak resistance Masters of the Castle. *Marzaon* with five hundred *Turks* Fortify'd himself in the Palace, more certain of the Danger, then the Cause, and Authors; The first light discovered the King, Commanding his men, who presently dispatch't a Trumpeter to *Marzaon*, to tell him, he had antient pretensions on that City, and now the Election of the Inhabitants, who under the Oppression of the *Bashaw*'s intrusion, were so ty'd up in their Voice and Liberty, as not to pronounce the name of their natural Prince; that he came to their help as Sufferers, but much more, as his own Subjects; that if he would leave the City, he would use him as a Friend; permitting him to carry away his Arms and Baggage, if not, Justice and Victory should give him a double Title to his own Subjects.

History of *India*. Dec. 6. Lib. 6. Cap. 1.

What the *Turks* do.

76. The *Turk* finding out the conspiracy of the *Arabs*, and wanting Strength and Provisions for his Defence, obey'd necessity, and March't out with Colours flying and Drums beating, to possess himself of a Castle eight Leagues off, designing from thence with Relief from *Bacora* to reduce the City to its former slavery; He began to fall upon the *Caravans* of *Adem*, which furnish't the City, which receiving water, and provisions from the Mountain, was in a few days brought to great Streights; for if any Provisions came in, they were few, dear, and stollen. The deplorable people with tears in their Eyes weigh'd in the same Scale Famine, and Tyranny, evils which only afford a miserable Choise. The Tyrant recruited his party with continual supplies, which the King could not with equal Force oppose,

They are Recruited.

oppose, and discoursing with the Magistrates on the ways of saving the City, they put him in mind of the Fame of our Victories against the *Turks*, and our Fidelity in protecting our Confederates. They resolv'd to dispatch a small Bark to the Governour of *Ormus*, who was then *Dom Manoel de Lima*, offering him a Fortress, and the Revenues of the Custom-house, withall letting us understand the danger the State would be in, if the *Turk* got footing in the City. The Inhabitants send to Ormus.

77. 'Twas reported *Marzaon* in a short time expected considerable Relief from *Balsora*, and if forborn till his Recruits arriv'd, would by open force fall upon the City; on which the King of *Campar* shewing himself a Souldier, in his Discourse and Courage, unwilling that Stock should take faster Root, resolv'd with three thousand Choise men to Besiege the Fortress, which with greater Resolution then Fortune he engag'd in, being Kill'd in the first assault. The *Arabs* seis'd with fear at the Death of their King, left the Siege to Bury the Body, though upon that occasion, Revenge had been more opportune then Piety.

78. The Vessel which went for *Ormus* at the entrance of Cape *Rosalgate* met with *Dom Payo de Noronha*, who with twelve small Galleys guarded that Straight, and understanding the *Arabs* pretensions, thought that Relief worthy some great Commander, and writ to the Governour of *Ormus*, that if he design'd not that honour for himself, not to refuse it him; *Dom Manoel* sent him two Ships more, and some select Souldiery, with them to go and secure the City whilst he was making greater Levies, and after an honourable reception, Counsel'd the King of *Campar*'s Embassadour to ask a Fleet of the Governour of *India*, who was one would not deny protection to the States friends, especially against the *Turks* whose Warr was look't upon as the Inheritance of our Arms. The Messenger meets with *Payo de Noronha.*

79. *Dom Payo* arriv'd at *Adem*, where he was receiv'd with what affection and greatness they could shew to *Dom Payo* arrives at *Adem.*

 their

their own Prince, and the City delivered him, as Defender and Governour; They planted our Colours, for which all vow'd solemnly to Dye, letting themselves Blood in their Breasts, Barbarous, but Loyal demonstrations and ceremonies, protesting they would hold out the City as a Member of the State, to which they were by obedience Vassals; by affection, Children; but *Dom Payo* so carry'd himself, as to forfeit the reputation of our Arms in the *East*; in favour to so great a Family we will omit the particulars of the Story, though by an other Pen written with more Liberty in ordinary History.

Behaves himself ill.

80. The Citizens of *Adem* though ill protected by *Dom Payo*, lost not their devotion to the State, holding out the City with only the name of *Portugal* in their mouths; and either not having or not desiring other protection, resolv'd to send one of the Blood-Royal to the Governour, to advise him of their condition, on whose extremities he might raise a new Name, by not sleighting the glory of helping the afflicted; that the Prince of *Adem* would receive Laws and his Crown from the State, to whom he would turn Feudatary; with a gratefull, and honourable Tribute.

The Inhabitants send to *Goa*.

81. *Dom John de Castro* was over-joy'd to hear, the report of his Name and Victories, reach't the Ears of Princes so remote, heightning not only their Reverence but Subjection; the message gave extraordinary content to *Goa*, seeing their Governours fortune bring the State the felicity of the first discovery of *India*, since where other Arms were scarce heard of, his were Obey'd.

The Governour rejoyceth.

82. The Governour gave the expedition to his Son *Dom Alvaro*, who had so well deserv'd in all he undertook, as it look't not like the election of a Father, but of a publick Minister; diverse old Cavalliers desir'd to accompany him, whom the Governour by a modest decree took off, commanding their stay in *Goa*, because he should want 'em for more important business, yet such was their eagerness on the expedition, as they look't

Sends his Son.

on

on the decree as a common grievance; the fault of those times seem'd to be the ambition of dangers; the Governour satisfy'd 'em, and was content to see such Emulation begot under his Discipline. He presently gave order for the Equipping and Victualling thirty Galleys, and made Commanders of 'em, *Dom Antonio de Noronha*, Son of the Vice-King *Dom Garcia*, *Antonio Moniz Barretto*, who went Governour of the Fortress to be made in *Adem*, *Dom Pedro d' Eca*, *Dom Fernando Coutinho*, *Pero de Attayde Inferno*, *Dom Joan de Attayde*, *Alvaro Paez de Sottomajor*, *Fernaon Perez de Andrade*, *Pero Lopez de Sousa*, *Ruy Diaz Pereira*, *Pero Botelho Porca* Brother to *Diogo Botelho*, one of the Infante *Dom Lewis*'s Family, *Alvaro Serraon*, *Luis Homem*, *Melchior Botelho* Over-seer of the Revenue, *Gomez da Sylva*, *Antonio da Veiga*, *Luis Alvarez de Sousa*, *Joaon Rodriguez Correa*, *Diogo Correa*, who came with the Embassadour of *Adem*, *Diogo Banho*, *Pero Preto*, *Alvaro da Gama*, and others.

With what Fleet.

83. But few days before the Fleet weigh'd, came to *Goa* an Embassadour from the King of *Caxem*, from whom his Neighbours the *Fartaques* had usurp't a considerable part of his Kingdome; He reigning on the *Southern* Shore of *Arabia*, and knowing *Adem* was to be reliev'd by our *Armado*, concluding that with the same Fleet we might restore him, writ to the Governour, that the Restitution of *Caxem* would not be less Laudable in the World then the defence of *Adem*; Represented what secure entertainment our Fleet had found in his Ports, reckon'd up those which at several times had Anchor'd there, on which he was suspitious to the *Turk*, offer'd also besides his Loyalty a reasonable Tribute. The Governour, considering that by those succours our Arms came into repute, and got friends to the State, ordered the same Fleet should countenance *Caxem*; the atchieving both the one and other design being but the same Voyage and expence; and because the Siege of *Adem* stood in need of speedy supplies,

An other Embassage from *Caxem*.

The Governour's answer.

ſupplies, the Governour fore-ſeeing the main Body of the Fleet would arrive too late, and ſo fruſtrate the aim and deſign, ſent away *Dom John de Attayde* with four Veſſels to make his way into *Adem*, and hold out the Siege till *Dom Alvaro*'s arrival. *Dom John de Artayde* ſet Sail, the freſh *North-weſt* Winds endammag'd one of the Ships, which arriv'd ſhattered, the reſt perſu'd their Voyage.

What paſt in *Adem*.

84. The Beſiegers and Beſieg'd in the mean time fought reſolutely in *Adem*, drawing Blood on both ſides; The weight of the Warr light upon ſome *Portugueſe* of *Dom Payo*'s Fleet, who ſhew'd from a mean Origine glorious Courage, ſo engag'd in the reſiſtance, as if they had defended their own Country, not a ſtrangers Dominion; theſe ſuffis'd to retard for many days the *Turks* Victory, and being Souldiers of Fortune, our Chronicles in ungratefull ſilence obſcure their Names, as if Virtue of neceſſity were to have noble Progenitors, and theſe were for their own Actions leſs honourable then others for other men's; I believe the great Ones have with injuring Nature ſet up new Laws, not making only Eſtates but Deſerts hereditary.

Turks arrive.

85. Things in *Adem* being (as we have ſaid) in that Contingency, there appear'd a Fleet of *Turks* of nine Galleys Royal, and ſome ſmall Veſſels, which fac't the City, and coming to Anchor out of the Bay, got to Shore, where they Pitch't their Tents and Fortify'd their Encamping, adviſing the *Baſhaw* to joyn 'em with his Army. The *Arabs* on ſight of ſo great numbers come againſt 'em, came remiſsly to the Defence, ſome Puſillanimous, others out of Heart, thought the Courage and Strength of the Enemy inſuperable, and at private meetings blam'd the King's ambition of dilating his Crown with the Blood of his innocent Subjects, not content with the fortune of his Predeceſſours; but the *Portugueſe* amongſt 'em, obſerving the brighteſt Fame work't out of difficulties, forc't on the *Arabs*, convincing the Reſiſtance to be neceſſary and poſſible,

offering

offering themselves afresh to be the voluntary Companions of their Fortune; enough to put new Courage in 'em, upon which they vow'd to Dye in their defence, not so much out of Obligation as Example.

86. The *Turks* Besieg'd the City, by raising two Batteries with pieces on 'em of an extravagant bigness, two amongst the rest (by them call'd *Quartaos*) carry'd a Bullet of four Palmes circumference, which made more Ruins, then Breaches in the Walls, and from the danger taught the Besieged discipline; who made their Retrenchments and Traverses within, by which they entertain'd, and blunted their assaults, and made the *Turk's* Victory doubtfull, and costly. But *Dom Payo de Noronha* (carry'd away by some resolute fatality) depriv'd the *Arabs* of the Victory, ours of the Honour, sending private Orders to all the *Portuguese* to come and joyn him, thus forsaking the defence of a Prince, a Friend, and Feudatory, not complying with the obligation of either his Birth or Office. Most of the *Portuguese* obey'd, only *Manoel Pereira*, and *Francisco Vieira*, two Souldiers of Fortune, said, the City was the Kings of *Portugal*, and they would lose their Lives in the defence; it appears, the Warrs of those times seem'd to require first Courage, then Discipline; these two held out the City till the last day, and gain'd more repute in its Ruins then the *Turks* in their Victory. Lay Siege. *Dom Payo* calls off our men.

87. As soon as the *Arabs* understood the *Portuguese* were Retreated, (all hopes of Defence being desperate) they began to parly; but the Prince commanded 'em to give over Treating, saying he had rather be beaten out, then give up the City; that the *Turks* should not without some stains of their Blood, win those Colours of the Kings of *Portugal*. Loyalty which deserv'd better Assistance from our Arms. The Enemy, knowing the Division and Coolness of the Inhabitants, continued his Assaults, which brought on again the Speech of a Surrender, which the Prince always broke What the *Arabs* do.

 off,

off, constant to himself, and the State; but danger, famine, and despair, prevail'd with some of the Inhabitants to give up a secret Gate to the Enemy, at which he entred the City. The Prince fighting with Royal, but Unfortunate courage, disengag'd with his Life, the Loyalry he had promis'd to the State; *Manoel Pereira*, and *Francisco Vieira*, sav'd a young Prince whom they carry'd to *Campar*, comforting the Subjects with that tender branch of its prostrate Trunk.

Dom John de Attayde's success.

88. *Dom John de Attayde*, (whom we left with three Ships at Sea) continued on his Voyage, and having favourable Winds, in few days saw the Coast of *Arabia*; He stood for the City *Adem*, and Rowing into the Harbour, got amongst the Galleys which were there at Anchor, but the *Easterly* winds yet reigning, got out to Sea again. The *Turks* on the sight of our Ships immediately weigh'd, and by the advantage of their Oars gave us so hot a Chase, that the two Ships commanded by *Gomez da Sylva*, and *Antonio da Veiga*, were almost under the Prow of their Galleys, and seeing it impossible to fly, much more to resist, ran their Vessels on the Shore which was near them, and by that means scap't with their Lives. *Dom John de Attayde* who was in the best Ship; bore up what he could against the Wind; seeing himself often lost, till by the Night coming on he stood for *Abexim*, under which Shore he carin'd his Ship in the Island of *Mete*, which lies o're against the Cities of *Barbara*, and *Zeila*; those who sav'd themselves by Land got to the protection of the King of *Campar*, where they found *Manoel Pereira*, and *Francisco Vieira*, who acquainted them with the success we have now related; they were entertain'd and provided of all things with plenty and affection.

Dom Alvaro's Voyage.

89. *Dom Alvaro de Castro* seeting Sail with the whole Fleet, and going before the *Easterly* winds, made a short Voyage, and got so farr as to recover the Islands of *Canecanim* where he met with *Dom John de Attayde* of whom he knew the loss of *Adem*, and how the *Turks* chas'd

chas'd him, from whose Galleys he had by the favour of the Night freed himself. *Dom Alvaro* with the Gentlemen and Souldiers of the Fleet, betray'd a just resentment at the News, valuing less the loss of that State, then the foil of our Arms, because both amongst Natives and Strangers the sinking in opinion is always Eternis'd. The King of *Campar*'s Embassadour, and Brother-in-law, who was in our Fleet, becomingly resented the Deaths of his Brother-in-law, and Nephew, yet was not a little comforted with the knowledge they were not in Arrerages to Honour or Loyalty, and on those considerations shew'd as strong a mind, as if he had been to calm an others sorrow. *Dom Alvaro* consulted with the Officers of the Fleet what was to be done, and all were of opinion, since the relief of *Adem* had been ineffectual, to divert their Arms in favour of the King of *Caxem*, (as the Fleet had instructions) on whom the Bordering *Fartaques* had surpris'd the Fortress of *Xael*, which commanded a Haven, the principal Scale of those few that petty King had; a design more advantagious then difficult. He calls a Council, and what he resolves:

90. *Dom Alvaro* commanded to Steer to *Xael*, and coming to Anchor in sight of the Castle, the *Fartaques*, out of either fear or friendship receiv'd peaceably our *Armado*; The Fort was Built of Turfs, with four so little Works, as five and thirty Souldiers, who were there in Garrison, were enough to Man it; These men on sight of our Fleet, sent out a Woman (who understood and spoke *Portuguese*) to ask for the Commander in chief and tell him, the *Fartaques* were friends to the State, that if we came to demand that Fortress, they would immediately quit it; many concluded the proposition acceptable, for of so few Enemies and without Name we could not expect Glory, or Booty; most Voted, that for the Authority of our Arms we should summon 'em to Surrender on discretion. The woman well understanding this resolution, and ill satisfy'd with our answer, reply'd, that the *Fartaques* knew how to defend Goes to *Xael*.

defend both their Lives and the Castle. The *Moors* upon that took down the white Flagg, and planted an other Red one, Ours immediately discharg'd some Canon-shot, but so at Rovers as to do no Dammage; *Dom Alvaro*, with all his men surrounded the Fortress, which he commanded should be Seal'd in diverse places, securing those who went on with his Musquets from below; and the charge being uninterrupted the *Moors* durst not appear. *Fernaon Perez* was the first, who began with a Ladder to clime, carrying with him his Colours which he planted and maintain'd on the Wall; almost at the same instant got up *Pero Botelho*, with the same hazard and fortune as the former, these clear'd the Scaling for the rest.

Resolves to Scale it.

91. *Antonio Moniz Barretto*, *Dom Antonio de Noronha*, *Dom John de Attayde*, and others, went to a Gate of the Fortress, which was stop't up with Bushes, and found it impossible to enter, till our men went on the inside and dis-ingag'd it; the *Fartaques* retir'd to two Works, whence with desperate Courage they defended themselves, refusing their Lives offer'd 'em by *Dom Alvaro*, which they seem'd willing to lose out of revenge, or to credit that force they could not resist; stoutness being even amongst these infidels the most Cardinal virtue. The *Moors* in fine fought till they all fell, such Barbarous obstinacy not deserving the name of Courage, where there was no hope of Victory or Revenge; of our men five Dy'd, the Wounded were above forty.

The *Arabs* Fight till they all Dye.

92. When the Fortress was gain'd, (an action more considerable to the Prince, then famous for us) *Dom Alvaro* delivered it to the King of *Caxem*'s Embassadour, who shew'd then his gratitude for so signal a favour, in Victualling the Fleet, afterwards, in holding faithfull correspondence with the State; and the Season of the year being almost spent, *Dom Alvaro* went to Winter at *Goa*, where he was receiv'd with applause above the Victory, a Ceremony, the Governour indulg'd as a Father, and *Dom Alvaro* pris'd as a Souldier.

The place is gain'd.

93. Lou-

93. *Lourenco Pirez de Tavora* came with five Ships in Company to the Barr of *Lisbone*, having had not only a short, but happy and prosperous Voyage; we told of *Dom John Mascarenhas*'s coming on them, full of fame and deserts; the news of *Dio* being immediately spread amongst the People, every one, according to his capacity judged of the patience of the Siege, and resolution of the Battail. The common people were endless in the praises of *Dom John de Castro*, as men without envy for persons, or fortunes, above 'em; the Gentlemen, and great Ones, abetted or consented to the universal Acclamations; an unusual virtue, to be able to endure the fame of Peers; and there was not one so ambitious, who coveted for himself a greater Name, or more illustrious Atchievements.

Lourenco Pirez arrives at Lisbone.

History of *India*, Dec. 6. Lib. 6. Cap. 7.

94. The King and Court put on their Robes, and appointed a day to give God thanks in the Chapel with Pious and Royal offerings; there was a Learn'd Sermon, in which were set forth the Praises and Virtues of the Governour. The King acquainted the Pope, and the greatest Princes of *Europe* with the Victory, who all gave him joy as for the most famous Action of the *East*; *Dom John de Castro* in his Letter to the King desir'd leave to return to the Kingdome, shewing how little Sollicitous he was of Dignities, who left the greatest, and that a total neglect might not be branded as a new ambition, begg'd of the King two Acres of ground which joyn to his Country-house at *Sintra*, and end in a little Hill, which to this day is call'd * *Monte das Alvicaras*. The King in the honours conferr'd on him, seem'd to consider his Services, and in his Reward respected his Fortune, all which is seen by his Letter, of which we here give you a Copy.

Rejoycing for the news of *Dio*.

What the Governour asks for the good News.

* The Mountain of good News.

The King Dom John *the Third's Letter.*

The King's thanks to him.

History of *India*. Dec 6. Lib. 6. Cap. 8.

95. "VIce-King and Friend, I the King heartily "salute you. The Victory God gave you "against the Officers of the King of *Cambaya*, was of "as eminent satisfaction to us, as 'tis fit we should have "for such, and so great a Conquest, and for so great "mercies and favours, as you in it receiv'd from our "Lord, for which he is to be ever prais'd; there is also "much due to the Prudence, and great Courage you "shew'd in that day, as to what you did in the great "and speedy Relief you sent to the Fortress of *Dio*, "exposing in so extravagant a Season your Sons to Sea, "by which is seen how much more predominant our "Service is with you, then the natural affection of a "Father, which we value, as 'tis reason we should, see-"ing, you not only Routed so great Forces of the Ene-"mies, but secur'd all *India*, by the great apprehensions "our Enemies have of so signal a Victory; which ser-"vice, there is as much reason we should Rank as it de-"serves, as we should have for it the requisite satis-"faction; we had no little discontent for the Death of "your Son *Dom Fernando*, both as he was your Son, "and as he gave proofs in that Age, what he would have "been in all his Life after; and since he Dy'd so ho-"nourably, and in so eminent service for God, and us, "you ought less to resent his loss, and give God thanks "he was pleas'd he should so Dye, as we know you did, "shewing, by your forgetting the Death of your Son, "your remembring what was suitable for our Service, "of which things we shall always be so mindfull, as not "only to impute 'em to you by our great satisfaction "for 'em, but by our special grace, which is now to have "a beginning in the rewards we conferr on you and "your Son *Dom Alvaro*, reserving the compleating "of

"of 'em for the end of your Service, which we are "confident, and take for granted, will be such, as that "hath been you have already rendered us, and in the "confidence and experience we have of it, though very "much desiring at present to comply with you in all "things, yet considering how much it is for our Service, "(and seeing by your Actions how much more you prise "that, then all other business of your own) we have "thought good not to give you leave to return as you "desir'd of us; and for that purpose recommend to, "and command you, to receive it well, and that you "will serve us in that Charge other three years, at the "end of which we will in God's name send you leave "to return, and we hope he will inable you so to "do; yet though it be so much for the advantage "of our Service, that you should continue serving us "for that time in those parts, if you think your return "necessary, we should be glad of your writing to us, "and expecting our answer. *Pero de Alcacova Carneiro* "writ it in *Lisbone* the 20th. of *October* 1547.

The King.

I believe the Queen *Dona Katherine's* Letter, requires our no less attention, where the Subscription is not only Royal but also the Discourse, giving judgment on the Actions of the Victory, with the Prudence of a Man, and Gallantry of a Souldier.

The Queen Dona Katherine's *Letter.*

96. "VIce-King, I the Queen heartily salute you. "I have read your Letter in which you give "us a particular account of what you have done, and "ordered in all those things you thought to be for the "service of our Lord the King, and for the defence and "security

"security of those Parts, and that all was so confor-"mable to what you are, and to the opinion his Majesty "hath of you, we have as much satisfaction, as 'tis "reasonable; both to see his Majesty is so well serv'd by "you; and for the signal honour you have purchas'd. "As to the great care and diligence, you upon your "Arrival employ'd in the repairing, and providing the "Fleet; 'twas a great beginning, and of absolute ne-"cessity for the remedying so weighty affairs as after-"wards presented; and we are assur'd how great soever "the pains you took in it were, your content of having "been so well employ'd, will be greater; you aim'd "right in the Warr you made upon *Hidalcaon*, because "by that was clearly seen the contrary to what you say, "is there the receiv'd opinion; that he could receive "no harm by a Warr with the *Portuguese*, (which must "be the reason he so often begun it) nor have any "benefit by Peace with 'em, which made him not care "to break it; and if he knew who you were, and how "much more prevalent honour then profit is with you, "he would not have made you the offer he did about "*Meale*; but the little impression it had on you, and "your evident undeceiving him, will make him know "it. As to the business of the Siege, and Warr of the "Fortress of *Dio*; the mercy of our Lord God was "eminent in the Victory he there gave you against so "great Force, and numbers, of the Enemies of his holy "Catholick faith, as were there from so remote Parts "met together, and 'tis an evident sign of his own Arms "upholding the State in those Countries; and for all, "we give him the praises, as are reasonable, and we ac-"knowledge to be due; and it much adds to the great "satisfaction, our Lord the King, and We have for so "great a Victory, to see with what prudence, and con-"duct you provided all things necessary for the obtain-"ing it; how stoutly you behav'd your self in the day "of Battail, and with what diligence you reliev'd that "Fortress, exposing for it your Sons in so Stormy wea-

"ther;

"ther; the Notion his Majesty and we have of all "these Actions, and of the great benefit which is the "consequence of 'em, is very proportionable to their "quality and greatness; and we hope his Majesty will "shew it so, in the honour and thanks he intends to re- "turn you, because all is your due; and he gave no "small sign of it, by his pleasure and satisfaction immedi- "ately to begin it, as you will see by his Letters to you "and your Son *Dom Alvaro*. We were not a little dis- "contented at the Death of your Son *Dom Fernando*, as "well for our knowledge how you must take it, as for "the loss of his Person, which (as he shew'd in that "Action) was eminently great; but we so well know "you, and your great Prudence and Virtue, as to be "certain, that at whatsoever time our Lord God should "take him to himself, you would conform to his Will, "and accept it at his Hand; especially it being then, "when for the defence of his Faith, and in so signal "Service for his Majesty, he Dy'd so honourably, and "was not wanting to the Obligation of being what "he was, which are very convincing reasons that you "ought so to take it, and very much less resent his "Death. As for what you sollicit us in, about your "return, in which your Wife *Dona Leonor* (whom we "were very joyfull to see, for the deserts of her Person "and Virtues, and out of the great affection we have "for her) hath spoke to us in your behalf, as in a bu- "siness she so much desires, we should be very glad if "we could in that gratifie your self and her with the "good liking and satisfaction of our Lord the King; "but for the good Service you have done his Majesty, "and the great miss might be there of your Person "in such a time, he hath thought good to make use of "you there for three years longer, as you will see by his "Letter; and we assure our selves, that for those con- "siderations you will take it well, and we very much "desire you it may be so, and hope in our Lord he will "give you health and vigour to perform it, and will

"assist and strengthen you in all your difficulties, be-
"cause the result of 'em is so much for his Service, and
"he knows the main design his Majesty hath in desiring
"it should be so, is because of his knowledge that his
"Service will by you there be unfeignedly promov'd;
"and by your remembring, amongst so many troubles
"and so important businesses, those things of Ours, you
"took into your care, it is evident, how great a desire
"you have in that, and all other things to serve us,
"which we so look upon as is reason; for what concerns
"*Diogo Voz* we have in an other Letter writ to you,
"what we desire should be done. We were very much
"pleas'd with that perfume of *Benjoim de Boninas*, and
"with all the other things you sent us by *Lourenco Pirez*
"*de Tavora*, all being so good, as they seem to be sent
"with that good Will which we esteem the most, and
"take all very well of you; and about those Servants
"of Ours, and Persons, who, (as you write us) have
"serv'd well there, and about those things, you think
"it necessary to provide, we will mind our Lord the
"King, as you desire, it should be done. That which
"his Majesty hath to look too, in the Rewards he
"ought to bestow on all those who have there serv'd
"him, is to take notice of what you have writ to him,
"and of what you desire, as 'tis reason he should; we
"take very well of you, the good Character you give
"his Majesty of those our Servants, who were present
"at the Action of *Dio*, and also the many Favours, and
"great Civilities, we know for our sake you shew'd
"them. *Pero Fernandez* writ it in *Lisbone* the 30th. of
October 1547.

The Queen.

The Letter the *Infante Dom Lewis* writ him, is not less considerable, as being from a Prince who knew how to make so profound an estimate of Deserts and Virtues.

The

The Infante Dom Lewis's *Letter.*

97. "HOnourable Vice-King. I receiv'd your "Letter which came in *Lourenco Pirez de* "*Tavora's* Fleet, in which you tell me you receiv'd mine "I sent by *Lewis Fiqueira*, and I take very well of you, "your telling me, the advice I gave you seem'd good "to you, and the more, your putting it in practice, "and, though I had not known you, I had sufficient "cause to believe it was so, by hearing what you do "there, and seeing you write so plainly your difficulties, "Poverty, and Abstinence, weapons by which are o're-"come the World, the Flesh, and the Devil, who reign "so absolutely in those parts of *India*, a Victory, grea-"ter then that of the King of *Cambaya*, or of all the "Force of the *Turk*; for which as long as you Live "you ought to fear nothing, but be confident in our "Lord God, that he will assist you, as he hath lately "done in the Defence and Battail of *Dio*, for which "Victory you have great cause to praise him, who hath "made you an Instrument of so much Service to him-"self, and to my Lord the King, of so much honour "to your Self, and to all the *Portuguese*; to the absent, "as to those who were present. And certain it is, that "in that expedition, from the first day you had the "News of the Siege of *Dio*, till that of yours and our "Victory, (according to my reach) you have done "what could be done, by a Stout, and Prudent Com-"mander, as well in your speedy Succours, as in expo-"sing your Sons as the marks of Fortune, to the dan-"gers of the Winter and Seas of *India*, that others "might less apprehend 'em, by which is clearly evinc't, "how much a greater share the Service of my Lord the "King, and the Obligation of your charge, have in "you, then the natural affections of a Father, which "are those most Tyrannically over-rule our Nature. "And by the patience you shew'd in the Death of your

"Son

"Son *Dom Fernando de Castro*, you have eminently "clear'd this opinion. It's certain I resented it for my "self and you, and by the certain signs I saw in him of "an extraordinary Courage took it for a very great "loss; and believe God design'd in that to recompence "him, by taking him out of this so troublesome Life "by so honourable means, and so much for his glory, "which ought to be no little part of your Consolation. "Your Son *Dom Alvaro de Castro* employ'd not his time "ill when through so many difficulties, and dangers he "reliev'd the Fortress of *Dio*, at that time, when its "only remedy was his Arrival, and, for his Behaviour "there, his falling on the Enemies Posts, and all the rest "of his Carriage, I do for my self, and you, give him "many blessings. And to return to your resolution of "venturing your Person, and the State of *India*, for the "relief of *Dio*, 'twas well taken, for had you not done "it, there had been the same hazard; and your arrival "at *Dio*, your ordering your Fleet, your commanding "the Landing of your men when the Battail was to be "given, and your way of Fighring, all this seems to "me to deserve that we now and ever give praises to "our Lord God, and that his Majesty should conferr "on you many honours, which he hath already begun "as you'l see concerning your Self and Son; He also "ought and will do the same to those Cavalliers, and "Gentlemen, who serv'd under you in that expedition, "especially to *Dom John Mascarenhas*, who behav'd "himself in the weight of that Siege like an honou-"rable Commander, and brave Cavallier. I was very "glad to see your manner of writing to his Majesty, "about the Service the Gentlemen, and Cavalliers who "went thither, did in the business of *Dio*, by which it "appears, you even scores with their deservings. Al-"ways do so for my sake, and be glad to praise Persons; "for it being certain, there will not want those men "who will speak ill of them, (which you ought to "punish where you find it) it is but reason the good "should

" should extoll them; that those you cannot there
" Reward, his Majesty may by your information do it.
" I spoke (as you writ to me) about your return,
" which his Majesty granted me not, and gave me for it
" two Reasons, and in my opinion, though you have
" many to countenance your desire of returning, his
" Majesty hath many more to desire your Service for
" three years longer in that Government, which you
" ought to be glad to do, to serve God, for the great
" mercy he shew'd you, and his Majesty for his confi-
" dence in you, and satisfaction in your Service; Rely
" on God for his giving you strength to grapple with
" the great difficulties and disorders of *India*, and I
" trust in him, that after such a performance you'l re-
" turn to fill these tops of the Rocks of *Sintra* with
" Chapels, and Trophies of your Victories, and that
" you'l visit and enjoy 'em in a profound repose. I
" speak not to you about particular businesses, because
" my Lord the King hath writ to you in what con-
" cerns his Service in answer to the general Letter
" you writ him, which came in a very good style, and
" well digested. Dated at *Lisbone* the 22th. of *Octo-
ber* 1547.

The Infante Dom Lewis.

98. 'Tis apparent by these Letters how well the Royal Family took the Services of *Dom John de Castro*, the King deny'd *Dom John* the leave he ask't to come and rest himself in the Kingdome for the good of his Country and the *East*, he added to his Government three years more, with the Title of Vice-Roy. He Liv'd not to enjoy, though deserve; this addition of honour; He had given him ten thousand *Crusades*, as a Gratuity towards the Defraying charges, and Letters Patents for his Son *Dom Alvaro* to be Admiral of the Seas of *India*, an employment he Computed by fewer Years then Victories.

99. The King *Dom John* by the advices of the Vice-Roy, understood, that the security of *India* requir'd always Forces ready, for all occurrences of the State, and that the defeat of *Cambaya*, (whose Ruine was an example for the rest) had created hatred as well as reverence in the Neighbouring Princes; on these and other considerations he sent this year for *India* six Ships, which parted in different Seasons. *Martim Correa da Sylva*, who brought a Commission for the Fortress of *Dio*, was Commander in chief of the first three which parted in *November*, the other Commanders were *Antonio Pereira*, and *Christovaon de Sa*; The Admiral Ship, having on the Coast of *India* adverse Winds fell off from her course, and not able to reach *Goa*, recovered *Angediva*, whence she sent to the Vice-Roy to provide her with necessaries, being forc't to Winter in that Port. *Christovaon de Sa's* Pilot knew better to shape his course, for as soon as he made the Coast of *India*, he bore up to get the Wind of *Goa*, and saw Land about *Carapataon*, whence he came directly for the Barr.

The King sends six Ships for *India*.

100. As soon as the Vice-Roy knew there was a Ship come in from the Kingdome, he gave orders for Landing the Sick, and went in Person to visit and provide for 'em. And certain it is, that amongst all the Excellencies of this extraordinary Vice-Roy, we may Rank his Charity in the Front, it not being a Customary virtue in a Souldier, much less in a publick Minister; He receiv'd his Letters, in which he found those honours and gratuities we have related, these he look't upon as payment, those as a recompence, for which the Gentlemen gave to each other the joy, as satisfy'd the Vice-Roy should continue his Government three years longer, in whom they knew the State would have a Man, the Soldiery a Father.

One comes to *Goa*.

101. *Dom John de Castro* found himself less spent by his Years then the Difficulties of so long a Warr, which made him succumb under the pressure of so perplex't a Solicitude; He fell Desperately ill, and his Sickness in few

The Vice-King falls Sick.

few days betray'd mortal Symptoms, which he, by the Vexatiousness of repeated accidents perceiving, unburdened himself of the weight of the Government: He call'd for the Bishop *Dom John de Albuquerque*, *Dom Diogo de Almeyda Freire*, the Doctor *Francisco Toscano*, Chief Chancellour of the State, *Sebastiaon Lopez Lobatto* his Auditor General, and *Rodrigo Goncalvez Caminha*, Overseer of the Revenue, to whom he delivered up the State, in Peace with the Neighbouring Princes, secur'd by so many Victories. He sent for the Magistracy of the City, the Vicar General of *India*, the Guardian of Saint *Francis*, *Frier Antonio do Casal*, Saint *Francisco Xaverius*, and the Officers of the King's Revenne, before whom he made this Speech.

Quits the Government.

102. "I am not asham'd Gentlemen to tell you, that "the Vice-Roy of *India* wants in this Sickness those "conveniencies the meanest Souldier finds in the Hos-"pitals; I came to Serve not to Traffick in the *East*, I "would to your selves have pawn'd the Bones of my "Son, and did pawn the hairs of my Beard, to assure "you I had no other Plate, or Hangings. There was "not this day Money enough in the House to Buy me "a Hen; for in the Fleets I set forth, the Souldiers fed "upon the Governours Salary, before the King's pay, "and 'tis no wonder for the Father of so many Children "to be poor. I request of you, during the time of this "Sickness, to order me out of the King's Revenue a "proportionable maintenance, and to appoint a Person "of your own who may provide me a moderate allow-"ance. And asking presently for a Missal, he took his Oath on the Gospel, he was not then Debitor one *Crusade* to the King's Revenue, or had receiv'd any thing from *Christian*, *Jew*, *Moor*, or *Pagan*, or for the carrying out the Authority of his Place, or Person, had any other Houshold-stuff then what he brought from *Portugal*, and that he had here spent the Money he had got in the Kingdome; that he had not where withall to Buy an other Quilt, then that they saw on his Bed; that he had only

He speaks to the Council.

The Oath he takes.

only made a Sword for his Son *Dom Alvaro* to return into the Kingdome, and set the Hilt with some Jewels of small value. That he desir'd they would enter a Protest of this, that if at any time the King found it otherwise, he might punish him for perjury. This Speech was writ in the City-Books, which, they who succeeded might read for their Instruction, with whom I believe the Memory is more pregnant then the Example.

103. As soon as the Vice-Roy perceiv'd himself summon'd to a sharper Conflict, avoiding the importune diversion of Human cares, he secluded himself with the Father Saint *Francisco Xaverius*, providing for so doubtfull a Voyage so secure a Pilot, who all the time of his Sickness, was his Nurse, Reconciler, and Governour; As he had got no Riches to make a new Disposal of, he made no other Will then that he left (at his coming to Govern *India*) in the Kingdome, in the hands of *Dom Rodrigo Pinheiro* Bishop of *Angra*, to whom he had Communicated it; and receiving the Sacraments of the Church, he gave up his Soul to God the sixth of *June* one thousand five hundred forty eight, in the eight and fortieth Year of his Age, and almost three of his Government of that State. The Riches he gain'd in *Asia* were his Heroick actions, which Posterity will read in this Book with a tender Memory. In his Study were found three pieces of small Money, and a Discipline which seem'd to have been often us'd, and the Locks of his Beard he had pawn'd; He ordered his Body should be Deposited in Saint *Francis* Church in *Goa*, thence to be Translated to his Chapel at *Sintra*; They immediately consulted on his Funeral, which was to be not less Compassionate then Solemn, deserving the Illustrious, and common Tears of the whole State.

He retires with the Father *Xaverius*.

His Death.

His Burial, and the grief at it.

104. After some years his Bones came to the Kingdome, where they were receiv'd with reverent and pious applause, as being the last benefit his Country receiv'd with his Ashes, and on the Shoulders of four of his

His Bones come to the Kingdome.

Grand-

Grand-children carry'd to Saint *Dominicks* Convent in *Lisbone*, where for many days were made costly Exequies; thence they were the second time Translated to Saint *Dominicks* Convent at *Bemfica*, where (though in an others Chapel) they remain'd some years in a decent Depository, till his Grand-child *Francisco de Castro*, Bishop, and Inquisitor General, made for them a Chapel, and place of Burial; for Design, Matter, and Adornment; but to the King's Monuments, not second to any; the relation of it will not perhaps seem tedious, out of respect to the Memory of the Grand-father, and Piety of the Grand-child.

Are Deposited in Saint *Dominicks* in *Lisbone*.

Translated to *Bemfica*.

105. Saint *Dominicks* Convent of *Bemfica* is two Miles from *Lisbone*, nam'd so, from a Neighbouring Village. 'Twas always in the possession of the Kings of *Portugal*, where for the freshness of the Air, they had a Country-house, which they went to for Diversion of business, or the exercise of Hunting. King *John* the First, finding himself indebted to God for so many Victories, amongst other Acts of Thanksgiving, gave this Palace to the order of Saint *Dominick*, with the Adjacent grounds, Gardens and Orchards, the twenty second of *May*, one thousand three hundred ninety and nine, for the Founding a Convent; which was not only Founded but Augmented by our Kings. The Founder oblig'd himself, by his Letters Patents (preserv'd in the Archives of the Convent) to protect, and defend the cause, the persons, and goods of the Religious, Sollicitous in God's cause, Couragious in his own. King *John* the Second endow'd it with a great Revenue, which the House now enjoys under the Name of the Fifth of the Islands, without imposing any new Obligation, which might render the Alms less Liberal, or Acceptable; the King *Dom Emanuel*, though Distracted with greater Cares and Buildings, left in the Sacrifices of this Temple, a Religious memory, ordering that twice in a Week should be Sung two Masses to the Angels, in the behalf of those who were at Sea; this was in that Age the Astrolabe

Where they now are.

of his Discoveries, and the Abetter of the Victories in the *East*. The Queen *Dona Katherina*, look't upon this House as her private Chapel, offering here from her own Oratory, Reliques of Veneration, and Value, amongst others, in a great Silver Cross a piece of the holy Cross, which offering from Royal hands doth assure the Certainty of so inestimable a present; Our Princes conferring on this House temporal and spiritual benefits. King *Philip* the Second, augmented with an honourable Alms, those it before enjoy'd. This Convent hath always been for the strictest observers of the Religion, who under the name of Recolets allow no Swerving or Indulgence from the first institution; hither as to a School of Virtues, use to retire the most eminent of the Order; some to avoid, others to be at rest after their Prelacies, in a holy leisure to be untaken up but by God, and to reform their Affections.

106. In this Convent, Illustrious for its Foundation, and Discipline, rest the Victorious Ashes of *Dom John de Castro*, in a Chapel, and Monument of a Religious greatness. The Chapel is Consecrated by the name of *Corpus Christi*, hath the great Door into the Cloister of the Convent, and over that in a Scutcheon of Relieve the Arms of the Founder; the wideness of the Door takes in forty Palmes, the height above seventy, a proportion the Architects name *Dupla*, and the work is *Dorick*. 'Tis only of one Isle of polish't Marble, the Pavement also is of diverse Colour'd and Polish't stones; there goes about it within, a well-ordered, and proportionable Pedestal, which sustains the Decency of an uniform Building; it contains six Arches (with Pilastres between) upon their Bases, and with their Capitals; there goes also a Cornish round about, it hath six Windows, proportionable to the rest of the Architecture. On the high Altar is a Tabernacle, (in which is always kept the blessed Sacrament, lighted by two silver Lamps) behind it an Altar-piece, both of Carv'd work, with great Flowers all Gilded, and on the top, a Picture

Picture of our Saviour's last Supper; behind the high Altar, and Altar-piece is the Quire for the Novices, for whose better Breeding, and Service of God, is made a House with twenty Cells, and diverse Offices which form the Body of a distinct Convent. The Roof of the Chapel above the Finishment of the Cornish is also of Stone, divided into Compartments with rich Mouldings. Of the six Arches which make the whole, the two first are on the plain of the Altar; on the Gospel-side is a Door goes up to the top of the Building, and the Founder's Lodgings; on the side of the Epistle, is another goes into the Sachristy. The other four are taken up with four costly Monuments, with Urns of Burnish't stones which rest on the Backs of Elephants of black Marble.

107. In the first Arch which joyns to the plain of the Altar, on the Gospel-side is the Monument of *Dom John de Castro*, in which before 'twas clos'd were laid his Bones with the following Epitaph.

D. JOANNES DE CASTRO XX. PRO RELIGIONE IN UTRAQUE MAURITANIA STIPENDIIS FACTIS; NAVATA STRENUE OPERA THUNETANO BELLO; MARI RUBRO FELICIBUS ARMIS PENETRATO; DEBELLATIS INTER EUPHRATEM ET INDUM NATIONIBUS; GEDROSICO REGE, PERSIS, TURCIS UNO PRÆLIO FUSIS; SERVATO DIO, IMO REIPUB. REDDITO, DORMIT IN MAGNUM DIEM, NON SIBI, SED DEO TRIUMPHATOR, PUBLICIS LACHRIMIS COMPOSITUS, PUBLICO SUMPTU PRÆ PAUPERTATE FUNERATUS, OBIIT VIII. ID. JUNII ANNO 1548. ÆTATIS 48.

Under

Under the Arch adjoyning to this, rest the Bones of his Wife *Dona Leonor Coutinho*.

108. On the Epistle-side of the Altar, under an Arch over against that where is *Dom John de Castro's* Monument, rests his Son *Dom Alvaro*, where his Bones were put in the same manner, on him is writ this following Epitaph.

D. ALVARUS DE CASTRO MAGNI JOANNIS PRIMO-GENITUS, CUI PENE AB INFANTIA DISCRIMINUM SOCIUS, PUGNARUM PRÆCURSOR, TRIUMPHORUM CONSORS, ÆMULUS FORTITUDINIS, HÆRES VIRTUTUM, NON OPUM: REGUM PROSTATOR: IN SINAI VERTICE EQUES FELICITER INAUGURATUS; A REGE SEBASTIANO SUMMIS REGNI AUCTUS HONORIBUS; BIS ROMÆ, SEMEL CASTELLÆ, GALLIÆ, SABAUDIÆ LEGATIONE PERFUNCTUS, OBIIT IV. KALEND. SEPTEMB. ANNO 1575. ÆTATIS SUÆ 50.

In the next Arch to this lies his Wife *Dona Anna de Attayde*, under the Body of the Chapel is made a Vault, with six stone Arches, in one of which is an Altar to celebrate Mass, the rest have Repartments for the Bones, and Bodies of the Dead.

109. The Bishop, Inquisitor General, Founder of this Chapel, gave (for the maintenance of those Religious who are to perform the Duties of it) to the Convent of *Bemfica* two hundred and forty thousand * *Reis* yearly, to be paid out of the Chamber of this City of *Lisbone*, which are thus distributed. One hundred

* The *Portuguese* keep their accounts in the least Money they have, which are *Reis*, whereof 400. made a *Crusade*, which is worth 3 s. 6 d.

dred and twenty thousand *Reis* for three Masses to be daily Celebrated; fifty (though given before) for the Anniversaries he shall appoint in his Will; forty, for the Fabrick and providing the Chapel; thirty, for supplying the necessities of those Religious men who reside in the Noviciate for the looking to, and cleaning the Chapel; which besides this, he Adorn'd with many rich and devout Pieces, and gave to the Sachristy all things necessary for Divine Worship, as well Ornaments for Holy-days as Work-days, Linning, Candlesticks of all sizes, Lamps, and other such like necessaries, all in aboundance and perfection.

110. *Dom John de Castro*, as Illustrious for his Family, as Virtues, was Born in *Lisbone* the 27th. of *February* of the year one thousand five hundred; He was second Son to *Dom Alvaro de Castro*, Governour of the House of *Civil*, and to *Dona Leonor de Noronha*, the Daughter of *Dom John de Almeyda* second Earl of *Abrantes*; Grand-child to *Dom Garcia de Castro*, who was Brother to *Dom Alvaro de Castro*, the first Earl of *Monsanto*, these two were Sons to *Dom Fernando de Castro*, Grand-children to *Dom Pedro de Castro*, and great Grand-children to *Dom Alvaro Pirez de Castro*, Earl of *Arrayolos*, and first Constable of *Portugal*, Brother to the Queen *Dona Inez de Castro*, Wife to King *Dom Pedro* the Cruel. This Constable, was Son to *Dom Pedro Fernandez de Castro*, call'd (in *Castile*) the Man of Warr, who coming into this Kingdome, begun here the Illustrious house of the *Castros*, which hath preserv'd it self in so much greatness; *Dom Pedro* by the Male line descended from the *Infante Dom Fernando*, Son to King *Dom Garcia* of *Navarre*, who Married *Dona Maria Alvarez de Castro*, the only Daughter of the Earl *Alvaro Fanhez Minaya*, the fifth Grand-child in descent from *Lain Calvo*, from whom this Family derives its beginning. *Dom John de Castro* when very young Marry'd *Dona Leonor Coutinho* his Cousin-German once remov'd, greater for her Quality, then Portion, with whom retiring to the Town of

Dom John de Castro's Family.

of *Almada*, he by an Antidated old Age avoided the ambition of the Court; He went to serve at *Tangiers*, where he gave the first, but extraordinary proofs of his Courage, though of his Actions there, we have more from his Fame then our Knowledge. He return'd to Court, re-call'd by the King *Dom John* the third, and the Kingdome being too narrow for his Gallantry went to *India* with *Dom Garcia de Noronha*; He accompany'd *Dom Estevaon de Gama* in his expedition to the Mouth of the Red-Sea, and made a Journal of his Voyage, a usefull and acceptable work to Sea-men. On his return to *Portugal* he retir'd to his Country-house at *Sintra*, recreating himself by Reading, in his Solitudes, and employments always Exemplary; He put on his Sword again to follow the Eagles of *Charls* the Emperour in the Battail of *Tunez*, where he rais'd his name with new Glory; when this design was over, hiding himself from his own Fame, he again retir'd to *Sintra*, knowing how to avoid, not keep himself from employments. The King *Dom John* made him Admiral of the Navy of the Coast, a Service where his Courage was answered by Success; He went last of all to Govern *India*, where, by the Victories we have related, he secur'd, and brought into reputation the State. When the designs of Warr spar'd him, he in a large Card describ'd all the Coast betwixt *Goa*, and *Dio*, marking the Flats, and Shelves, the height of the Pole in which the Cities lye; the depth of Water, Anchoring, and Creeks which form the Havens; the Trade-winds, and Nature of those Seas; the force of the Currents, the swiftness of Rivers, disposing the Lines in different Tables, all, with so minute and exact Geography, as only this Work might serve to make him Famous, if he were not so eminently, for his great Fortitude. He look't the same in his streights at Home, and prosperity in the *East*, appearing always the same Man in diverse Fortunes; his Ambition was to deserve all things, and ask nothing; He equally did reason and justice to all men, unbyast in his

his Punishments, but so Justifiable, that the Complaints were more against the Law then Minister. He was free to the Souldiers, sparing to his Children, shewing more civility in his Office, then Nature; He us'd with a great deal of Ceremony the Actions of his Predecessours, honouring even those he put not in practice; without prostituting his Civility, he preserv'd his Respect. He appear'd above the Great ones, and Father of the Meanest; such was his Life, as by that, more then by Punishments, he reform'd extravagancies; his first Zeal was always in God's cause, then in the States; he past no Virtue without Reward, some Vices without Punishment; amending not a few, some by Favours, others by Clemency. The presents he receiv'd from the Princes of *Asia*, he put to the King's Revenue, a Virtue all prais'd, few imitated; the maimed Souldiers found him Sollicitous in their Cure, and Compassionate of their Condition; He oblig'd every one, yet seem'd obnoxious to all; He kept the Souldiers (as what would prove the Ruine of the State) from Merchandizing; He set upon no Action, which he did not atchieve, being ready in Execution, mature in Counsel: amidst the employments of a Souldier, he preserv'd the virtues of a Religious man, was frequent in visiting Temples, a great honourer of Church-men, mercifull and liberal to the Poor; had great Devotion to the Cross of Christ, which he Reverenc'd in its Figure, by a low inclination without any difference of time or place; and so Religiously was he fir'd with the Worship of this most holy Representative, as he rather chose to Build a Temple to its Memory, then raise a House to his Posterity, leaving it on his Fatherly blessing to his Son *Dom Alvaro*, that if he found in the favour, or justice of the King, any recompence for his Services, he should with that Build a Convent for the *Franciscan* Recollets in the Mountain of *Sintra*, and name the House *The invocation of the Holy Cross. Dom Alvaro de Castro*, Heir apparent to the virtues of so pious a Father, gave order for

John de Barro's Hist. of *India*, Dec. *6*. Lib. 1. Pag. 4.

for Building the Convent, not so great for the Majesty of the Pile, as for the Sanctity of the Penitents who Inhabit there. Being the first time sent from King *Dom Sebastian* Embassadour to Pope *Pius* the Fourth, he obtain'd of him to priviledge the Altar of the Convent for all Masses, and on the day of the Invention of the Cross, Plenary indulgence to all those who pray'd for the pressing necessities of the Church, and designedly for the Soul of *Dom John de Castro*; so singular and unusual a grace as we have not known granted to Soveraign Princes. It is apparent, the Fame of his Victories was as loud in *Italy*, as that of his Virtues, attested by so Illustrious a testimony from the Vicar of Christ; for these and other Virtues we believe he now enjoys in Heaven nobler Palmes in a more eminent Triumph. He had three Sons, who all expos'd themselves to the dangers of Warr, as their Fathers blessing; *Dom Miguel* the Youngest, who in the Reign of King *Dom Sebastian* went to the *Indies*, and Dy'd in the Government of *Malaca*; *Dom Fernando* burnt in the Mine at *Dio*; *Dom Alvaro*, with whom he seem'd to share his Palmes and Victories, the Son and Companion of his Fame, who returning to the Kingdome without any other Riches then the Wounds he receiv'd in the Warr, Married *Dona Anna de Attayde*, Daughter to *Dom Lewis de Castro*, Lord of the House of *Monsanto*; He was a particular Favourite to King *Dom Sebastian*, entrusted by him in the greatest Affairs and places of the Kingdome, went on diverse Embassies to *Castile*, *France*, *Rome*, and *Savoy*: Was of the Council of State, and sole Superintendent of the Exchequer, and in the midst of so eminent Offices, Died Poor, though he Deceast a Favourite.

His Children.

The praise of *Dom Alvaro de Castro*.

The END.

An Index of the most Observable things in this History.

A.

Adem.

Dom Affonso de Noronha.

Agacaim.

Dom Alvaro Bacaon.

Dom Alvaro de Castro.

INDEX.

Dom Antonio de Atayde.

Antonio do Casal.

Antonio Correa.

Antonio Moniz Barretto.

Goes

INDEX.

The

INDEX.

Is

INDEX.

Where

Goga.

INDEX.

INDEX.

Dom John de Castro.

Puts

Dis-

INDEX.

He

INDEX.

Malucos.

INDEX.

Rumecaon

INDEX.

Rumecaon.

INDEX.

INDEX.

The

INDEX.

FINIS.

By the Composers not current Reading the Copy, some Faults have crept into the Impression; the mistake of one Letter in some Tenses, and the putting *Or* instead of *Nor* to answer neither happens often, but is easily Corrected, as are the mistakes in names of *Persons* and *Places*.

Errata.

PReface, p. 2. l. 36. read *petentem*, p. 11. l. 35. read *nor 'leays*, and so throughout the Book, p. 13. l. 4. read *but in Peace*, ibid. l. 7. read *strove*, p. 14. l. 10. read *his Hight*, p. 15. l. 1. read *affrightning the place*, p. 16. l. 36. read *have own'd it*, p. 33. l. 3. read *ran*, p. 37. l. 8. read *an Altar-peice*, p. 76. l. 6. read *to punish*, p. 102. l. 29. read *Spear*, p. 134. l. 36. read *Sentinells*, p. 160. l. 15. read *Bramaluco*, p. 168. l. 32. read *came*, p. 173. l. 25. read *your Company*, p. 195. l. 8. read *Zamaluke*.